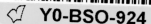

AUDIOVISUAL: UTILIZATION, PRODUCTION, AND DESIGN.

by
les satterthwaite
arizona state university
tempe, arizona

KENDALL/HUNT PUBLISHING COMPANY
2460 Kerper Boulevard   P.O. Box 539   Dubuque, Iowa 52004-0539

Originally entitled *Graphics: Skills, Media, and Materials*

Printed in the United States of America
10 9 8 7 6 5 4

INTRODUCTION:

This publication is intended to provide students in introductory media courses with answers to questions that are commonly asked about media. These questions fall under the general categories of selection/evaluation, production, operation, and utilization.

Selection involves the question, "Where can I find what instructional materials already exist?" This relates to the wealth of instructional materials that are available from commercial and free/inexpensive sources. We will explore these sources for each of the media that we treat.

Production involves the question, "If I can't find what I want how can I produce the materials I need?" Our emphasis will be in the area of graphics. Basic skills of mounting, lettering, and illustration will be explained and applied to the construction of both simple and complex media. While graphic skills are not normally considered in the production of photographic and electronic media we will cover such concepts as hand drawn slides and filmstrips, graphic "flats" for photo copy, and even the production of graphic motion pictures that do not require a camera.

Operation is concerned with the question, "Now that I have the message I need, how do I deliver it to the intended audience?" However, rather than deal with the many brands and models of a given piece of hardware we will deal with the general characteristics of a certain type of media. Through this approach it is hoped that you will be able to generalize to the particular brand and model of equipment that you will be using.

Utilization is the process of answering the question, "Now that I have the message and the delivery system how do I fit it into my instructional system?" While there are as many different teaching-learning strategies as there are teachers, they can be grouped into the following five categories. First the presentation of information to large groups of learners. In some instances this would be done simultaneously; in others the presentation might be individually—to one learner at a time until the entire group has been covered. The second instructional strategy would be interaction. In this strategy the instructional materials are designed to stimulate a discussion—an interaction between the students. The third instructional strategy would be independent study. This is a situation in which the instruction designs the materials to present information, require a response, and provide feedback as to the accuracy of the learner's response. The fourth stragegy is drill and practice. This allows the learner to drill until mastery of the content is achieved. The last strategy involves self-evaluation. The learner interacts with the media and ascertains his own progress through the instructional system.

This publication is intended to explore the selection/evaluation, production, operation, and utilization of a wide range of instructional media and materials.

CONTENTS:

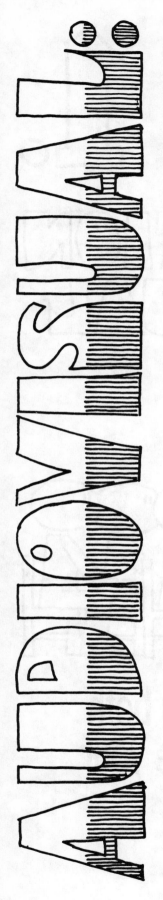

AUDIOVISUAL: UTILIZATION, PRODUCTION, AND DESIGN.

CHAPTER 1.

AN INTRODUCTION TO AUDIOVISUAL EDUCATION

AV Education is a process utilizing both media and materials to enhance your classroom communications.

WHAT IS AUDIOVISUAL EDUCATION?

The field of Audiovisual Education began with the outset of World War II. It was necessary to quickly and effectively train large numbers of men and women to survive in a modern war situation. It was discovered that motion pictures were an important tool that could be used for the effective transmission of information. Soon film producers had gone to war, and the training camps were filled with examples of mediated instruction. As the war progressed new media were introduced into the classroom. Overhead projectors, opaque projectors, slide projectors and filmstrip projectors were introduced, and message materials were designed for these media.

Public educators noted the astounding success of media and their related materials in military training and decided to adopt and adapt these tools for use in the public classrooms. Soon a major new industry was born. Hardware and software producers found the public education market so lucrative that companies were developed just to fill the perceived needs of this fast growing market. This was the era of the producer, distributer and media specialist. Schools added specialized staff who could assist the classroom teacher to make more effective use of these materials and their delivery systems. The media specialists taught teachers how to use the new "teaching tools" and how to acquire these new instructional materials. The emphasis was on production and service.

Soon the materials producers had almost saturated the markets, and there arose a different type of problem. With so many similar instructional materials to choose from, the teachers needed to be able to select the best of what was available and to make effective use of it in the classroom. Now the media specialist put on another hat and became concerned with the selection and evaluation of these materials and the techniques to deliver them effectively to their students.

But the hardware producers were not asleep. As each new communication system was developed, its potential for classroom use was explored. There was educational radio, educational television, programmed instruction, and on and on and on. Each was heralded as the panacea for the ills that beset American education. Obviously none of them really succeeded in totally solving education's problems. However, as each new media was added, it expanded the role of the school media specialist.

The concept of programmed instruction forced those who were in education to take a much closer look at the process of learning. In this exploration a divergent approach was born—educational technology. The educational technologist became concerned with the process of analyzing and evaluating instructional problems and solutions. Now we have new media such as computers, video discs, teleconferencing, and we also have a new approach. This text will seek to explore both the new and old media and the techniques for increasing their effectiveness in the classroom. We will also look at the process whereby media can be used to enhance various types of classroom communications.

THE MODEL:
ANALYSIS
SPECIFICATION
PRODUCTION
EVALUATION

AN INSTRUCTIONAL MODEL THAT INCORPORATES MEDIA

There are probably as many models of the process called instructional development as there are instructional developers. It seems that each person prefers his individual variation or his own way of picturing the model for development of predictable materials. Basically, these models begin with a problem that needs a solution and ends with a product that solves the problem. They are normally divided into four major phases or stages: 1) the analysis stage that begins with the problem and ends with instructional objectives, 2) the specifications stage that begins with the objective and ends with the specifications for the desired end product, 3) the production stage that begins with the specifications and ends with the selection and/or production of instructional materials to meet these specifications, and 4) the evaluation stage that begins with the prototype product and ends with an evaluation of its effectiveness in assisting the learners to attain the objectives we started out with. But it's not quite that simple; there are many substages to consider.

1. WHAT IS THE INSTRUCTIONAL PROBLEM?
   A. How are the learners performing now?
   B. How do you want their behavior to change?
   C. What skills/information do they need?
   D. What are the behaviors desired and in what sequence?
2. HOW CAN WE HELP THE LEARNERS ATTAIN THESE OBJECTIVES?
   A. Develop descriptions of the content and audience.
   B. Determine how to motivate, instruct, and provide appropriate practice.
   C. Determine the best media to deliver the above.
   D. Determine what the materials for these media should look and sound like.
3. WHAT MATERIALS CAN BE FOUND/PRODUCED TO DO THIS?
   A. Are there appropriate commercial or free/inexpensive materials, and where can I find them?
   B. Do these materials meet the specifications, or can they be adapted to meet the specifications?
   C. Can we produce materials to these specifications if we can't find what we want?
4. DID THE PROPOSED SOLUTION TO THE PROBLEM WORK?
   A. Were the materials delivered effectively?
   B. Did the learners attain the objectives?
   C. If the learners did not attain the objectives—
      1) Can I modify the delivery?
      2) Can I modify the materials?
      3) Can I modify the objectives?

This is the process we will follow: 1) analysis, 2) specifications, 3) production, and 4) evaluation. Through an exploration of this process we will examine other concerns related to developing predictable instructional materials.

THE PROBLEM:

PRESENT BEHAVIOR

⬇

DESIRED BEHAVIOR

Given a blank diagram
the learner will
label the four stages of
the water cycle.

(conditions)
(learner)

(behavior)

WHAT'S THE PROBLEM?

Instructional problems are all around us. The textbook selection committee decides on a new text, and the implication is that you will "teach" your students the content in that text. The school board passes a resolution that your school will join the "back to basics" movement, and the implication is that you will redesign your curriculum to emphasize the basics. Or perhaps you have noticed the need to repeat instructions to students in your classroom—they don't listen. These are all instructional problems. Either you feel the need to teach a given concept or idea (internal needs), or you are faced with pressures to teach a given concept or idea (external needs).

Once you have identified the instructional problem, what is the next step? First, take a good look at your students. Can your students do what they need to do without additional instruction? Surprisingly, it is often possible to modify learner behavior by simply telling them what is expected or by changing the environment in which they perform. However, if you evaluate the learners' present behavior and find that it does not meet your goals, you should begin the process of instructional development.

First, we need a clear, concise statement of exactly what we want the learners to be able to do. In short, we prepare appropriate instructional objectives for the learners, the content, and the goals. A well-stated instructional objective must communicate well and has four basic elements or components. First, the well-stated instructional objective must describe something the learner will do. It must be *learner* oriented. A statement such as, "To teach the importance of the water cycle," is a goal statement describing what you will do (teach), not what the learner will do. Secondly, a well-stated instructional objective must describe what the learner will *do*. It describes a behavior that we can observe and measure. Here words like "understand," "know," etc. must be replaced by precise verbs that mean the same thing to everyone. Vern Gerlach suggests the INDOC system that keys to verbs such as "identify," "name," "describe," "order" and "construct." These enhance our communications and ensure that everyone will have the same meaning from the objective.

In addition to the two required elements of a well-stated instructional objective, they may also contain two other elements. A well-stated instructional objective *may* describe the conditions under which the behavior will occur. In many instances these conditions or "givens" may determine the difficulty level of obtaining the objective. A well-stated instructional objective *may* also contain the standards you require for the successful attainment of the objective. These standards may represent quantity, quality or even time considerations that you feel are important to the attainment of the objective. When standards are not included in an objective, the assumption is that the students will perform at a 100% level.

This first step of the development process begins with a problem and ends with the creation of appropriate instructional objectives. It may also include the ordering and sequencing of these objectives into logical patterns. Now we know where we are going, and we are ready to move into stage two of the process—developing the instructional specifications that will describe the instructional materials that are necessary to aid the learners in the attainment of these objectives.

SPECIFICATIONS:

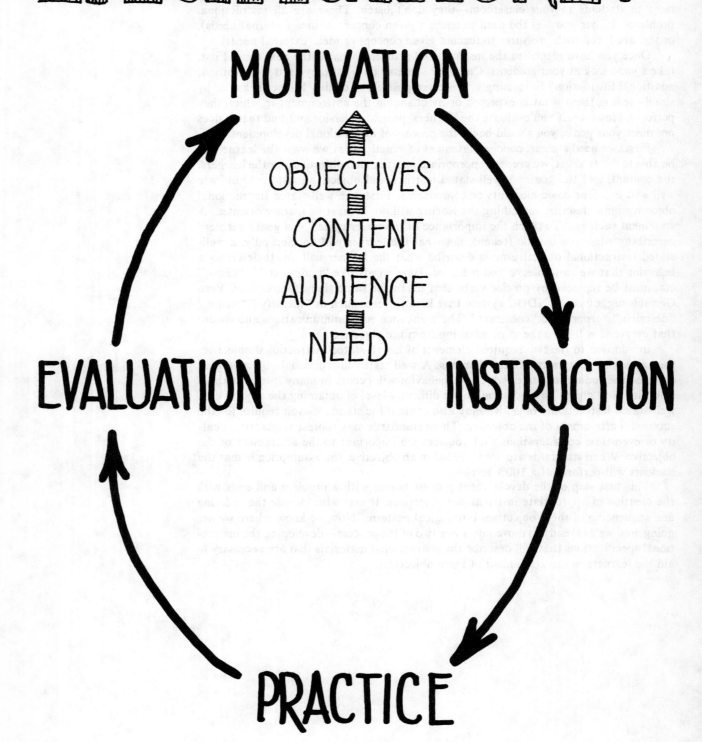

MOTIVATION

OBJECTIVES

CONTENT

AUDIENCE

NEED

INSTRUCTION

EVALUATION

PRACTICE

HOW CAN WE ASSIST THE LEARNERS
TO ATTAIN THE OBJECTIVES?

Once we have identified the need and prepared the objectives that we want the learners to attain, we are ready to prepare the specifications for the instruction necessary to assist them. To prepare these specifications we need to know our content and our audience. Obviously, we had some idea of our content and audience when we prepared our instructional objectives, but now is the time for preciseness (and possibly modifying our objectives). We want to prepare an audience description and a content outline. Both of these require some degree of research, and a logical place to begin this research is with our client. What does the text have to say about the content, what does the board mean by "basics"? etc. We should use all of the print and non-print resources at our command within the time constraints placed upon the developmental process. The content outline should be in an "outline" format. It should describe what is to be included and the order and sequencing of the materials. The outline format will allow the effective communication to others and is much more readable than a paragraph. It is not unusual that as the content outline and the audience description are developed, it may be advisable to modify the instructional objectives we began with.

When we have completed our three documents: 1) the audience description, 2) the content outline, and 3) the instructional objectives, we are ready to deal with other aspects of the specifications. We must make some media and instruction decisions. What media will be best for "motivating" the learners? How can we develop a positive attitude toward the content and the desired outcomes? What media will be most appropriate for delivering the factual information to the learners—"instructing" them? It must be appropriate to the content, the audience, and the objectives. What media will be best for providing the learners with appropriate "practice"? If practice is necessary for successful mastery of the information, how can we provide it effectively and efficiently? What is the best media for "evaluating" the learners' end performance? How can we be sure that the learners have attained the objectives that we have set for them? These four components: 1) motivation, 2) instruction, 3) practice, and 4) evaluation, form the pattern of our teaching and may require the use of media to be effective.

Media decisions require a knowledge of the characteristics of the various media. Which are best for motivation? Which are best for presentation, interaction, independent study or other aspects of instruction? Are some media better suited for practice than others, and if so, do they meet the needs of the audience, content, and objectives? And, finally, is media necessary for evaluation? If the concepts to be evaluated are primarily visual (recognizing colors, shapes, animals, etc), then perhaps media must be considered as part of the evaluation process.

In this stage of the process we have described the audience, the content and the objectives. We have also made choices as to the most appropriate media for motivation, instruction (in all its forms), practice, and evaluation. We have some idea of what the proposed instructional materials should look and sound like, and now it is time to move to stage three and select and/or produce the materials to meet these specifications. In many models the specification stage may be much more precise and may include roughs, scripts, storyboards and/or treatments, but since we may want to utilize free/inexpensive materials, we will maintain a little more freedom at this stage.

ACQUISITION:

INEXPENSIVE

EDUCATORS
PROGRESS
SERVICE...

COMMERCIAL

NICEM INDEXES

PRODUCTION

AUDIENCE
CONTENT   } SPECS { SKETCHES
OBJECTIVES }   STORYBOARD } SKILLS
                       SCRIPT

THE ACQUISITION OF APPROPRIATE MATERIALS

We have the problem and the objectives developed in stage one of the process. We have the technical specifications including audience, content, and media choices developed in stage two, and now we are ready for stage three in the development process—acquiring the instructional materials for the media we have selected. At this point, perhaps we had best make a distinction between media and materials. We will define instructional media as the delivery systems, the hardware that actually delivers the information to the learners. However, an overhead projector is not "content." The instructional materials, the software, are the messages, the content for motivating, instructing, providing practice, and even for evaluating. The overhead transparency is an example of an instructional material, and it is delivered to the audience via an instructional media, the overhead projector.

Our concern now is the acquisition of instructional materials for the media we have selected. Basically, there are three sources for this acquisition: 1) we can acquire existing commercial materials; 2) we can acquire existing free/inexpensive materials; or 3) we can produce these materials locally by applying various production techniques. The term "commercial" is used to describe the massive collection of instructional materials that are offered for sale by manufacturers of these products. However, there are so many manufacturers of instructional materials, it is necessary to have a unified listing, and this is provided in the NICEM Indexes. The NICEM Indexes are grouped according to media types, such as the NICEM Index to 16mm Films or the NICEM Index to Video Tapes. In these indexes the materials are clustered according to topics, and so if your objective deals with "The Water Cycle" and you have decided that a film is most appropriate to motivate the students, you can look under "Water Cycle" in the NICEM Index to 16mm films to see what is available. Utilizing the information in the appendix of these Indexes, you can either send off for preview copies or for producers' catalogues that will provide a more detailed description of the products.

But all too often cost is a major factor in selecting instructional materials, and so you need to be aware of the Educators Progress Service publications. These are listings of materials, that are produced by industry, that *may* be useful in the classroom. The "Educators Guide to Free Films" or the "Educators Guide to Free Science Materials" may contain materials that you could either use as is or modify to meet your instructional specifications.

If you can't find materials that are appropriate to your audience, content, or objectives, you can always produce them yourself. This production process normally involves the development of a "blueprint" in the form of a rough sketch or storyboard script and then the application of either simple or complex production techniques. The bulk of this text will deal with the various production techniques that will allow you the option of designing and producing your own instructional materials.

We began this stage of the process with the technical specifications that describe the media we would use to motivate, instruct, provide practice for, and evaluate our audience. It ended with the selection and/or production of the materials that would be appropriate for these media. Now we are ready to deliver the instruction and determine its effectiveness.

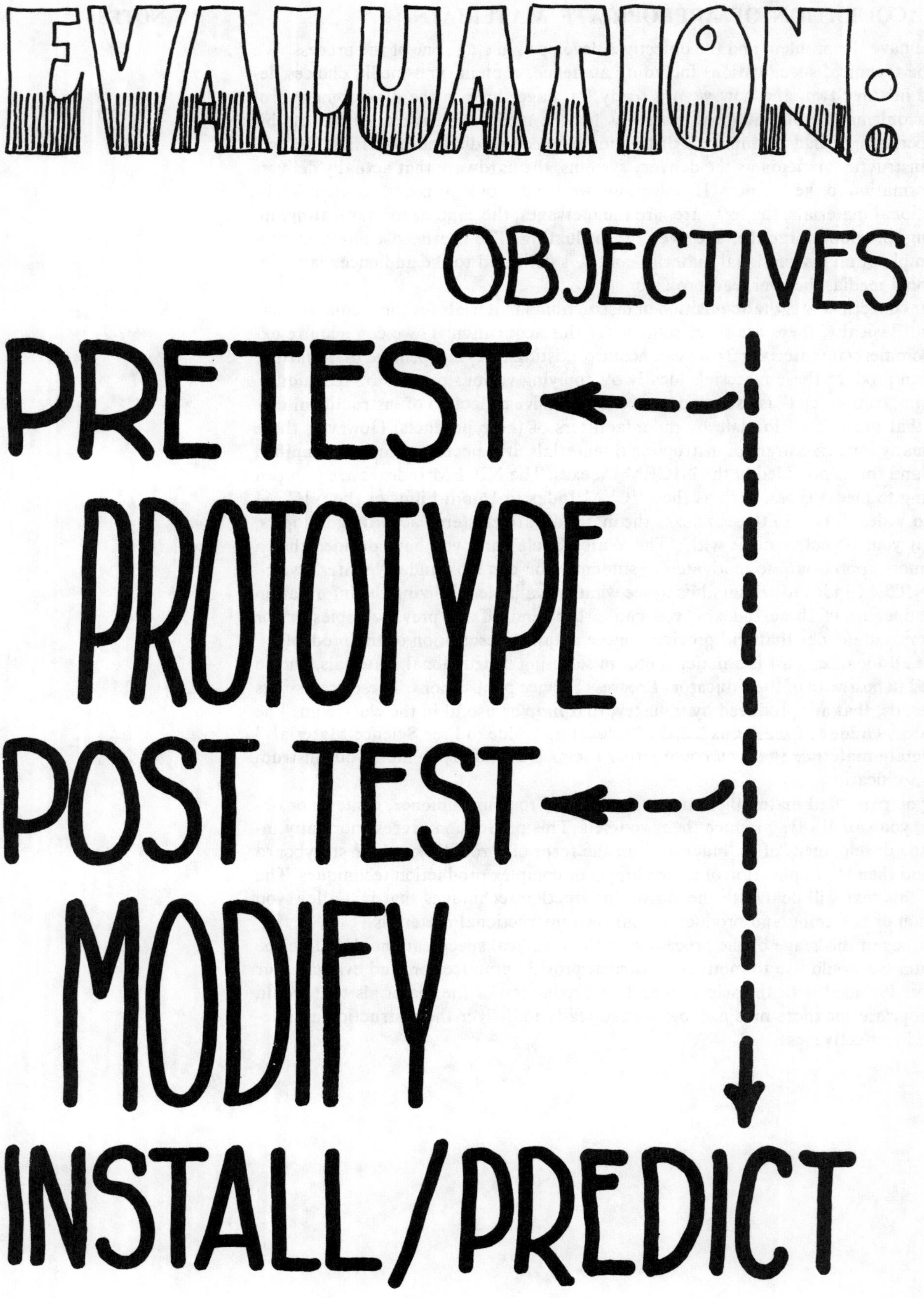

EVALUATION:

OBJECTIVES

PRETEST ←---

PROTOTYPE

POST TEST ←---

MODIFY

INSTALL/PREDICT

DID OUR SOLUTION WORK?

We have reached the point where we are ready to try out our instructional materials and strategies on the audience. It has been a long process. We have gone from an instructional problem to objectives, from objectives to specifications, from specifications to the end product, and now we are concerned with the effectiveness of the instruction. We must keep in mind the possibility that this product may only be a prototype and that the results of our evaluation may determine that it is necessary to redo segments, if not the whole unit.

While our first concern is the delivery of this information to the intended audience, we must also be concerned with the determination of the learning that will take place as a result of this instruction. This means that we must develop a pre- and a post-test. The pretest will determine where the learners are before the instruction, and the post-test will determine where the learners are after instruction. Obviously, the difference in scores between the pre- and the post-test will determine the amount of learning that has taken place. In constructing the pre- and post-test, it is essential that we keep our minds on what we are trying to measure—the objectives. Ideally, there will be one or more questions on the test that relate specifically to each objective or subobjective we have written. If there is a direct relationship between the objectives and the test questions, we will be able to identify those subareas that need improvement. It is also essential to remember that the objectives guide both the instruction and the evaluation. If the objective is to, "Name the three forms that water can take," then the test questions should also require the student to "Name the three forms that water can take." It is not reasonable to substitute a question such as, "Water can take which of the following forms? a) liquid, b) solid, c) gaseous, d) all of the above, e) none of the above." This latter question is an identifying activity, not a naming activity.

Once we have added our pre- and post-tests to the instructional materials we are going to use, we are ready for the evaluation—that is, we are ready for the evaluation if we know how to operate the hardware, the media, that will deliver the instruction to the learners. There is no value in having a motion picture to motivate the learners if no one knows how to operate the motion picture projector properly. So equipment operation is a skill that must precede the evaluation.

Administer the pretest to the sample learners. Ideally, this should be a little before you present the information. A pretest that immediately is followed by the instruction may provide a "set" for learning that is not built in to the instructional system. With the pretest given, you are ready to deliver the information by motivating the learners, instructing the learners and providing appropriate practice. With the completion of the delivery of the information, you are ready to administer the post-test. Next we score the pre- and post-test and analyze the resulting data in terms of the attainment of each of the objectives and/or subobjectives. Here we can determine which objectives were attained and the degree of their attainment. If it meets our criteria, then the program can be installed into our instructional system. If it does not meet our criteria, we can examine the objectives, the motivation, the instruction, and the practice to see what modifications can be made to ensure better scores on the next use of the instructional program. We now have hard data to guide our modifications and to ensure that we have a highly predictable product.

SAMPLE PLANNING DOCUMENTS

Your name _____ Your lab instructor _____

Your client _____

TOPIC: The Water Cycle

I intend to teach a unit on the four stages of the water cycle. This is especially important since water is a *reusable* natural resource and vital to life on this plant Earth.

CONTENT OUTLINE:

    I. Introduction and motivation
       A. There is no new water in the world.
       B. We must use the same water over and over again.
       C. Natures purification system is called the water cycle.
   II. The four stages in the water cycle
       A. Evaporation
       B. Condensation
       C. Precipitation
       D. Percolation
  III. The evaporation stage of the water cycle
       A. Heat changes liquid water into water vapor (gas).
         1. Heat from the sun is the primary energy source.
         2. There are other techniques (wave action, transpiration, etc.).
       B. The heated water vapor rises into the atmosphere.
  IV. The condensation stage of the water cycle
       A. The rising vapor cools and condenses (gas into liquid or solid).
       B. Different forms at different levels
         1. In the upper atmosphere it forms clouds.
         2. In the lower atmosphere it forms fog.
         3. On the ground it forms dew.
   V. The precipitation stage of the water cycle
       A. Droplets form around particles (hydroscopic neclei).
       B. When sufficiently heavy, they fall as precipitation.
         1. Rain, showers, drizzle, thunderstorms
         2. Snow, sleet
         3. Hail
       C. The precipitation falls to earth.
  VI. The percolation stage of the water cycle
       A. Some water flows along the earth's surface.
         1. Brooks to streams
         2. Streams to rivers
         3. Rivers to oceans
       B. Some soaks down into the earth.
         1. Ground water
         2. Artesian wells
 VII. The process repeats itself.

AUDIENCE DESCRIPTION:

The target audience for this program is sixth grade students in Arizona. Since Arizona is so dependent on water, there should be an interest in water utilization and preservation. However, the students are generally uninterested in science topics.

INSTRUCTIONAL OBJECTIVES:
Learners will:
DESCRIBE THE FORM AND FUNCTION OF THE WATER CYCLE.
GIVEN A BLANK DIAGRAM, LABEL THE FOUR STAGES OF THE WATER CYCLE.
NAME THE THREE FORMS THAT WATER CAN TAKE.
DESCRIBE HOW WATER CHANGES FROM LIQUID TO GAS.
DESCRIBE HOW WATER CHANGES FROM GAS TO LIQUID.
DESCRIBE HOW WATER CHANGES FROM LIQUID TO SOLID.
DESCRIBE HOW WATER CHANGES FROM SOLID TO LIQUID.
NAME TWO FORMS OF LIQUID PRECIPITATION.
NAME TWO FORMS OF SOLID PRECIPITATION.

INSTRUCTIONAL MEDIA TO BE USED:
FOR MOTIVATION:

I will use a segment of the film "WATER" which shows a stream and the surrounding area drying up through time lapse photography, and the trigger question, "What happened to the water?" Then I will use a plain glass of water and point out that it is millions and millions of years old (perhaps even dinosaurs bathed in it), and yet it is drinkable today because of nature's purification system, the water cycle.

FOR INSTRUCTION:

I will present the concept of the water cycle using overhead transparencies because they are excellent presentation tools and because I can add and subtract information through overlays. It will also allow me to control the pacing during this crucial first presentation. I will then show the film "WATER" to show the process in a real world setting apart from the graphic diagram of the water cycle in the transparencies. I will need to provide a good introduction since the film is set in the Midwest and the class is from Arizona.

FOR PRACTICE:

I will provide the students with a duplicated handout of the diagram of the water cycle and ask them to label the stages. The opposite side will contain the same diagram with the stages labeled and with a brief description of the activities in each stage. The students may keep this practice material for reference.

FOR EVALUATION:

I will use a printed test of my own construction that will include diagrams of the water cycle and pictorial representations of various forms of precipitation, as well as the questions.

LESSON PLAN:

I will begin with the *film clip* to arouse their interest in the topic and then use the glass of water (realia) to get across the point that there is no new water in the world. I expect this will generate some questions, and I will use the questions to lead into the concept of the water cycle. The transparencies will begin with a blank diagram of the water cycle and then, through overlays, introduce each phase of the water cycle in sequence. With the overhead transparencies I will be able to have the room lights on and can write names or draw diagrams on the chalkboard to enhance the presentation or answer questions.

When we have completed the cycle, I will show the complete film "WATER" (10 min.) and introduce it by pointing out that it was shot in the Midwest and there will be some differences between there and Arizona. After the film is over, I will point out the differences as we discuss the film.

The practice activity should only take a few minutes, and when it is completed I will have them check their answers by turning the paper over. I will let them keep the practice materials as reference to study for the test. As a possible follow up activity I would like to construct a bulletin board with just the blank diagram of the water cycle and have students collect pictures representing various stages. Ideally, they would put the pictures in the appropriate position (i.e. pictures of rain in the precipitation stage, pictures of streams in the percolation stage, etc.).

POSSIBLE TEST ITEMS:

1. Name two forms of solid precipitation. (snow, hail)
2. Name two forms of liquid precipitation. (rain, drizzle, showers)
3. Describe how water changes from solid to liquid. (heat melts it)
4. Describe how water changes from liquid to solid. (cold freezes it)
5. Describe how water changes from gas to liquid. (forms around nuclei)
6. Describe how water changes from liquid to gas. (heat makes vapor/steam)
7. Name the three forms that water can take. (liquid, solid, gas)
8. Label the four stages of the water cycle on the blank diagram provided. (evaporation, condensation, precipitation, percolation)
9. Describe the form and function of the water cycle. (A cyclical process that repeats itself in four basic stages: 1) evaporation, 2) condensation, 3) precipitation, and 4) percolation. The water cycle is nature's way of purifying the limited amount of water that we have in the world.)

CHAPTER 2

MOUNTING INSTRUCTIONAL MATERIALS:

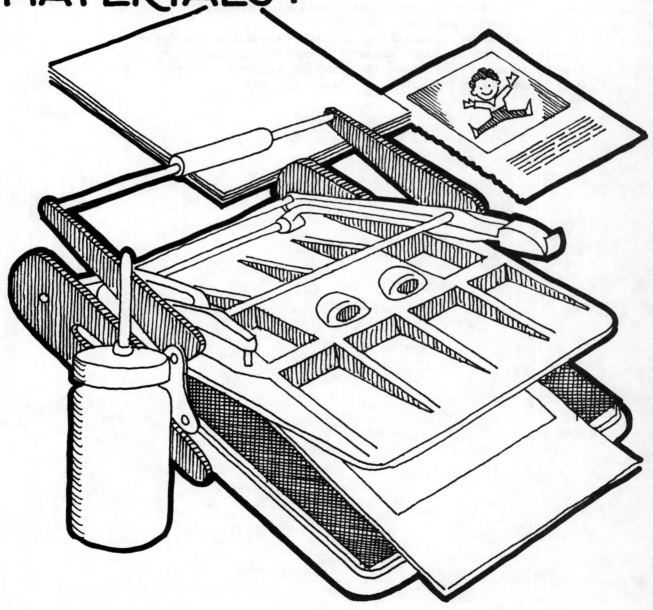

MOUNTING INSTRUCTIONAL MATERIALS:

This section begins our exploration of the basic graphic skills of mounting, lettering, and illustration. Mounting seems to be a logical place to begin since we often need to protect and present visual materials that are collected from a wide variety of sources. This leads us into the first question. WHY IS MOUNTING IMPORTANT, WHAT PURPOSE DOES IT SERVE?

One major purpose of mounting techniques is *preservation*. Visual materials that have been collected will soon lose their instructional value if they are not protected by being adhered to either a rigid or a flexible backing material. We can further improve on this protection through lamination, which is the process of covering the visuals with a transparent coating. A second important reason for mounting materials is *presentation*. Many of the instructional media that we will explore require some sort of mounting, often in a specific format. The materials must meet the needs of the delivery system, and mounting is one of the techniques we have that will produce materials suitable for these media. A third reason for mounting instructional materials is *manipulation*. Part of the mounting process removes the visual from its original environment (perhaps a magazine) and places it in a more appropriate format for instruction. In some cases we can add other visual elements to modify the meaning of the visuals, and it is quite possible through picture manipulation to literally create your own visuals from existing components. Thus mounting is a technique that will allow us to preserve, present, and manipulate visual materials for instruction. WHAT DO WE MOUNT?

Recognizing that very few students are accomplished artists who can sketch, draw or paint the exact picture they want, we will rely primarily on *tearsheets*. Tearsheets are simply pictures that have been torn from magazines, newspapers, direct mail or any other source. These tearsheets come in many variations. They are printed in different sizes on different types of paper. The same ad may run in TIME and in READERS DIGEST. Because of the difference in format size we can sometimes find the same pictures in different sizes. Sometimes the ad is printed on newsprint (newspaper) and sometimes on high quality coated papers (magazines). These size and paper variations mean we must match the appropriate mounting technique to the visual materials. WHAT DO WE MOUNT THESE TEARSHEETS TO?

Mostly, we will mount the visual to a rigid backing such as railroad board. However, occasionally we will desire a flexible backing such as cloth. Again, the right mounting techniques must be selected based upon the desired backing. WHAT DO WE MOUNT WITH?

We will concentrate on the more professional adhesives but will offer you a variety in terms of cost. For example, rubber cement is a professional mounting adhesive that is relatively inexpensive, while MT-5 dry mount tissue is a mounting adhesive that is relatively expensive. The MT-5 is easy to use, but the rubber cement requires more of your time and energy. Other special-use mounting materials will be introduced to meet specific needs. Chartex is used to provide a cloth backing to the visual materials; Fotoflat is used where excessive heat might damage photographs or other delicate visuals; and Sealamin lamination film is to be used when it is desirable to cover the visual with a transparent coating for additional protection.

RUBBER CEMENT MOUNTING:

   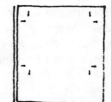

SELECT　TRIM　POSITION　REGISTER

—TEMPORARY— | —PERMANENT—

 　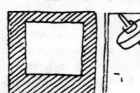

TURN　APPLY R.C.　　APPLY R.C.　DRY

POSITION　ADJUST　BURNISH　　WAX PAPER　VISUAL

 　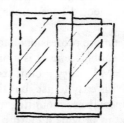

CLEAN　USE　　REMOVE　BURNISH　USE

RUBBER CEMENT MOUNTING

Rubber cement is a professional yet inexpensive adhesive used to join two surfaces. It is best used to adhere tearsheets to a rigid backing such as railroad board. There are two techniques (temporary and permanent), but they both begin at the same point—selecting an appropriate visual. For effective rubber cement mounting the tearsheet should be printed on the thickest possible paper. Lightweight paper may often cause the picture from the reverse side to bleed through. Once you have an appropriate visual, you need to trim it down to the proper shape and size. While a paper cutter can be used for this purpose, the blades are often dull, resulting in something less than a clean cut. I prefer a single-edged razor blade and a ruler with a metal edge. With the picture trimmed, position it on the backing and determine an appropriate arrangement. Register the location by making light pencil marks at the corners of the visual. These will be erased later, so make them light and slightly away from the edge of the visual. Then separate the visual and the backing and you are ready to begin the mounting process.

TEMPORARY RUBBER CEMENT MOUNTING

For temporary (3–12 months) rubber cement mounting the first step is to apply an even coat of rubber cement to the back of the visual. Make sure you place the visual face down on a surface that will not be damaged by an application of rubber cement. Then using the brush in the rubber cement dispenser, coat the back of the visual. Do not go back over areas where you have already applied rubber cement, or bumps and distortions will occur that can create problems. Try to avoid getting rubber cement on the front of the visual as it may remove the ink when you rub it off later. Now, with the rubber cement still moist, reposition the visual, using the registration marks as your guide. You can make small adjustments in placement while the rubber cement is still moist. When it is in place, burnish it down with a brayer or your hand to ensure complete contact with the backing material. Let it dry and remove any excess rubber cement from around the visual by rubbing it lightly. Once it is cleaned, the visual is ready for use.

PERMANENT RUBBER CEMENT MOUNTING

For permanent rubber cement mounting the process is quite different. Here we apply rubber cement to the back of the visual (as in the temporary rubber cement process), but we also apply it to the surface of the backing material. For the backing material use the registration marks to ensure a complete coat in the area where the visual will be placed. Then we let these two rubber cement coated surfaces dry completely. When these dry coats of rubber cement come in contact, they will be permanently adhered, so to allow us to reposition the visual where the registration marks indicate it should be, we cover the backing with overlapping sheets of household wax paper. The wax paper is translucent, so we can see the marks and reposition the visual. Then, holding the visual in place, slip one sheet of wax paper out and then the second. Burnish the visual down to the backing with a brayer or your hand, making sure not to scuff or damage the visual. Clean off any excess rubber cement by rubbing it lightly. Make sure you erase the registration marks and generally clean up the mounting. You now have a permanent rubber cement mounted visual that can be successfully used for a long time.

In this process make sure that your rubber cement is diluted to the proper consistency. If the rubber cement is too thick it will cause bumps; if it is too thin it may not adhere successfully.

MT-5 DRY MOUNTING:

SELECT	TURN	COVER	TACK	AREA TACK

—STANDARD | IRREGULAR—

TURN	TRIM	CHECK	TURN	TRIM

POSITION	TACK	TACK	POSITION	COVER	TACK

225° 225°

COVER/COOK	USE	COVER/COOK	USE

MT-5 DRY MOUNTING

MT-5 is a dry adhesive that is used to bond two adjacent services together permanently. The process is quite simple, but the cost is relatively high. The process begins with the selection of the visual to be mounted. The key is to select a visual that will not be damaged by heat and pressure. Obviously, the visual must communicate the concept you are concerned with, but if heat and/or pressure will damage the visual, find another mounting technique. Once you have an appropriate visual, turn it face down on a clean surface and cover it with dry mounting tissue. Then either tack the tissue to the back of the visual by applying heat (use a tacking iron) in the center, or do what is called *area tacking*. Area tacking is simply tacking in a number of areas behind the important visual element. Now we are ready for the trimming process.

STANDARD MT-5 DRY MOUNTING

A standard MT-5 dry mount is one that is trimmed into a square or rectangular format. Turn the tacked visual over on a surface that you can cut on. While you may trim the visual with a paper cutter or scissors, I prefer a single-edged razor blade and a ruler with a metal edge. Now trim the visual into the size and format (rectangular) that you desire. Position the trimmed visual onto the selected backing material in the location desired. Holding it in place, lift one corner of the visual, exposing the tissue underneath. With the tacking iron tack the tissue to the backing material. Lift the diagonally opposite corner of the visual and tack the exposed tissue to the backing. This diagonal tacking will help to eliminate any wrinkles when the materials are heated in the dry mount press. Cover the visual with clean newsprint and place it in a dry mount press set at 225 degrees. Close the press and cook the materials for 1–3 minutes. The mounted visual is permanently bonded to the backing. If the humidity is high in your area you may want to begin the process by placing the visual into the dry mount press to remove excess moisture.

IRREGULAR MT-5 DRY MOUNTING

An irregular MT-5 dry mount is one that is trimmed into an irregular shape to conform to a specific visual element. In this case you begin with a visual that has been area tacked. Now trim the visual into the size and configuration that you desire. In the example on the opposite page everything is trimmed away except the apple. Place the trimmed visual onto the backing materials and cover with a scrap of newsprint. Apply the tacking iron to the newsprint and let the heat penetrate to adhere the tissue under the visual to the backing. Cover with clean newsprint and place in a dry mount press that has been preheated to 225 degrees. Close the press and cook the visual for 1–3 minutes. If you are mounting more than one cutout, mount each separately, especially if they overlap each other. You now have a permanently mounted visual that can be used to create the specific impression or communication what you desire.

FOTOFLAT DRY MOUNTING:

 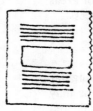   OR

SELECT   TURN   TISSUE   TACK   AREA TACK

— STANDARD   IRREGULAR —

TURN   TRIM   CHECK   TURN   TRIM   CHECK

POSITION   TACK   TACK   POSITION   COVER   TACK

180°   180°   

COVER/COOK   USE   COVER/COOK   USE

FOTOFLAT DRY MOUNTING

Fotoflat is a wax based dry adhesive that bonds two surfaces together with less heat than MT-5 dry mounting tissue. This means we can mount visuals that otherwise might be damaged by the heat (225 degrees) and pressure of the dry mount press. Actually, Fotoflat can be adhered using a home iron set at rayon temperature. Begin the process with an appropriate visual. Turn it face down on a surface that will not be damaged by heat and tack the tissue to the visual once in the center or use the area tacking technique. Now you are ready for the trimming process.

STANDARD FOTOFLAT DRY MOUNTING

A standard Fotoflat mount refers to one that is trimmed in either a square or a rectangular format. This type of mounting begins with the single tacking process to adhere the tissue to the visual. Turn the visual over onto a surface that will not be damaged by cutting. Trim the visual into the size and format desired. Normally a square or rectangular format is used for the standard Fotoflat dry mount. Then position the visual onto the backing in the location desired. Normally, more space will be left below the visual than to the sides or top. With the visual in place lift one corner of the visual, exposing the Fotoflat below. Then tack the exposed tissue to the backing. Repeat this process on the diagonally opposite corner. This diagonal tacking will allow the materials to expand when heated and avoid any wrinkling. With the Fotoflat tissue tacked to the visual and also to the backing, simply cover it with clean newsprint and cook it. You may place it in a dry mount press that has been preheated to 180 degrees, or you may simply iron it on with a home iron set at rayon temperature.

IRREGULAR FOTOFLAT MOUNTING

The process of irregular Fotoflat mounting begins with "area tacking." Then the visual is trimmed to the desired shape and size. When the visual is positioned where you want it on the backing, it must be with newsprint to tack it in place since area tacking does not allow the lifting of a corner of the visual. When it is tacked to the backing, it is then mounted by either cooking it in a dry mount press set at 180 degrees or by using a home iron set at the rayon temperature setting.

Fotoflat dry mounting tissue has some characteristics that are unique. First, it is a dry adhesive that can be mounted at a relatively low temperature (180 degrees). This allows visuals that might otherwise be damaged by the high heat of MT-5 dry mounting tissue to be permanently mounted. However, this brings us to the second unique characteristic of Fotoflat. While it is a permanent dry mounting process, it is also possible to remove the visual after it has been mounted. You can reheat the mounted visual and while it is still hot slip a razor blade between the visual and the backing and peel the visual away from the backing material. Fotoflat is another of the family of dry mount adhesives and is used to bond two adjacent surfaces using heat and pressure.

OVERSIZED MT-5 OR FOTOFLAT MOUNT

ORIGINAL   TURN/TACK   TURN   TRIM

SELECT BACKING AND POSITION VISUAL.

TACK   COOK HALF   COOK HALF   INSPECT

OVERSIZED DRY MOUNTING.

Sometimes it is desirable to mount very large materials. Maps, posters, enlargements on newsprint or other oversized visuals may be successfully mounted to either rigid backing materials or even to cloth using dry mount adhesives. For mounting these visuals to a rigid backing such as railroad board or even wood, you should use MT-5 dry mount tissue or Fotoflat. To mount these materials to cloth backing you should use Fotoflat or Chartex, which we will explore in the next few pages. While both MT-5 and Fotoflat do come in rolls up to 36″ wide, it is more common to stock the 11 × 14″ sheets, so this is what we will discuss.

First turn the oversized visual face down on a clean surface that will not be damaged by heat. Place sheets of either Fotoflat or MT-5 onto the back of the visual so that they touch but do not overlap. Tack the tissue to the visual by applying heat (tacking iron) directly onto the tissue. While it may be enough to tack the tissue once in the center of each sheet, you can also tack at the edges where they are butted together. It is essential that you ensure there are no wrinkles created by this tacking, as they will transfer to the visual when heat and pressure are applied.

When the back of the visual is completely covered with the dry mounting tissue, turn it over and trim the visual and tissue to the desired size. There are a number of tools that can be used in this trimming process: scissors, paper cutters, and single-edged razor blades. I personally prefer the single-edged razor blades. When these are combined with rulers with a metal edge, it is relatively easy to make clean straight cuts and to ensure that the visual and tissue backing are trimmed to the same size.

Position the trimmed visual/tissue sandwich onto the desired backing and tack it in place at diagonally opposite corners. Now we come to a major problem, adhering the visual to the backing. The dry mount press is normally too small to mount these oversized visuals. If you are using MT-5 dry mount tissue it is best to use the dry mount press, and you will need to put the visual into the press a part at a time. When you do this, make sure that each time you put it into the press you are overlapping a portion that has previously been adhered. This will insure a successful mount without wrinkles. If you are using Fotoflat dry mount tissue you can also use the dry mount press. However, it must be set at 180 degrees for the Fotoflat and not the 225 degrees used for MT-5. But Fotoflat can also be adhered using a regular home iron set at the rayon temperature setting. Just cover the visual with a clean newsprint and simply iron the visual to the backing.

As with any dry mounting process, you can ensure success in moist climates if you will dry the visual out before you begin the mounting process. Just place it into the dry mount press after covering it with clean newsprint, or cover it with newsprint and iron out any excess moisture. This process will result in a permanent mounting of an oversized visual to a rigid or cloth backing.

CHARTEX DRY MOUNTING:

FLUSH EDGE CHARTEX MOUNTING

 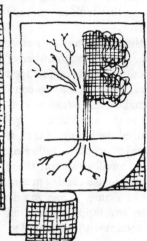  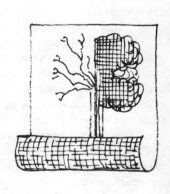

BACK & TACK   TRIM   ADHERE   UTILIZE

EXPOSED EDGE CHARTEX MOUNTING

THE PINE TREE

SELECT   TRIM   SELECT/ADHERE   UTILIZE

CHARTEX DRY MOUNTING

Chartex dry mounting is used when it is desirable to adhere a visual to a cloth backing. In this case the Chartex is both the adhesive and the backing material. Actually, Chartex is a cloth that has been coated on one side with a wax adhesive similar to that used in the Fotoflat dry mounting tissue. This means that for any Chartex mounting you will need: 1) the visuals to be mounted, 2) the Chartex that you will mount it to, and 3) the tools necessary to trim and adhere the visuals to the Chartex. There are two different ways that Chartex can be used. First, the flush edged Chartex mount, and secondly, the exposed edge Chartex mount. Let's begin with the flush edged Chartex mount.

In this application we simply want to adhere the visual to a cloth backing, and we do not care about the final size of the mounted visual. Normally visuals used in the Chartex process are large, but the real key is the selection of a visual that will not be damaged by heat or pressure. Place the visual down on the Chartex. Make sure that the adhesive side of the Chartex is toward the visual. Generally speaking, the adhesive side will be smoother, but if you're not sure, apply a little heat to check its adhesive quality. With the visual in place over the Chartex, apply a little heat with a tacking iron or a home iron set at the rayon temperature. To avoid damaging the visual it is advisable to place a scrap of newsprint over the visual during this tacking process. With the visual temporarily adhered to the Chartex, you can now trim the visual/Chartex sandwich to the desired size and format. There are a number of tools that can be used for this trimming, but it is essential that the visual and the Chartex be trimmed to exactly the same size—no exposed edges. Then cover the trimmed sandwich with clean newsprint and either place it in a dry mount press that has been preheated to 180 degrees or simply iron it on with a home iron set at the rayon temperature.

There are some slight variations when you desire an exposed edge Chartex mount. This is commonly desirable when you want flip chart pages of a common size but you are using visuals that are a variety of sizes. First, determine size of flip chart page that is desired. Then trim the visuals to the desired size and format. Place the trimmed visuals onto the trimmed Chartex in the positions that are desired. While you can tack them in place with a tacking iron, it is relatively easy to just hold them in place and iron them on. However, you may need to cover the visual, as the home iron may damage the surface. Just use a clean sheet of newsprint, but make sure that you do not iron beyond the edge of the visual as this will cause the newsprint or the iron to adhere to the exposed Chartex. The mounted visuals can be attached to a flip chart and used quite successfully.

Chartex is a very versatile adhesive, and visuals that are backed with this material can be folded or rolled. They can even be mounted to window blinds for pull-down charts or maps. It is an excellent material to preserve large maps or charts that are used over and over.

Wet Mounting

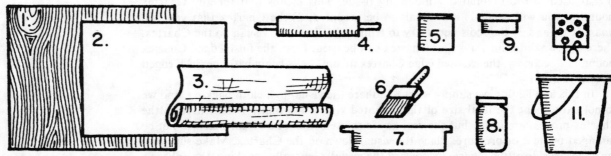

EQUIPMENT & MATERIALS: 1.) WET MOUNT BOARD, 2.) VISUAL, 3.) MUSLIN, 4.) ROLLING PIN, 5.) WALLPAPER ADHESIVE, 6.) PAINT BRUSH 3-4 IN., 7.) PAN, 8.) WHEAT FLOUR, 9.) THUMB TACKS, 10.) SPONGE, & 11.) BUCKET.

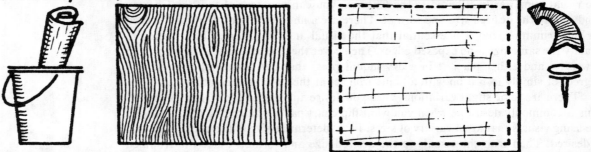

1. SOAK THE MUSLIN AND SMOOTH IT ON THE MOUNTING BOARD.

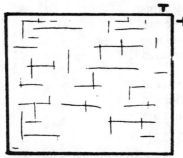
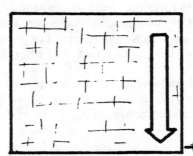
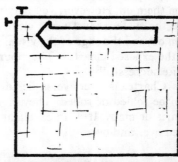

2. TACK ONE CORNER, STRETCH & TACK THE ADJACENT ONES.

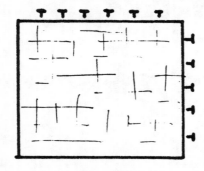
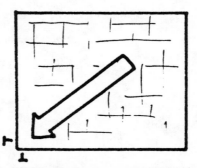
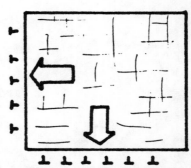

3. TACK BETWEEN.   4. TACK 4TH CORNER.   5. TACK BETWEEN.

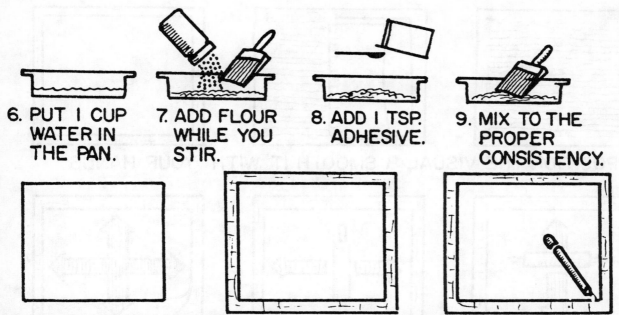

6. PUT I CUP WATER IN THE PAN.

7. ADD FLOUR WHILE YOU STIR.

8. ADD I TSP. ADHESIVE.

9. MIX TO THE PROPER CONSISTENCY.

10. THE VISUAL IS POSITIONED ON THE STRETCHED MUSLIN & REGISTER IT WITH A PENCIL.

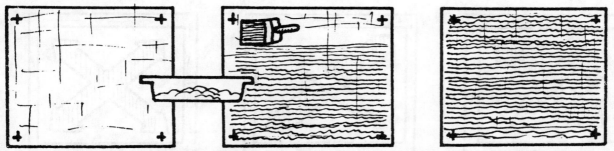

11. APPLY A SMOOTH, EVEN COAT OF PASTE TO THE MUSLIN.

12. SOAK THE VISAL LIBERALLY WITH WATER. FOLD IT IN HALF FOR MOVING TO THE COATED MUSLIN.

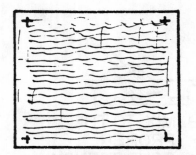 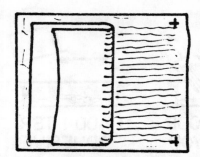 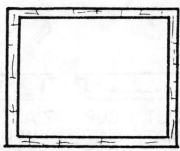

13. POSITION THE VISUAL & SMOOTH IT WITH YOUR HANDS.

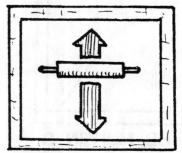 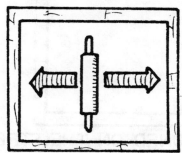 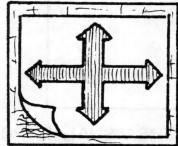

14. ROLL IT LIGHTLY IN A "PLUS" FROM THE CENTER OUT.

15. THEN ROLL IN AN "X", AGAIN FROM THE CENTER OUT.

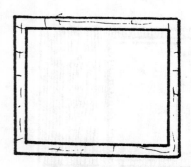  

16. COVER THE EDGES WITH STRIPS OF NEWSPRINT & THEN ROLL BEYOND THE EDGES IN A "STARBURST" PATTERN.

17. REMOVE THE NEWSPRINT, CLEAN MUSLIN, & DRY.

The Display Easel

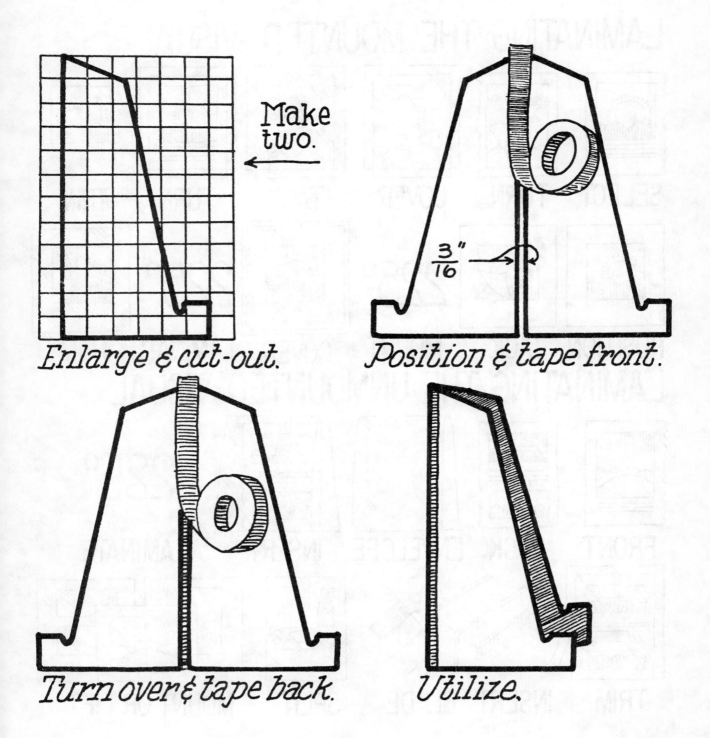

Make two. ←

Enlarge & cut-out.

3"/16

Position & tape front.

Turn over & tape back.

Utilize.

LAMINATION, SEALAMIN FILM:

LAMINATING THE MOUNTED VISUAL

SELECT	TURN	COVER	TACK	TURN	TRIM

 225°  225°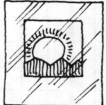

POSITION	TACK	MOUNT	COVER	LAMINATE	TRIM

LAMINATING THE UNMOUNTED VISUAL

 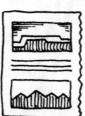 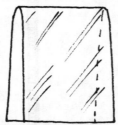 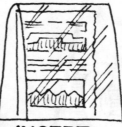 225°

FRONT	BACK	ENVELOPE	INSERT	LAMINATE

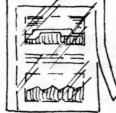 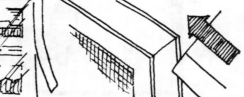 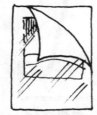 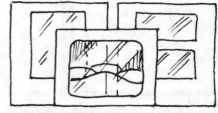

TRIM	INSERT	BLADE	SPLIT	MOUNT OR LIFT

34

LAMINATION, SEALAMIN FILM

The process of lamination is used when the additional protection of a transparent covering is desirable. While there are a number of different laminating films on the market and there is even special laminating equipment available, we will concentrate on laminating with Sealamin laminating film and using the dry mount press.

LAMINATING THE MOUNTED VISUAL

Often it is desirable to laminate a visual that has been mounted to a rigid backing such as railroad board. It is essential that the *mounting* process be done with MT-5 dry mounting tissue. The additional heat (225 degrees) may damage either rubber cement or Fotoflat mounts. Also, the visual must be selected with the heat and pressure in mind. Once the visual is selected, turn it face down on a clean surface, cover it with MT-4 and tack it in place. Turn the visual/tissue sandwich over and trim it to the desired size and format. Position it on the backing material and tack it to the railroad board by lifting a corner and tacking the exposed tissue to the backing. Then lift the diagonally opposite corner and tack that exposed tissue to the backing. Cover the tacked visual with clean newsprint and place in a dry mount press at 225 degrees for one to three minutes. If you are in a moist climate, you should dry the visual out before the mounting process. After the mounted visual has cooled, cover it with Sealamin laminating film. While Sealamin does come in a variety of widths, the common format is a roll that is 11 1/8" wide. This will work quite nicely with the standard 11 × 14" railroad board. Make sure that the dull side of the Sealamin is down (toward the face of the visual) and that there is approximately a 1" overlap at the top and bottom. Fold these over and tack them to the back of the backing. Then cover the visual with clean, smooth newsprint and place in a dry mount press that has been preheated to 225 degrees. Cook the lamination for 3–5 minutes. Trim away any excess lamination film, and you have successfully laminated a mounted visual.

Laminating an unmounted visual is even simpler. Dry the visual out in the dry mount press. Make an envelope of laminating film, and with the dull surface inside, insert the visual to be laminated. Note that you should not trim the visual you are laminating at this time. Place the materials into a newsprint envelope and cook in a dry mount press at 225 degrees for 3–5 minutes. If you want to use the visual as is, you can just trim the lamination down to the desired size and use it. However, if you want something a little different, you can split the page. By inserting the dull corner of a single edged razor blade between the two layers of laminating film, you can often separate the corners of the visual. Then simply grasp these corners, and with a smooth steady pull you can split the page so that you end up with the front page in one hand and the back page in another. This works best with visuals printed on heavy paper stock. These split pages can then be mounted to railroad board with Fotoflat, or they can be soaked in water to produce lifted overhead transparencies, which we will cover in more detail in the transparency section.

LAMINATION, PRESSURE FILM:

LAMINATING THE MOUNTED VISUAL

  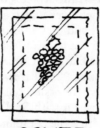  

SELECT   TURN   COVER   TACK   TURN   TRIM

 225°

POSITION   TACK   MOUNT   PEEL   ADHERE   BURNISH

LAMINATING THE UNMOUNTED VISUAL

  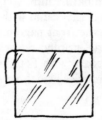 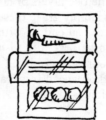 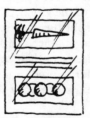 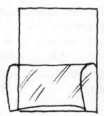

FRONT   BACK   PEEL   ADHERE   BURNISH   PEEL

ADHERE   BURNISH   TRIM   INSERT   SPLIT   MOUNT

LAMINATION, PRESSURE FILM

Many times it is desirable to mount materials that might be damaged by an application of heat and pressure. In this case, where the Sealamin laminating film is inappropriate, you can use a type of pressure sensitive film. Basically, this material is a sheet of acetate that has been backed with an adhesive similar to rubber cement. There are many brands of this pressure sensitive laminating film, and a good rule of thumb is the more costly they are, the better they are.

LAMINATING THE MOUNTED VISUAL

One advantage of the pressure sensitive laminating film is that the mounted visual can be adhered with any mounting technique. On the opposite page we are showing it mounted with MT-5 dry mount tissue, but it could also be mounted with rubber cement, Fotoflat or even Chartex. Select the appropriate visual and turn it face down on a clean surface. Cover it with the MT-5 (as shown) or Fotoflat or apply a coating of rubber cement. If you are using a dry adhesive, tack it in place then turn it over and trim the visual to the desired size and format. If you are using rubber cement, the visual is trimmed before you apply the rubber cement to the back of the visual. Then position the tissue-visual sandwich on the backing and tack it in place at diagonally opposite corners. Place it in a dry mount press that has been preheated to the appropriate temperature (180 degrees for Fotoflat or 225 degrees for MT-5). When the visual is mounted you are ready to laminate it with the pressure sensitive laminating film. First, cut a sheet of the film slightly larger than the backing material. Next, peel away the paper that is adhered to the adhesive side of the laminating film. This needs to be done carefully. Then, beginning at the top, apply the laminating film to the mounted visual and follow by burnishing it carefully.

LAMINATING THE UNMOUNTED VISUAL

In some instances you may want to protect images that are printed on opposite sides of the same page. DO NOT TRIM THE VISUAL. Simply cut two sheets of laminating film slightly larger than the visual; peel away the backing of one and adhere it to the front of the visual to be laminated. Then peel away the backing from the second sheet of laminating film and adhere it to the back of the visual. It is advisable to burnish each side separately. Burnish until the frosted appearance has disappeared completely throughout the surface of the visual. Last, you can trim the visual and laminating film to the desired size and format. While you can stop at this point, it is possible to go one step further. If it is desirable to see both sides of the visual at the same time, you can split the page. WARNING: THIS WILL WORK BEST WITH VISUALS THAT ARE PRINTED ON HEAVY PAPER. Insert the dull corner of a razor blade between the two layers of laminating film and separate them. With the corners separated, grasp the corners, and with a slow, steady pull separate the front from the back. You will end up with the front in one hand and the back in another. This split page can be mounted with Fotoflat, or it can be used to produce overhead transparencies through the lifting process described in the overhead section.

Passe Partout Preparation

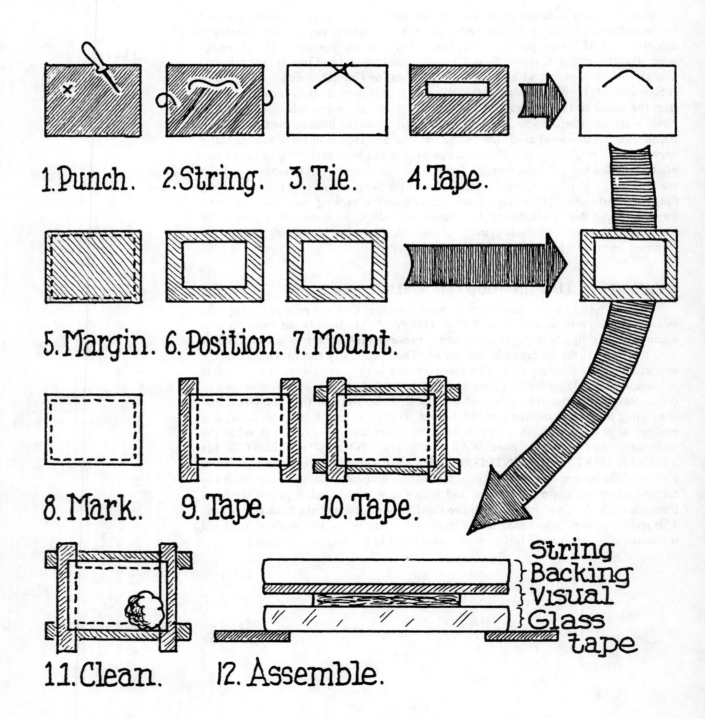

1. Punch. 2. String. 3. Tie. 4. Tape.

5. Margin. 6. Position. 7. Mount.

8. Mark. 9. Tape. 10. Tape.

11. Clean. 12. Assemble.

String
} Backing
} Visual
} Glass
tape

The process of Passe Partout is used when it is desirable to mount visual materials behind glass for wall hanging. Basically, it is framing a picture with tape.

This page of verbal information is related to the series of diagrams on the following pages. It is suggested that you familiarize yourself with both the written instructions and the visualization of these instructions before you actually begin the process of Passe Partout. It is hoped that once you have become quite familiar with the process, the visual portion will serve as a quick reference during the actual production.

Passe Partout framing occurs in four stages: (1) preparing the backing, (2) preparing the visual, (3) applying the tape and assembling the components, and (4) cutting and folding the corners.

STAGE ONE: *Preparing the backing*

Select a heavy backing material the same size as the glass. Punch two holes with an ice pick or awl. Thread string through the holes and tie it with a square knot on the other side. Apply tape over the string on the inside portion of the backing materials. Naturally, the orientation of the backing must fit the orientation of the visual to be mounted.

STAGE TWO: *Preparing the visual*

Select a backing board the same size as the glass. Position and mount the visual to this backing, making sure that you remember that there will be a margin of tape around the edge. This margin is usually about 1/4″. You may use any mounting technique you desire. You may even decide to cut a mask to fit over the visual.

STAGE THREE: *Preparing the glass*

Using china marking or grease pencils, mark the margins on the glass. Cut strips of tape about 2″ longer than the sides and apply them to the side opposite the margin marks, which you can use as a guide. It is usually best to lay the tape on the working surface with the sticky side up and then apply the glass to the tape. Apply the sides first, then the top and bottom. Clean off the margin lines before you assemble the components. Place the visual on top of the glass with the visual down. Then place the backing on the top with the hanging string up. The next two stages are the most difficult and will require the most effort on your part.

STAGE FOUR: *Cutting and folding the corners*

Beginning with the lower right hand corner, make your first cut. It is parallel to the side and extends from the corner. The second cut is also parallel to the side but is out from the glass a distance equal to the thickness of the components (glass, mounted visual, backing). The third cut extends from the second cut and is parallel to the bottom of the glass. It will allow you to remove the portion of tape shown in step 16. Repeat this process with the lower left hand corner. Turn the components around 180° and cut the two top corners just as you did the two bottom corners. Your finished product should look like the drawing in step 17. Now we will fold the corners. Beginning with the sides (18), fold the right side over. You will have to hold the components tightly and use some pulling pressure to fold the tape over. Then fold the left side over. Next (19) fold in the flaps at each of the four corners. The final step is to fold over the top and bottom pieces of tape.

Passe Partout: cutting corners

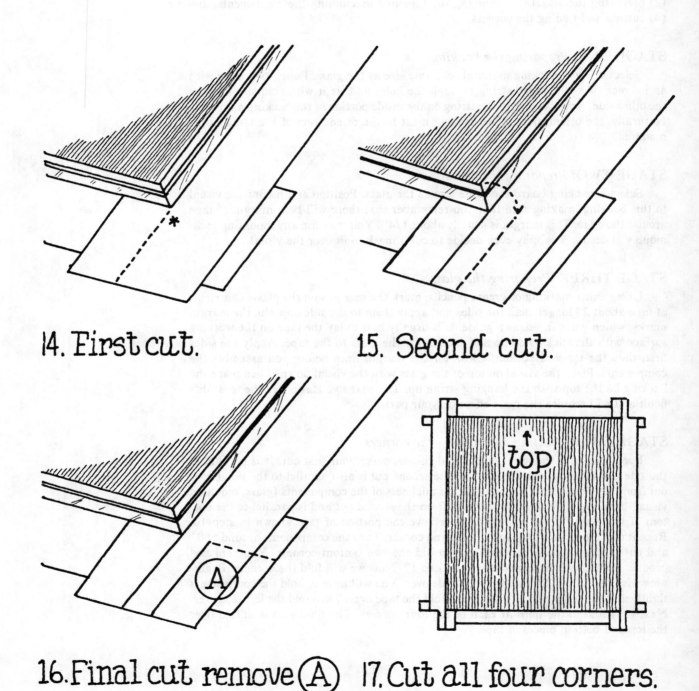

14. First cut.

15. Second cut.

16. Final cut remove Ⓐ

17. Cut all four corners.

Passe Partout: folding corners

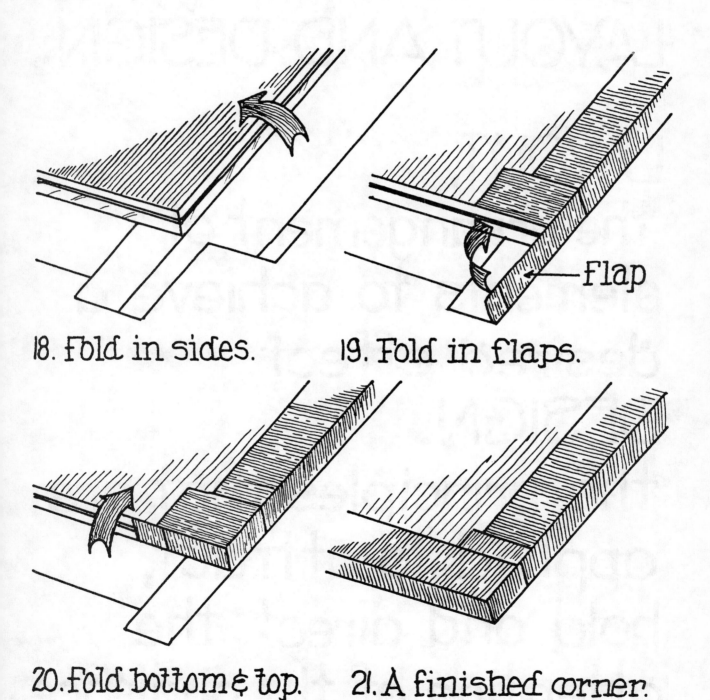

18. Fold in sides.

19. Fold in flaps.

Flap

20. Fold bottom & top.

21. A finished corner.

CHAPTER 3

LAYOUT AND DESIGN:

LAYOUT,
the arrangement of
elements to achieve a
desired effect.
DESIGN,
the principles that are
applied to attract,
hold and direct the
attention of the audience.

LAYOUT AND DESIGN

Layout and design are two activities designed to improve the effectiveness of your communications within the classroom. The term "layout" refers to the arrangement of the elements of the message to achieve a desired effect. The term "design" refers to the principles that are applied to attract, hold, and direct the attention of the audience. Thus you use design principles to arrive at a layout that will more effectively get your message across to your audience. In our society we are bombarded by a confusion of often conflicting messages; some we attend to and some we ignore. With the application of appropriate design principles and the evolution of related layouts, your messages should have a higher reliability in terms of attracting, holding, and directing the attention of your intended audience. Remember that the first 10 seconds of exposure to any message is vital. It is during this brief time that the audience makes up its mind to attend to or ignore what you have to say. Why do **you** watch the TV commercials or look at the ads in the magazines or newspapers? The same principles that are used to "grab" you can also be used to grab your audiences. Once you have their attention, how do you hold the audience? It's not enough to get their attention, our job is to transmit information, and this requires time. Can the physical arrangement of elements within a display hold the attention of the audience regardless of the content? Well, many people feel that it can, and there seem to be principles that will assist you in this effort. The next concern is that the members of the audience *read* the message the way you intend for it to be read. Again there are principles whereby you can literally control the way in which the members of the audience read your message.

To begin this process we first must become aware of the elements in the layout that we can manipulate. These normally consist of the headline, the visual or visuals, and the copy or captions. By the arrangement of these elements we can begin to achieve the effects we desire. In simple, static visuals this arrangement of elements is achieved through the development of a series of thumbnail sketches to select the desired configuration. The selected thumbnail is then transferred to a rough and finally to a comprehensive or the final art.

The selection of an appropriate arrangement is often determined by the application of appropriate design principles. The few that we will explore include balance, stimulus differential, grouping/separating, and sequencing. These are but a few of the design principles that can be used, but they are some of the more common. The application of these principles of design and the development of appropriate layouts will go a long way toward making your visual message materials more effective and your communications more predictable.

THE ELEMENTS OF A LAYOUT:

HEADLINE

VISUALS

COPY

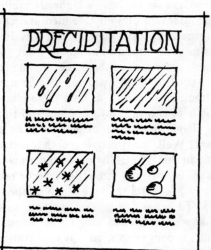

{ EQUAL EMPHASIS ON THE ELEMENTS RESULTS IN A POOR LAYOUT, USE SIZE FOR EMPHASIS.

DEVELOPING A LAYOUT:

THUMBNAILS:

A SERIES OF SMALL ROUGH SKETCHES OF DIFFERENT IDEAS FOR LAYOUTS. SELECT ONE.

ROUGHS:

ENLARGE THE SELECTED THUMBNAIL TO THE PROPER SIZE OR RATIO.

FINAL ART:

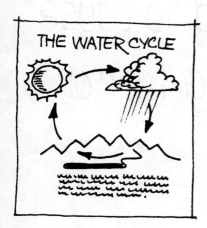

THE WATER CYCLE

POLISH THE VISUAL AND ADD ACTUAL HEADLINES AND BODY COPY. A FINISHED PRODUCT.

PRINCIPLES OF GOOD DESIGN:

BALANCE: The arrangement of elements to achieve stability.

STIMULUS DIFFERENTIAL: That which is different in the environment is attended to.

GROUPING/SEPARATING: Principles of proximity used to cause items to be perceived as together or apart.

SEQUENCING:

GOOD BALANCE IN A LAYOUT:

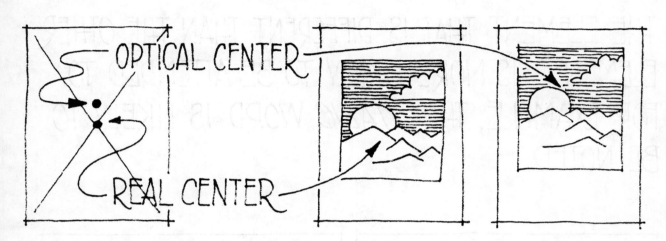

OPTICAL CENTER

REAL CENTER

FORMAL BALANCE

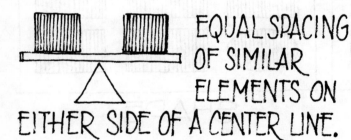

EQUAL SPACING OF SIMILAR ELEMENTS ON EITHER SIDE OF A CENTER LINE.

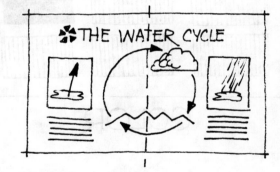

THE WATER CYCLE

INFORMAL BALANCE

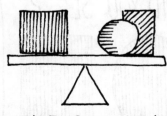

THE ARRANGEMENT OF UNEQUAL ELEMENTS ON EITHER SIDE OF A CENTER LINE.

THE WATER CYCLE

47

STIMULUS DIFFERENTIAL:

THE ELEMENT THAT IS DIFFERENT THAN THE OTHER ELEMENTS IS MORE LIKELY TO BE ATTENDED TO. FOR EXAMPLE, THE *ITALIC* WORD IS LIKELY TO BE NOTED.

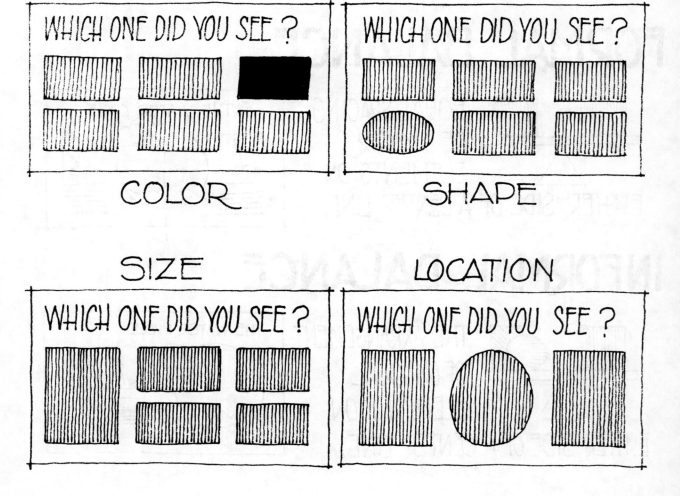

COLOR

SHAPE

SIZE

LOCATION

48

ORGANIZING THE ELEMENTS:

USING PROXIMITY

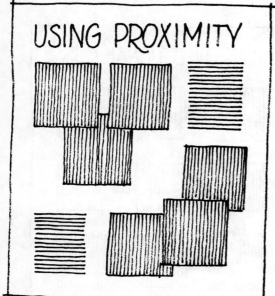

USING SHAPE

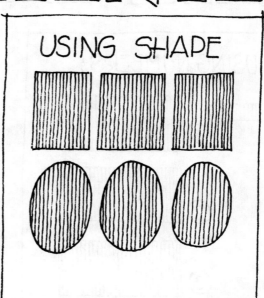

WHICH ELEMENTS IN THESE DISPLAYS APPEAR TO BELONG TOGEATHER? WHY?

USING COLOR

USING BACKGROUND

SEQUENCING THE ELEMENTS:

USING NUMBERS:

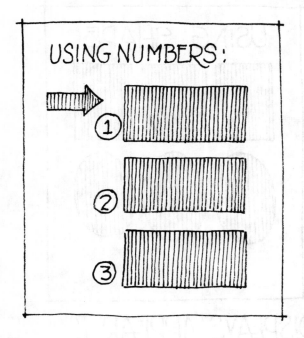

USING DIRECTIONAL CUES

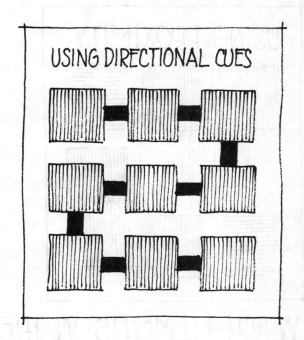

USING THE VISUALS

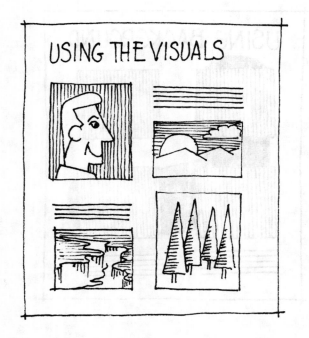

USING DESIGN ELEMENTS

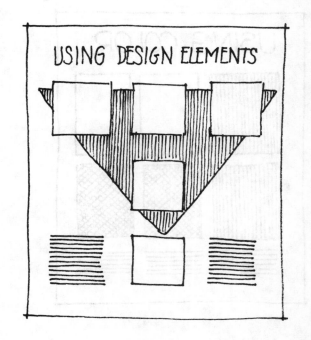

50

CHAPTER 4

LETTERING TECHNIQUES

CHAPTER 4
LETTERING TECHNIQUES

ABCDEFGHIJKLMNOPQRST

LETTERING TECHNIQUES

Lettered materials are an excellent supplement to visualized instructional materials. While a picture may be worth a thousand words, a single word or line of lettering may serve to make the communication more precise. Visual materials are often open to multiple interpretations, and the captions or body copy that is provided can direct the audience to read the visuals the way you want them read.

Our first concern is with the equipment and techniques necessary to form the individual letters that make up the words that we want to use to direct the audience in how to read the visual materials. There are literally millions of lettering techniques, and we only have space to deal with a few of them. Our concern is to pick the right technique to fit the size of the letters desired and to fit our pocketbook. This brief chart may be of some assistance in selecting the proper lettering system.

	Lettering sizes	Approximate costs	Unusual Characteristics
Hand lettering with the Speedball	1/2″–5″	Low	Requires practice
Hand lettering with feltpen	2″–7″	Low	Requires practice
Cutout lettering used as stencils	1″–5″	Moderate	Many available
Cardboard/plastic stencils	1″–8″	Moderate	Various styles
Unistencil	5″–24″	Very low	Single style
Wrico stencils	1/2″–6″	Moderate	Best for larger lettering
Mechanical lettering The Leroy system	1/16″–2″	Expensive	Excellent quality
Mechanical lettering Letterguide system	1/16″–3″	Expensive	Variations
Dry transfer	1/8″–5″	Very expensive	Multitude of styles and sizes

So the first step in the process is to identify the lettering technique that meets the particular needs you have. For very large posters and banners you may need to use the Unistencil developed by Harvey Fry. For small lettering for handouts and transparencies you may need to use the mechanical Leroy sytem or, if you can afford it, the expensive Dry Transfer system.

But whatever system you select, you also need to make sure that the lettering you produce is readable. There are a number of factors that determine if lettering can be easily read by the intended audience. The spacing of the letters, words, and lines of lettering makes a great difference in readability. The size of the lettering is also important in terms of readability. The style of the letters and the contrast between the color of the lettering and the background will influence this readability of the captions, headlines and body copy that you produce to supplement the visual elements within your instructional materials. The next few pages will deal with these readability factors and how to use them effectively.

READABILITY
* SPACING:

EQUAL DISTANCE

MECHANICAL SPACING
OPTICAL SPACING

EQUAL AREA

LINE SPACING

KEEP TO HEIGHT OF CAPITAL LETTER OR LESS.

* SIZE:

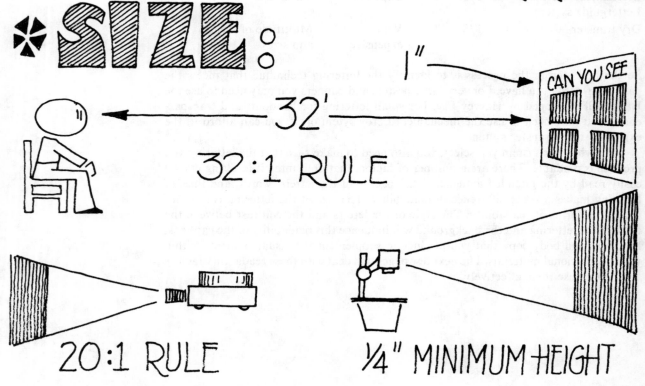

1"

CAN YOU SEE

32'

32:1 RULE

20:1 RULE

¼" MINIMUM HEIGHT

READABILITY

*STYLE

Mistral

𝕺𝖑𝖉 𝕰𝖓𝖌𝖑𝖎𝖘𝖍

Optima

Palace Script

Playbill

Pretorian

PROFIL

QUENTIN

Franklin Gothic Cond. Reverse

Futura Light

Futura Medium

Futura Demi Bold

Futura Bold

Futura Bold Condensed

Futura Extra Bold

Futura Medium Italic

Futura Bold Italic

Gill Extra Bold

*CONTRAST

DARK LETTERING IS BEST AGAINST A LIGHT COLORED BACKGROUND.

LIGHT LETTERING IS BEST AGAINST A DARK BACKGROUND.

SHADOWED LETTERS CAN BE QUITE EFFECTIVE ALSO.

HAND LETTERING, THE SET-UP:

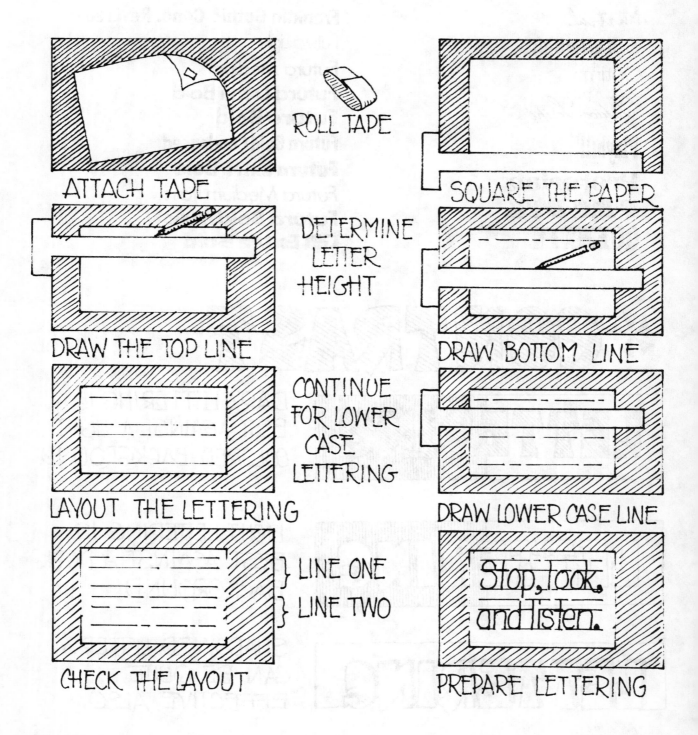

ATTACH TAPE

ROLL TAPE

SQUARE THE PAPER

DRAW THE TOP LINE

DETERMINE LETTER HEIGHT

DRAW BOTTOM LINE

LAYOUT THE LETTERING

CONTINUE FOR LOWER CASE LETTERING

DRAW LOWER CASE LINE

CHECK THE LAYOUT

} LINE ONE
} LINE TWO

Stop, look, and listen.

PREPARE LETTERING

HAND LETTERING, THE SET-UP

Hand lettering with either the Speedball pens or felt pens is one of the least expensive types of lettering you can produce. However, like most things that don't cost a lot, it does require practice and the development of skills on your part. Preceding the actual formation of the letters, it is necessary to organize the materials to be lettered and to prepare guide lines for your lettering. The opposite page suggests one approach that has proved successful.

You will be using a drawing board and a T-square for this process, and your first concern is attaching the materials to be lettered to the drawing board. Pins or thumb tacks can be used, but they damage both the visual and the drawing board. I suggest you use masking tape. If you just tape across a corner of the visual to be lettered, you will probably damage the edges when you remove the tape. I suggest that you take the masking tape and make a roll with the sticky sides out. This is then placed under the visual, where its removal will not create damage. Make sure that when you adhere the visual to the drawing board you line up the visual so that its edges are parallel to the drawing board. Use a T-square for this purpose. Hold the head of the T-square tight against the edge of the drawing board and then align the bottom edge of the visual with the T-square.

Next, determine the size of letters you desire and where you want them to appear on the finished product. On the opposite page we are going to letter a simple phrase, "Stop, look, and listen." We want to use both upper case (capital) and lower case letters, and we want the lettering to appear in two equal lines. First we draw the top and bottom of the capital letters, making sure to draw these lines lightly as we will want to erase them later. We also make sure that the space between the lines of lettering is less than the height of the capital letters. In the example we are using "tight" line spacing.

Since we are using lower case lettering, we will also need to add guide lines for the tops of most lower case letters. In the example I want them to be quite large, so they are above the middle of the upper case guide lines.

With the guide lines in place we can now sketch in the actual letters. This must be done lightly, because these will be erased with the guide lines. If the sketch does not come out exactly as we want in terms of spacing, we *do not erase and redo*. The erasing will distort the surface of the paper and create problems when we ink in the letters. Rather, we adjust when actually inking in the lettering.

At this point our lettering should be parallel; the guide line will have seen to that. We have a good idea of where the actual letters will need to go. We have done the guide lines and the letter sketches very lightly so that we will be able to erase them without damaging the finished lettering. Now we are ready to actually ink in the letters, and to do this we may use either the Speedball pen system with India ink or the felt pen system with various colored felt pens. The next few pages will provide directions for this.

SPEEDBALL HAND LETTERING:

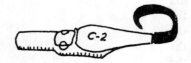 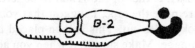 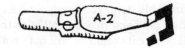

  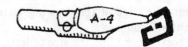

SPEEDBALL TIPS COME IN DIFFERENT SIZES AND STYLES.

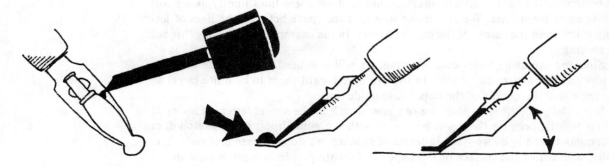

LOADING AND USING THE SPEEDBALL PEN TIPS.

CLEANING THE SPEEDBALL PEN TIPS WITH PAPER.

SPEEDBALL HAND LETTERING

The Speedball system consists of a variety of pen tips, pen holders and black or colored India inks. With practice it can produce high quality hand lettering that will enhance your visual materials. The Speedball pen tips come in different shapes and sizes. The shapes are designated by a letter code printed on the brass portion of the pen tip. The A style pens are square and are excellent for specialty alphabets. The B style tips are round and produce excellent Gothic lettering. The C style tips are chisel shaped and produce Roman style letters. The sizes of the pens are designated by a number code from 0–6. In this case the larger numbers produce smaller (thinner) lines. Thus a B–O pen will produce a very broad line while a B–6 will produce a very narrow line. Pick the right tip for the type of lettering that you want to produce.

The Speedball tips actually come in two parts that are crimped together. The steel part is the pen nib that transfers the ink to the paper, and the brass part forms a reservoir which holds the ink. Do not dip the pen directly into the ink supply. This will cause a bead of ink to form on the tip, that will transfer to the paper as an unwanted blob. Rather, use the dropper-stopper that is part of the ink supply. Load a supply of ink into the stopper by depressing then releasing the rubber portion on the top. Then hold it over the space between the steel and brass portion of the Speedball pen and deposit a drop or two of ink into the pen's reservoir. This will need to be refilled if your lettering is of any length or size. It is advisable to do this loading over a piece of scrap material rather than your visual, as sometimes the ink drops on through rather than remaining in the reservoir.

The Speedball pen is used a little differently than most lettering pens. For the best results you want the tip of the pen to be flat on the paper. This may mean a slight adjustment in the manner in which you normally hold the pen. It is suggested that you practice with the pens before you do your final inking on the visual. With practice comes proficiency.

The Speedball pens are expensive and should be cared for. When you buy them, they may have been coated with a film of oil or other preservative. This needs to be removed for the ink to flow through the pen properly. I have found that simply passing the tip of the pen through the flame of a match will effectively burn away the oil. If it is a used pen tip you may need to scrape off the excess ink (especially in the reservoir) with the dull edge of a single-edged razor blade. Be especially careful not to bend the brass portion of the pen tip. To avoid having to scrape off excess dry ink you should clean the pen tips after each use. I do not suggest washing, as this tends to rust and carrode the tips. Rather, I simply use a scrap of notebook paper and insert it between the steel and brass parts and draw it through, removing the excess ink. It's a little messy, but it will leave the pen tip ready for the next use.

SAMPLE SPEEDBALL ALPHABETS:

ABCDEFGHIJ

KLMNOPQRS

TUVWXYZ &!?

abcdefghijkl

mnopqrstuvw

xyz 1234567890

ABCDEFGHIJKLMNOPQ
RSTUVWXYZ 123456789
abcdefghijklmno
pqrstuvwxyz AB
CDEFGHIJKLM
NOPQRSTUVW
XYZ 1234567890
script ABCDEFGHIJ
KLMNOPQRSTUVWXYZ 3
EEE RR SSS gg GGG

FELT PEN HAND LETTERING:

BROAD TIP

FINE TIP

CHISEL TIP

ROMAN

GOTHIC

ROMAN

BROAD TIP PEN LETTERING STYLES

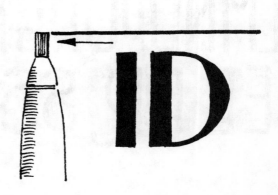

FELT PEN HAND LETTERING

Felt pens come in a variety of tips and colors. As shown on the opposite page, the more common pen tips are: 1) the broad tip, 2) the fine tip, and 3) the chisel tip. The fine tipped pens are becoming more and more common and are available from standard to extra fine point sizes. The broad and chisel tipped felt pens will produce a good quality of Roman style lettering from 1″ to 6″ tall. The fine tipped felt pens will produce a Gothic style of hand lettering; the size will depend on the fineness of the tip size.

In addition to variations in pen style and size and the colors that are available, the felt pens also come with two different types of ink. The permanent ink will normally mark on any smooth surface (including acetate) and leave a permanent image. The water color inks will not adhere to acetate quite as well, but they work quite well on paper for lettering purposes. If your concern is with hand lettering on paper or railroad board, you will want to make the selection on the basis of cost and quality of the color and line.

Selecting an appropriate surface for the lettering is also very important. Because both the water based and the permanent inks are liquid, you need to be concerned with how this liquid will react to the paper surface that you are lettering on. If the surface is slick then the ink will not penetrate into the paper and you should get lettering with nice clean edges. If, on the other hand, you use a porous paper such as newsprint the ink will penetrate into the paper, which will act like a blotter, and the edges of the lettering will be rough and difficult to control. Try the pens on a sample of the paper you will be using before you do any actual lettering.

While there is no real "trick" to using the fine tipped felt pens, proper lettering with the broad tipped and chisel tipped pens may need some practice. Notice the shape of the broad tip shown on the opposite page. Holding the felt pen so that the angled edge is parallel to the guide lines will produce a Roman style of lettering that has nice square tops and bottoms. In the example next to this you can see that it is also possible to hold the pen tip at somewhat of an angle to the guide lines and produce a more distinctive type of Roman lettering.

One other problem that you should be aware of in felt pen hand lettering is the fact that many of the lighter colors of ink are transparent. This means that guide lines and sketch lines will show through them and be next to impossible to erase. However, with practice you can even develop the skill necessary to do the lettering directly— without resorting to the guide lines and sketch letters we spoke of in the hand lettering set-up selection. This is perhaps the least expensive type of lettering that is available to you, and while it does require practice to master, it is well worth the effort in terms of the professional captions, headlines, and copy that you can produce.

SAMPLE FELT PEN ALPHABETS:

ABCDEFGHIJKLMNO
PQRSTUVWXYZ USING A FINE TIP FELT PEN.

ABCDEFGHI
JKLMNOPQ
RSTUWXY

USING BROAD TIP FELT PEN.

64

abcdefgh
ijklmnopq
rstuvwxy

abcdefghijklmn
opqrstuvwxyz
italics *serif* etc.

Be consistent in your letter formation.

CUTOUT LETTERING:

TYPES OF CUTOUT LETTERS:

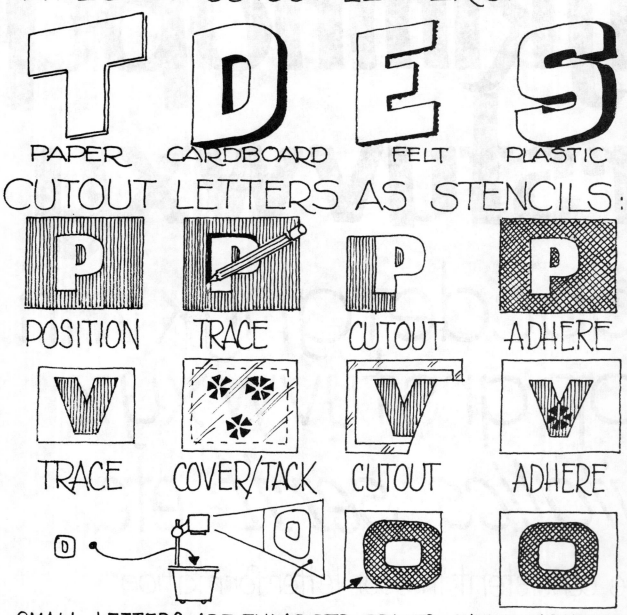

T PAPER **D** CARDBOARD **E** FELT **S** PLASTIC

CUTOUT LETTERS AS STENCILS:

P POSITION **P** TRACE **P** CUTOUT **P** ADHERE

V TRACE **V** COVER/TACK **V** CUTOUT **V** ADHERE

O ... **O** ... **O**

SMALL LETTERS ARE ENLARGED, TRACED, CUTOUT, ADHERED.

CUTOUT LETTERING

Cutout letters are, as the name implies, letter shapes that have been cut from a variety of different materials. There are inexpensive cutout letters made from construction paper, slightly more expensive letters cut from cardboard, and expensive letters cut from felt, wood, or plastic. These cutout letters can be used directly or they can be used as stencils to produce other lettering. Using them directly is simply a matter of selecting the appropriate letters and adhering them to the surface you desire. This is rather expensive, and so we will concentrate on the use of cutout letters as stencils.

One way to use cutout letters as stencils is to place the letters in the configuration you desire and trace around them onto the surface. Then remove the cutout letters and ink in the pencil lines. You may want to color in the letters or leave them open; this is a simple and inexpensive way to produce medium to large lettering.

A second way to use cutout letters as stencils is to prepare them for rubber cement mounting. Simply position the letters desired onto the surface you want the letters to be cut from (construction paper, railroad board, etc.) and trace them onto this surface. Then cut the letters out, turn them face down and apply a coat of rubber cement. Then reposition them on the backing you desire and adhere them in place. This means that the original cutout letters can be used over and over again, and the copy letters can be produced from any desired materials.

If a more permanent adhesion is required you might use one of the dry adhesives (MT-5 or Fotoflat). Place the cutout on the surface you want the letters to be cut from (any surface that will not be damaged by heat and pressure) and trace the letter. Turn the material over and tack the dry mount tissue to the back. Use the area tacking technique to ensure that when you cut the letters out they will match with the tissue underneath. Once the letters are tacked to the materials, cut them out and position them on the backing. Tack them in place and either cook them in the dry mount press at the proper temperature for the adhesive you are using or iron them on if you are using Fotoflat. A very interesting effect can be created by using gift wrapping paper or wallpaper from sample books that the local wallpaper store is finished with. You can also cut out letters from complementary colors or patterns and mount them so that the bottom letter creates a shadow effect. If you want to do this, I suggest you cut out the pairs of letters at the same time to ensure that they are identical.

In the next few pages I am providing you with some sample alphabets that you can use to produce your own cutout letters. Just make a thermal transparency of these pages (see the overhead section) and project them onto the materials you desire. Trace the letters and cut them out. This way you can use these alphabets over and over and can produce cutout letters of almost any size you want.

CUTOUT ALPHABETS:

FOR TRACING AND ENLARGEMENT

ABCDEFGHIJ
KLMNOPQRS
TUVWXYZ

ABCDEFGHZ
JKLMNOPQI
RS TUVWXY

68

ABCDEFGHI
JKLMNOPQR
STUVWXYZ

ABCDEFGHIJ
KLMNOPQRS
TUVWXYZ

STENCIL (CARDBOARD OR PLASTIC)
LETTERING:

① DRAW A GUIDELINE
② LINE UP LETTERS

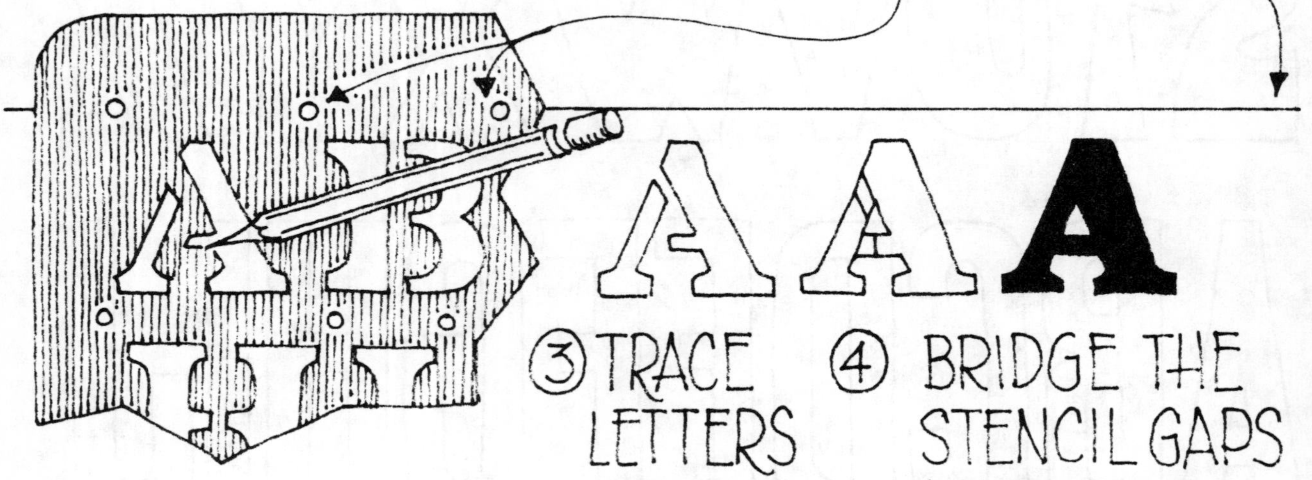

③ TRACE LETTERS WITH A PENCIL.

④ BRIDGE THE STENCIL GAPS AND COLOR AS DESIRED.

A's REGISTRATION

T's REGISTRATION

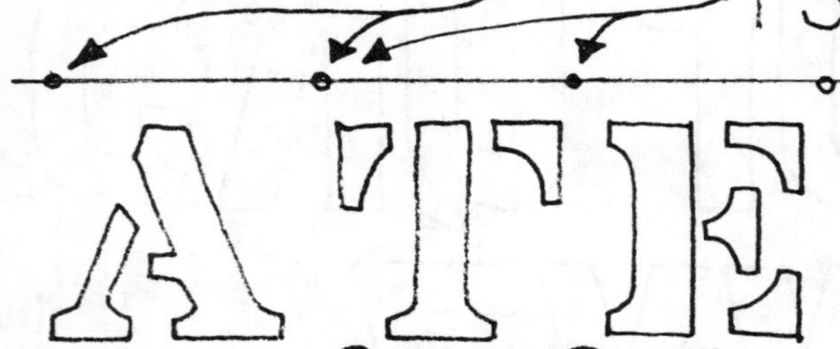

MECHANICAL SPACING

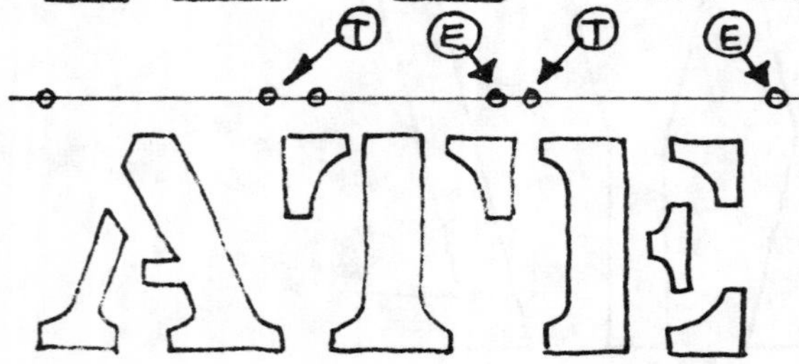

OPTICAL SPACING

STENCIL LETTERING

A moderately priced lettering system is the collection of plastic or cardboard stencils that is available at most stationery or art supply stores. These consist of sheets of plastic or cardboard with the letter shapes die cut from them. You may have to punch out the elements of the letters, but once you have, you have a system that will allow you to produce medium to large sized letters quite inexpensively.

When you examine these stencils you will notice that there are sets of small holes to the upper right and left of each letter. These holes are used to register the letter and, in many cases, to provide mechanical spacing. Because of these registration holes it is only necessary to draw a single guide line on the materials to be lettered. This line should be slightly above the top of the line of lettering that you desire. With the guide line on the materials, place the stencils over the material and line up the two registration holes of the first letter with this guide line. Then trace the letter with pencil (you will ink it in later). You will notice that the letters have the characteristic stencil configuration—they are not complete. You can either use them as is or bridge across the gaps to create a more complete letter.

With the first letter traced, you simply move to the next letter. If you want mechanical letter spacing, you will have to mark the registration holes on the first letter. Then position the second letter so that the left registration hole corresponds to the mark from the right registration hole of the first letter. Both registration holes must dissect the guide line. Now simply trace the second letter. Continue with this process until you have traced all of the lettering you want. Now you can ink the outline of the letters and color them in as desired. Erase the guide line and you have completed your lettering.

The technique described above will produce mechanical spacing that is similar to the example on the opposite page. If you prefer the optical spacing (and most people do), there is a slight modification of the process that is required. After you have traced the first letter, you use the registration marks of the second letter to align it but not to space it. Here is where the plastic stencils have a definite advantage. Now you can adjust the letters so that they are separated by an equal area rather than the equal distance used in mechanical spacing. Other than this the process is the same: trace the letters, ink the letters and erase the guide lines.

Cardboard and plastic stencils come in a variety of sizes and alphabet styles. Gothic and Roman are the most common styles, but there are some specialty alphabets available. Generally, the stencils do not go below 1″ and they are not easy to find above 6″ in height. But even with these limitations this type of stencil lettering can, with practice, produce professional looking lettering for your instructional materials.

THE UNISTENCIL SYSTEM:

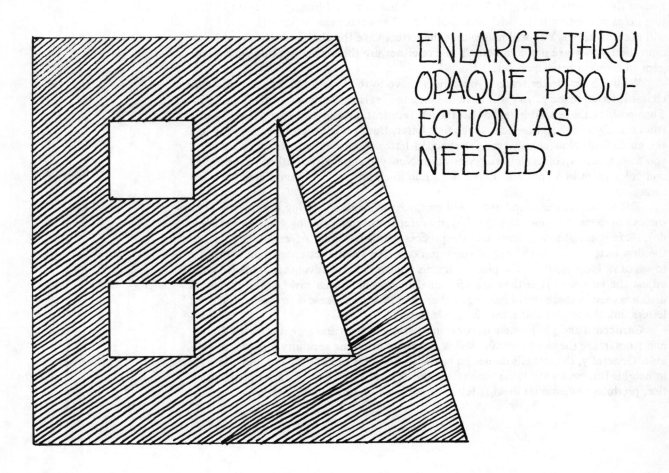

ENLARGE THRU OPAQUE PROJECTION AS NEEDED.

STENCIL   TRACE   ADAPT   OR   MODIFY

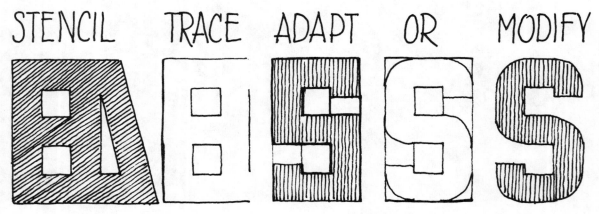

UNISTENCIL

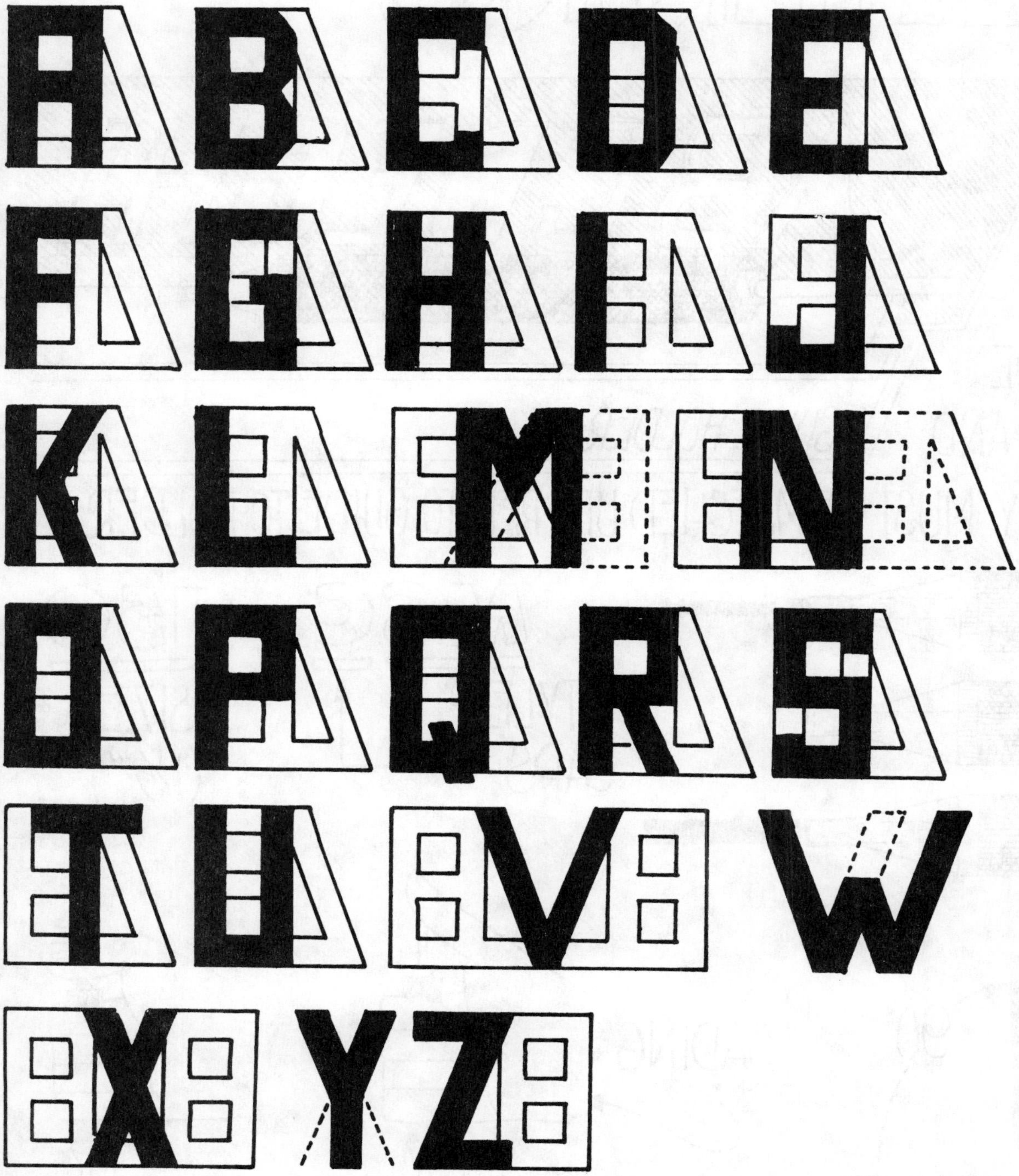

ABCDE
FGHIJ
KLMNO
PQRS
TUVW
XYZ

73

WRICO STENCIL LETTERING:

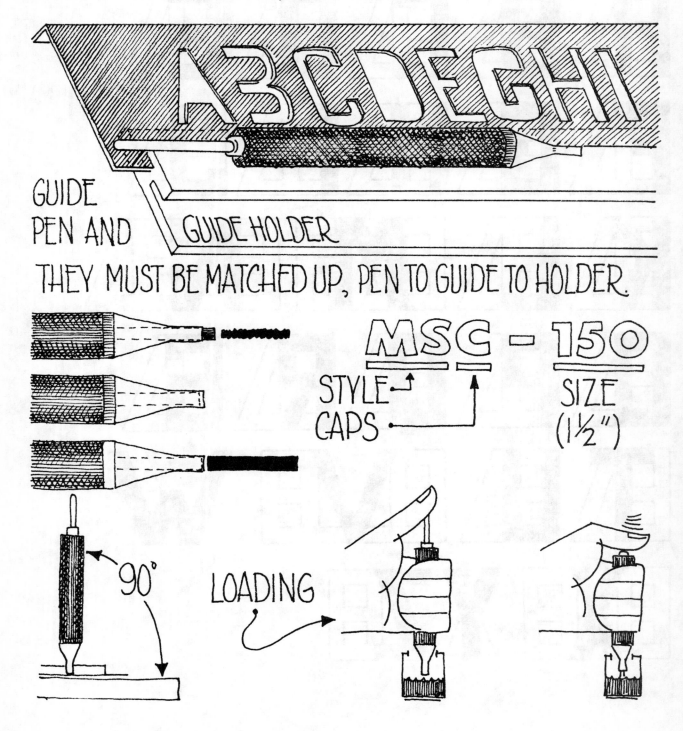

GUIDE PEN AND GUIDE HOLDER

THEY MUST BE MATCHED UP, PEN TO GUIDE TO HOLDER.

MSC - 150

STYLE →
CAPS →

SIZE (1½")

90°

LOADING

WRICO STENCIL LETTERING

Wrico lettering is actually a system of pens, guides and guide holders that is used to produce professional, medium to large format lettering. The key to success is to match the right pen to the guide and to select the right guide to produce the size and style of letters that you desire. Let's begin with the Wrico guides. These are large plastic (usually green) units with the letter cut out of them. Each guide has a code number that identifies the style, type and size of the lettering that is produced with that particular guide. In the example shown on the opposite page we have a Wrico guide with the code number MSC-150. The first letter or pair of letters tells what the style of the letters created by this particular guide is. In this case the MS style of letter is a common Gothic style letter. The last letter tells whether this guide will produce capital (C), lower case (L) or numerals (N). The number tells you the size of the letter that will be produced. In this case 150 means 1 1/2″. A good way to decipher this part of the code is simply to place the number over 100. Thus 150/100 = 1 1/2″, 100/100 = 1″ and 50/100 = 1/2″. So we know that the guide with the code MSC-150 will produce 1 1/2″ capital letters. Also on the guide you will find an indication of the size of pen that *must* be used. It will say "Use with brush pen B." The pens are designated by a letter: the A's produce narrower lines while the E's produce wider lines— use the pen that is called for on the guide. The pen is identified with a letter stamped on the steel tip.

In addition to the guide and the pen you will also need the guide holder. This is an aluminum sheet that is used to keep the Wrico guide off the surface that you are lettering on. If you do not use a guide holder the guide will smear the lettering as you slide it back and forth. The guide holder has one side for guides that are flat and a higher side for guides that have a bend at the top edge.

Now that you have all of the equipment, you are ready to begin the lettering process. First, we need to load the pen with India ink. This is done by depressing the plunger at the back of the pen and extending the brass tip into the ink supply. The ink will fill the grooves in the brass tip, and now all you have to do is adjust the tip so that the lines will be even on both edges. In the diagram on the opposite page you can see the effect if the tip is beyond the steel portion of the pen: the line is ragged and uneven. If the brass tip is too far inside the steel portion of the pen, the ink will not flow. There is a collar on the plunger of the pen that should be rotated until the ink flow is just right. Then place the guide in the guide holder and, holding the pen at a 90 degree angle to the paper, produce the letter. Note that some of the letters in the guide are not complete. For example, the B requires a vertical stroke that can be created using the vertical part of the letter D. Note that in the top part of the A and the D you just go around the edge; you do not try to fill in the open areas of the stencil. As with any other letter system, a little practice will allow you to produce professional looking lettering.

MECHANICAL LETTERING:

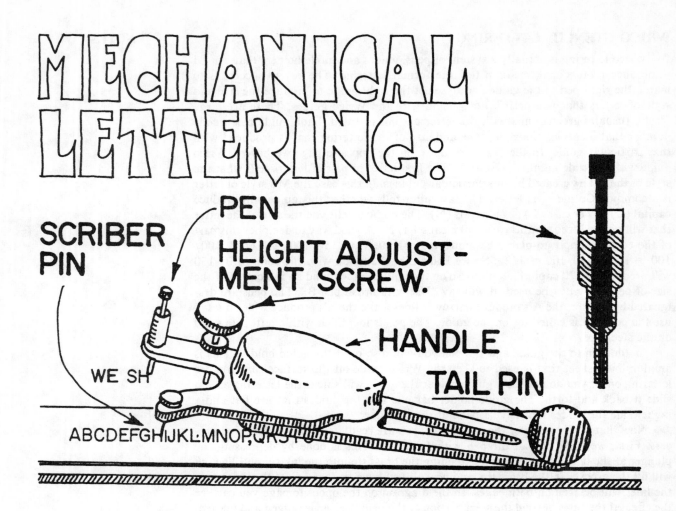

SCRIBER PIN

PEN

HEIGHT ADJUST-MENT SCREW.

HANDLE

TAIL PIN

WE SH

ABCDEFGHIJKLMNOPQRSTU

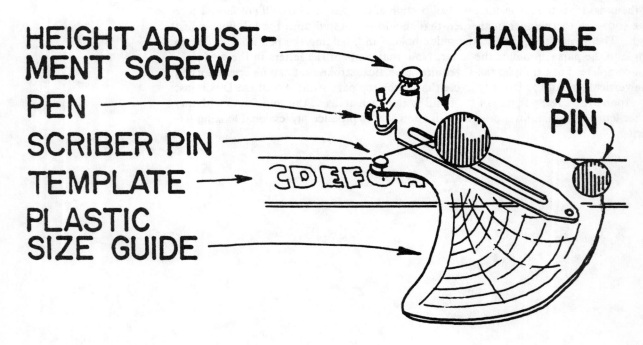

HEIGHT ADJUST-MENT SCREW.

PEN

SCRIBER PIN

TEMPLATE

PLASTIC SIZE GUIDE

HANDLE

TAIL PIN

CDEF

MECHANICAL LETTERING

There are a number of different mechanical lettering systems that can be used to produce very professional small to medium sized lettering. We will concentrate on two: 1) the Leroy system and 2) the Letterguide system. Both of these systems use a mechanical linkage between the template and the paper to transfer the letters.

The Leroy system consists of the Leroy scriber, the pen and the templates containing the engraved letters. The tail pin of the scriber fits into the tail pin slot of the template, and the scriber pin fits into the engraved letters. Tracing the letters transfers them to the paper through the pen that is placed in the upper arm of the scriber. The pens are coded and should be used as indicated on the templates. These pens come in two parts, the reservoir and the plunger. The reservoir is filled with ink, which flows through the pen as the plunger is raised when its tip hits the paper. This is why it is necessary to carefully adjust the height adjustment screw on the scriber so that the pen tip is riding properly on the paper.

The Leroy templates come in a wide variety of alphabets and sizes. Since the Leroy scriber will only reproduce the letters on the template, it is necessary to have a different template for each size of letter as well as for each style of letter desired. There is one adjustment that you can often make with the basic Leroy scriber. By adjusting the angle of the top arm of the scriber you can transform vertical letters into italics (slanted). But one of the basic disadvantages of this system is the fact that the necessary equipment is quite expensive.

The Letterguide system is a little more flexible. It has the same basic components: 1) the scriber, 2) the templates and 3) the pen. However, in this case the scriber can be adjusted to vary both the height and slope of the lettering produced from a single template. There is a plastic top on the Letterguide scriber, and by loosening the handle you can move a little red dot on the end of the scriber to any point along the grid. You can select smaller letter sizes, larger letter sizes, and a variety of slope angles. A second variation in the Letterguide system is the nature of the letters in the templates. While it is possible to interchange Leroy and Letterguide templates, those made specifically for the Letterguide system are usually open faced. This means that they produce an outline letter that can be filled in solid at a later time.

The major advantages of these mechanical systems is their ability to produce very professional small lettering. They are ideal for lettering overhead transparencies and map and chart work. However, like any lettering system they require practice to be able to develop the proficiency to use them effectively and efficiently. Even though their cost is high, they are a valuable addition to the collection of lettering tools for the graphic artist.

OTHER LETTERING SYSTEMS:

OTHER LETTERING SYSTEMS

There are probably a thousand different lettering systems that we have not had the time and space to discuss. Some of these should at least be alluded to in passing. However, most of them are so expensive that they only have a place in the more professional graphics shops.

DRY TRANSFER LETTERING

Dry transfer lettering is basically a set of black (or colored) letters that have been printed on the back of a wax coated paper or a plastic sheet. You can place the letters over the area where you want them and, by applying pressure from the top of the sheet, you will transfer the letters to the materials underneath. This is a very simple, professional lettering system and its only real drawback is cost. Not only do the sheets of dry transfer letters cost a great deal but they have a limited number of each letter and, for example, when you run out of "e's" or "a's" you have to buy a new sheet. But if you can afford it, there are thousands of alphabets in a wide range of sizes that can be used to produce professional headlines, captions and even body copy. There are also symbols and shading sheets available in this system that increase its utility.

PHOTO LETTERING SYSTEMS

There are a variety of photo lettering systems that photographically print letters onto strips of acetate and/or paper. These lettered strips can then be pasted up for photocopy or thermal copy purposes. Again the major drawback is the initial cost of the system and the fonts of letters that are used in the process.

RUBBER STAMP LETTERING

Rubber stamps are another system for producing letters for your headlines, captions and body copy. These rubber stamps can be either individual letters or printing blocks that contain entire sets of words or paragraphs made up of individual small rubber letters. These systems require frequent washing to maintain the elasticity of the rubber, and they deteriorate quite rapidly unless cared for. Many sizes and styles of letters are available, and you can use stamp pads with a variety of colors of ink to produce the letters.

Even these do not exhaust the variety of lettering systems that can be used by the graphic artist. As you may have noticed, there are a number of inexpensive lettering systems such as hand lettering and the plastic or card board stencil systems. There are also a number of very expensive systems such as the Leroy and the dry transfer systems. The major problem in lettering is to match the system with your needs and with your budget. In the next section we will look at some of the effects that you can create using the inexpensive hand lettering techniques.

CHAPTER 5
PICTURE WORDS AND OTHER LETTERING IDEAS:

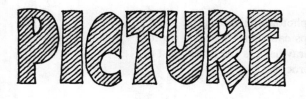

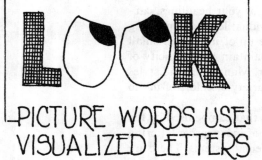

PICTURE WORDS USE VISUALIZED LETTERS

OR GRAPHIC LETTERS

OR MANIPULATED LETTERS TO ADD IMPACT TO THE PRINTED WORDS.

PRICES drip :

FIRE FIRE FIRE FBI

UTILIZATION

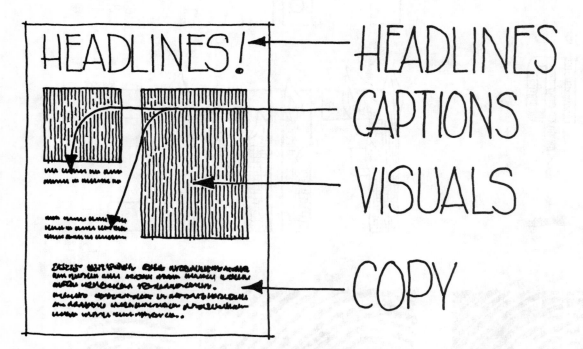

HEADLINES SET THE STAGE AND ARE OFTEN QUESTIONS. CAPTIONS "EXPLAIN" THE VISUALS AND INFLUENCE ITS DECODING. COPY IS USED WHERE LARGE AMOUNTS OF WORDS ARE NEEDED.

JUSTIFICATION:

THE SIMPLEST TYPE OF
JUSTIFICATION IS "LEFT".
THE LEFT MARGIN IS
MADE EVEN.

JUSTIFICATION IS A LITTLE MORE
DIFFICULT WHEN THE RIGHT
MARGIN IS MADE
EVEN.

CENTER JUSTIFICATION IS
THE MOST DIFFICULT,
BUT MANY CONSIDER
IT THE MOST ATTRACTIVE.

CALLIGRAPHY

The
*Italic Way
to
Beautiful
Handwriting*
*Cursive &
Calligraphic*
Fred Eager

COLLIER BOOKS
A Division of Macmillan Publishing Co., Inc.
NEW YORK
COLLIER MACMILLAN PUBLISHERS
LONDON

Project VII
Simple Roman Capitals

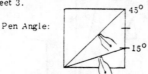

LESSON 32: No matter what you do with capitals, now or later, the essential forms you learned in the Block Capitals must be there. These Simple Roman Capitals appear to be dressed-up versions of Block Capitals. They approach the appearance of the Classic Roman Capitals which have served as a standard for capitals since the First Century A.D.

The pen-angle for Roman Capitals is usually flatter—about 15°. But watch for the places where it changes to 45° for the diagonals, and still steeper than 45° for certain vertical strokes in M and N. Roman Capitals should be upright.

TRACE and COPY one letter, then practice it on separate paper. Then the next letter, and so on. Use Guide Sheet 3.

Pen Angle:

1. Pen angle begins at 45° and flattens as it curves out at the bottom for the serif.
2. Pen angle is 45°, flattens for the serif and cross-stroke. Simply turn the pen in your hand.

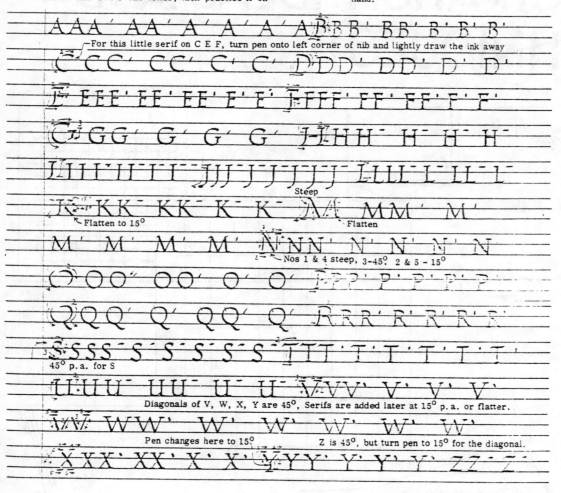

For this little serif on C E F, turn pen onto left corner of nib and lightly draw the ink away

Steep

Flatten to 15°   Flatten

Nos 1 & 4 steep, 3–45°, 2 & 5 – 15°

45° p.a. for S

Diagonals of V, W, X, Y are 45°, Serifs are added later at 15° p.a. or flatter.

Pen changes here to 15°   Z is 45°, but turn pen to 15° for the diagonal.

GS3

69

CHAPTER 6
ILLUSTRATION IDEAS AND TECHNIQUES:

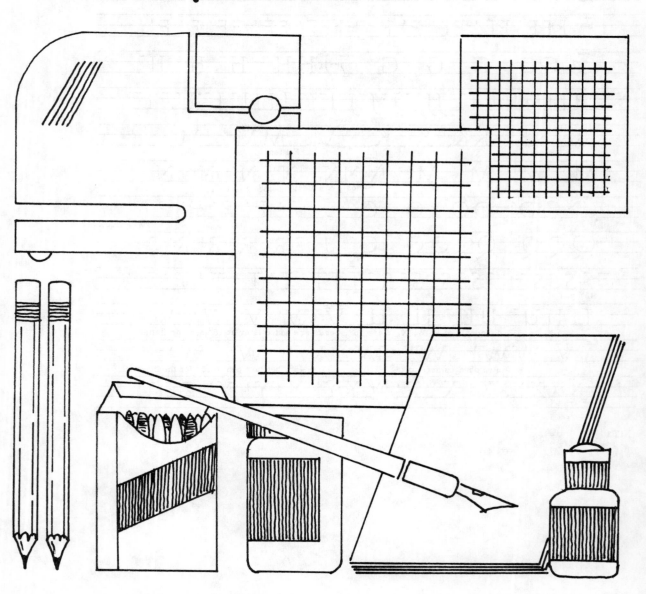

ILLUSTRATION IDEAS AND TECHNIQUES

The term "illustration" as used in graphic media production refers to the pictures, design and embellishments that you will use to enhance your communications. We recognize that at this stage you probably do not have the sketching or cartooning skills to create your own visuals, so the emphasis in this section will be the copying, modifying, and manipulation of existing visuals, which we call tearsheets. These tearsheets form the beginning point of the process of illustration, so perhaps we should spend a few moments considering them.

We are blessed in our society with a profusion of tearsheets that can be copied, modified, or manipulated to create visual materials that are suitable for illustrating our instructional materials. All you have to do is to look through the magazines or newspapers that are mailed to your home and you can find examples. Also consider junk mail as a possible source of illustrations. Often it is well illustrated, and these visuals can be transformed into suitable instructional materials. The problem is one of selection and storage. The term tearsheet is descriptive of the process of collecting these materials. Simply tear the visual from its original source. It is important that you do not trim the visuals to a desired size and format but rather leave them just as they were printed in the original source. In many of the mounting and illustration techniques you need extra space around the edges of the desired illustration.

Basically there are two classes of illustrations that you will find. The first are the photographs. These were originally photographs of people, places and things, that were screened for printing. This simply means that they were photographed through a process that changed the continuous tone images of the photos into a halftone image suitable for mass production printing. The second class of illustrations is the high contrast line drawings. As the name implies, these are visuals that are composed only of lines— there are no shades of grey. For many of our illustration techniques you will want to begin the process with an original that is a line drawing. The problem of translating a continuous tone image into a line drawing is usually one that requires a degree of artistic skill that is beyond most beginners.

Once you have begun your collection of tearsheets, your next problem will be that of organizing them so that you have easy access to the specific one that you want. I find that the standard file folder is an excellent storage system which allows me to classify the visuals in a way that is appropriate for my particular use. The final classification system that you use is a function of the content you teach and your particular needs. It might be a simple classification such as "animals" or you might want to break it down further into "wild animals" and "domestic animals." Or for your purposes you might have a separate file for each type of animal: "horses," "dogs," "birds," etc. With this type of filing system you can locate the specific visuals that you need, and through the various illustration techniques we can copy, modify or manipulate these to meet the media needs.

COPY TECHNIQUES: TRACING

ORIGINAL

ACETATE

CLIPBOARD

PROTECT

TRACE/COLOR

THE COPY

OVERHEAD

OVERLAY

ORIGINAL

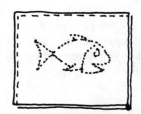

PAPER

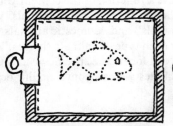

CLIPBOARD

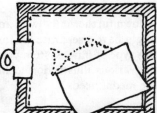

PROTECT

TRACE/COLOR

THE COPY

MOUNTING

AS MASTER

88

COPYING TECHNIQUES: TRACING

In many instances you will want to transfer an image from one surface to another. This is especially true when you are creating visuals as originals for overhead transparencies. There are a number of tracing techniques that can be used in this transfer process. We will examine just two: tracing using acetate and tracing using tracing paper.

TRACING WITH ACETATE

One of the first considerations is the nature of the original for this tracing. Unless you are skilled in sketching or cartooning, it is best to begin with a line drawing. Even these line drawings range from the simple line drawings of a coloring book to the complexities of an etching. Pick the one that meets both your skills and your illustration needs. Select an appropriate sheet of acetate and cover the visual. Since the acetate is transparent, you will be able to see the visual quite well. To maintain registration it is advisable to fasten the visual to the acetate somehow. You can use paper clips but I prefer to use a clipboard. This provides a good tracing surface as well as the mobility that is desirable during the tracing process. When you are working with acetate, it is essential to avoid getting fingerprints on the materials. Fingerprints are grease, and it is difficult to make the tracing materials work on grease. A scrap sheet of newsprint to rest your hand on will prove quite useful. Then select the medium that is appropriate for the desired end product. You can use India ink and pen for crisp lines or felt pens for color. Simply trace the image onto the acetate. It is best to put the outline on one side and, if you want to add solid colors, to do the coloring on the opposite side of the acetate. The resulting tracing can be used immediately as an overhead transparency, or it can be used as an overlay over a mounted visual or other illustration by simply taping it to the mounted visual.

TRACING WITH TRACING PAPER

In some instances you will want to transfer the image onto tracing paper for later mounting or as an original for thermal or diazo transparency production. Again, the first step is to select an appropriate line drawing from your tearsheet file. Cover it with tracing paper. The tracing paper is translucent and will allow you to see the visual below. Use a clip board to maintain registration and proceed to trace the visual onto the tracing paper. There are a number of tracing medium that can be used for this process, and you should select the one that meets your particular needs. It is also wise to protect the surface during the tracing with a scrap of clean newsprint. When the copy is finished you can mount it as you would any other visual. However, it is best to use white Fotoflat, as the other adhesives may discolor the visual. If you have used an appropriate tracing medium you can also use the tracing as an original for thermal or diazo transparencies.

These tracing processes are used to transfer a transparency to another surface without damaging the original. The results can be used for mounting, or as transparencies or transparency masters.

COPY TECHNIQUES: CARBON

ORIGINAL CARBON PAPER CLIPBOARD

TRACE CHECK COMPLETE COPY

ORIGINAL PAPER CARBON UP CLIPBOARD

TRACE CHECK COMPLETE REVERSAL

COPY TECHNIQUES: CARBON

With this tracing system we have increased our ability to transfer images from tearsheets onto a wider variety of surfaces. In some situations it may be desirable to transfer the image onto railroad board, wood or metal, and this technique will allow you this capability. It uses a common material called carbon paper. A major disadvantage of this process is that it generally damages the original since you draw directly on it. This can be avoided by making a Xerox copy and using the copy as the master.

Again we begin with our original. It should be a line drawing, and it should be only as complex as you can handle. Next, select a sheet of good quality carbon paper and place it under the original with the carbon side down. There are special carbon papers that will allow you to make transfers to wood, metal and cloth as well as to the railroad board. The next step is to place the original/carbon sandwich onto the surface to which you want the image to be transferred. In most cases you will have to use paper clips or other fastening devices to register the visual to the materials, but if it is possible, you will find that the clipboard is best. Now draw directly on the top of the original with a good ball point pen. These pens come in a variety of pen tip sizes, and you should use the one that produces the line image that you desire. Note that this will damage the original, and so it should either be expendable or a Xerox copy of one that you do not want destroyed. It is also advisable to check the progress of the tracing process periodically by lifting the visual/carbon section up to reveal the tracing underneath. I find that if I use a ball point pen with a different color of ink, such as red or green, I am less likely to miss sections of the tracing. Complete the tracing, and you have now transferred the original image to a different surface.

In some instances you may want to make some changes in the original; a common desired change is to flip the image right to left. For instance, if you have a person looking to the right in the original, it may be desirable to have the person looking to the left in the finished copy. This can be done quite easily by following this modification of the tracing process.

Begin with the desired original. Place a sheet of notebook paper under the original. Then place a sheet of carbon paper at the bottom of the stack, with the carbon side of the paper up. Register the sandwich with paper clips or a clipboard and proceed to trace the original with a suitable ball point pen. Check during the tracing process to make sure that you are copying all of the necessary lines. Note that the image will appear on the bottom of the sheet of notebook paper. When it is completed the copy will be a mirror image of the original; it will be reversed right to left. It is only possible to do this with notebook paper, as the heavier materials such as wood, metal, etc. will inhibit the pressure. But with this technique you can transfer an image to paper and at the same time reverse the image.

MODIFY THROUGH PROJECTION:

OPAQUE PROJECTION ENLARGEMENT

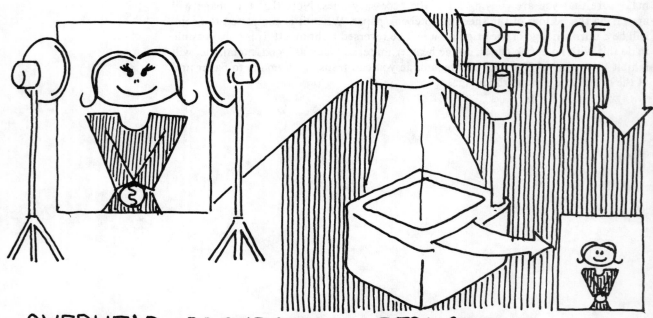

OVERHEAD PROJECTION REDUCTION

MODIFY THROUGH PROJECTION

Sometimes it is desirable to modify the size of the original illustration. There are a number of techniques that you can use to make the copy either larger or smaller than the original illustration. The use of projection equipment is one of the easiest, but it is also the most costly since it requires some sort of projection device. In this section we will look at the use of the opaque projector as a means of enlarging visuals, and at the overhead for both enlarging and reducing the size of illustrations.

There are some limitations on the original. First, it should be a line drawing with the degree of complexity that you can effectively deal with. With practice you will be able to enlarge even the most complex visuals. Second, the original visual must not be larger than 10 × 10″. The standard opaque projector has an aperture that measures 10 × 10″ and it will not project visuals larger than this. There are smaller, less expensive opaque projectors such as the Maganajector, which has an aperture of 3 × 3″, that are excellent for enlarging small visuals such as the panels from comic strips.

The visual is inserted into the projector, and the image is then projected onto the surface to which you wish to transfer the image. This may be railroad board, paper, cloth, or even a wall (if you want to make a mural). Adjust the size of the image by moving the projector closer to or further from the materials and possibly adjusting the position of the lens in the projector. Then simply trace the projected image. One disadvantage of the opaque projector is that the image is not very bright, so it is best to work in a darkened room. Another problem that you might have is determining what portion of the image you have already traced. Simply move into the beam of light, and this will show you what you have and have not completed. The result will be an enlargement of the original.

You can also produce an enlargement with the overhead projector, but this requires that the original be a transparency. However, you can reduce the size of a large visual through reverse opaque projection that can make larger originals smaller. The large original is placed on a wall, and the overhead is projected and focussed onto the original. Then the overhead is turned off. Lights are used to illuminate the original, and the room lights are turned off. Now the overhead will work in reverse. The image will be reflected from the original through the optical system of the overhead down onto the stage of the projector. If you place a sheet of paper onto the stage of the overhead, you will see an image that you can trace. A limitation of this process is the image size of the overhead (10 × 10″). This means that the final copy will be 10 × 10″ or less. However, this will provide you with the capability of reducing the size of large visuals, and the overhead projection system is commonly available and relatively inexpensive. The lighting system is the only additional expense necessary.

MODIFY THROUGH GRID SQUARE:

ORIGINAL

¼" APART

¼" APART

IDENTIFY

DETERMINE COPY SIZE

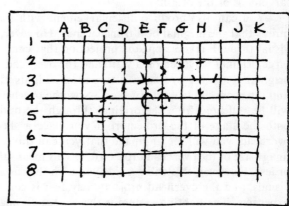

ENLARGE THE GRID

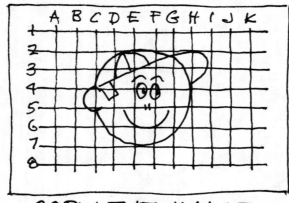

COPY THE IMAGE

ERASE THE GRID

MODIFY THROUGH GRID SQUARE

The grid square system can be used to enlarge and reduce the size of original visuals and has the advantage of being very inexpensive. The only tools that are needed are a yardstick and a pencil. The process is rather complicated, but that's the price you pay for an inexpensive technique.

Begin with a suitable original. Normally this should be a simple line drawing. If it is one that you wish to preserve, you will want to cover it with a sheet of acetate first. If it is not valuable, you may continue the process directly on the original visual. First draw a series of parallel vertical lines (normally 1/4″ apart). Then draw a series of parallel horizontal lines (also 1/4″ apart). This provides a 1/4″ grid that covers the original drawing. Now we need to identify these lines with numbers and letters. Normally I number the horizontal line and use letters for the vertical lines.

The next step is to determine the desired size of the enlargement. Let's assume that your original visual is 6″ tall and you want the enlargement to be 18″ tall. This means that you want an enlargement that is three times the size of the original. Now you put a grid onto the copy material that is three times the size of the grid on the original. If the lines on the original were 1/4″ apart, the grid on the copy should be 3/4″ apart. Make sure that when you draw this grid you do it lightly in pencil since it will need to be erased later. Number and letter the copy grid in the same way that you did the grid on the original (vertical lines with letters and horizontal lines with numbers).

Now you are ready to transfer the image. Note the points where the original crosses specific lines. For example, the brim of the hat peaks at H2. Make a mark on the copy grid and continue this process until you have identified and marked all the points where the original drawing crosses the grid lines. Then simply connect the lines, using the original as your guide. Once you have transferred the image in pencil, you simply ink it in and then erase the grid. The resulting enlargement should bear a striking resemblance to the original.

The process of reduction is just the reverse of this. You begin with a large original and put a large grid on it. Then you determine the desired size of the reduction and put a grid that size on the copy. Again transfer the points at which the original drawing crosses the lines on the grid to the copy grid and connect the lines.

It is even possible, with this system, to distort the original by varying the distances between the vertical lines (to create a thinner copy) or the horizontal lines (to create a wider copy). I have seen some remarkable effects with this system. However, the major advantage of the grid square technique is the low cost of the materials and tools. The disadvantage is the time that it takes to produce a quality copy using this process.

MANIPULATION: THE CUTOUT

THE COMPLETE CUTOUT   TO SUBTRACT   TO ADD

A SIMPLE AMPUTATION   NOT JUSTIFIED   JUSTIFIED

THE CUTOUT USED TO CREATE DIFFERENT MEANINGS.

  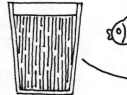  

IS YOUR WATER PURE?

CUTOUTS USE TO CREATE NEW VISUAL.

MANIPULATION: THE CUTOUT

The term manipulation refers to another way in which we can make changes in the original tearsheets. In this case manipulation gives us the capability of creating a totally new visual from the elements in existing visuals. The process begins with selecting elements from existing visuals and then recombining them into new configurations. The basic tool is the cutout. It is best to use MT-5 as the adhesive, so you may need to refer back to the section in Mounting that deals with the irregular cutout.

There are different types of cutouts. The easiest to work with are the complete cutouts, elements in the original that are complete within themselves. On the opposite page we can see that the apple in the original visual is all there. This complete element can be cut out from the original and used to hide unwanted elements in a visual, such as the package of cigarettes in the first picture, or to add information such as the insertion of the apple in the bowl of fruit in the second example. There are also amputated cutouts that can be used in this process. The second example on the opposite page shows a young girl that in the original is cropped at the shoulders. When this element is cut out, that amputation forms a straight line that does not appear right when it is mounted. However, by justifying this amputation with an appropriate background or some other logical reason for the straight line, these amputated cutouts can also be used effectively.

The cutout can be used to create different meanings by adding it to another original visual. It can also be used to create new visuals by taking elements from different sources and rearranging them into new patterns. In the examples on the opposite page, the young man takes on new meaning when it is mounted against the mountains or the sea or the design elements. In the bottom example the glass of water and the visual of the fish are cut out and combined as a sort of visual joke. This manipulation technique is limited only by the visuals that you can find and the imagination that you can bring to the process.

There are some tricks to this process. First, as I mentioned, it is best to work with MT-5 dry mounting tissue as the adhesive. Note that you need to do area tacking and be very careful in the trimming process. When you are mounting the final manipulation, do it in slow stages. Mount the base visual down first, and then mount each additional element one at a time. The additional time in the press will not damage the ones that went into the press the first time. It is also important to look at the size relationships of the visuals as well as how well they fit together in terms of style and color. The more time you spend selecting just the right set of visuals, the better your end product will be. Try your hand at this process and you will be both pleased and surprised at the results.

MANIPULATION: SPLICE MOUNTS

REMOVE STAPLES

SEPARATE PAGES

TRIM THE PAGES

TACK FROM FRONT

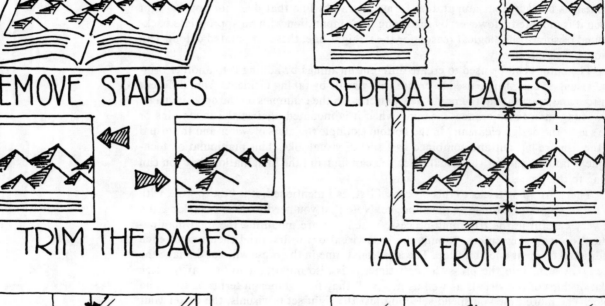

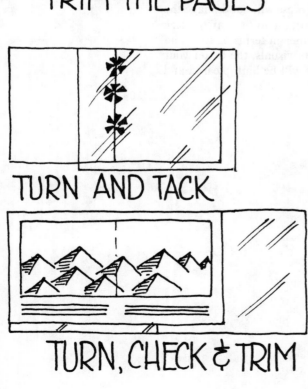

TURN AND TACK

ADD TISSUE, TACK

TURN, CHECK & TRIM

MOUNT

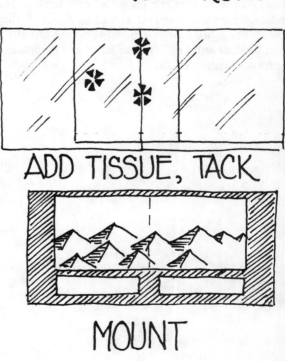

MANIPULATION: SPLICE MOUNTING

Many times you will find what is usually referred to as a two-page spread. This means that the visual extends from one page of the magazine to another. It is difficult but possible to preserve even these visuals for your instructional uses through what is referred to as the splice mounting process.

If you remember, we indicated that your tearsheets should be torn from the magazine, but here we need a quite different process. To remove the visual from the magazine you should first remove the staples in the spine of the magazine. The edges of the separate pages are trimmed as carefully as possible. Note that even though this is an MT-5 process, we begin by trimming the edges of the visual that are to be joined. Then a sheet of MT-5 dry mount tissue is placed on a work surface, and the visuals are placed on top of the tissue. Make sure that 1) the visual is properly aligned and 2) the tissue extends over the splice. Now tack the visual from the top. However, make sure that the tacking takes place outside the area of the visual you want to preserve. This is necessary because often in this tacking process the material on the table top adheres to the tissue and will need to be trimmed away as part of the final process. With the visual temporarily adhered to the tissue, turn it over and tack, making sure to bridge across the splice; add additional tissue as required and tack it in place to make sure that all of the visual is covered with dry mount tissue. Now turn it over and check to make sure that the edges of the visual match. Trim away the excess and then mount the visual to the desired backing using a dry mount press preheated to 225 degrees.

Often you will find that the colors of the two pages do not match. If it is distracting, you may want to clean up the colors with the use of Mongol colored pencils. This process is not used very often, but when a desirable visual appears on two separate pages of a magazine, this is the only reasonable way to preserve them.

OTHER ILLUSTRATION IDEAS:

OTHER ILLUSTRATION IDEAS

The techniques that we have suggested for copying, modifying, and manipulating visual materials are just a few of the techniques that can be used to assist in the effective visualization of your various units of instruction. There are other techniques and materials that will also enhance your visual communication process. For example, photography is an obvious way to acquire visuals specific to your needs; this will be covered in a later section. An interesting tool has been developed by the PHANTOM LINE GRAPHICS CO. (955 Foothill Drive, Providence, Utah 84332). This simple apparatus, shown on the opposite page, consists of a mirrored sheet of acetate that allows you to see the reflected image of the visual and to copy it on a sheet of paper that is placed below the mirror. While I did not have a great deal of success with it, many of my students find it a great way to copy existing visuals.

Another source of potentially useful visuals that we should also consider are the various companies that produce clip art. While this covers many content areas and can take many forms, the one that I am most familiar with comes in small booklets and can be used as pasteups, originals for enlargement, and for other appropriate applications. Initially designed for the paste-up artist who is producing materials for the printing process, these can be a valuable addition to your illustration collection.

There is also a process called photosketching that helps to translate photographs into line drawings that are suitable for a wider range of purposes. Beginning with a photographic print on paper, you simply draw the image with a good quality of India ink. Leave out as much detail as is necessary and emphasize those elements you desire. When the ink is completely dry, the photograph is placed into a Farmers Reducer solution.

Solution #1	Potassium ferricyanide, 1 1/4 oz.
	Water to make 16 oz. of solution
Solution #2	Hypo, 16 oz.
	Water to make 64 oz. of solution

Mix the above solutions extra strong (normal solution is about one oz. of number 1 to four oz. of number 2 in a quart of water. The print is placed in this bleaching solution until every trace of the photographic image disappears. Rinse the print in clean water and then fix it in a hypo solution. Wash and dry as you normally would for any photographic print. The result will be a line drawing that is remarkably similar to the original photograph.

There are many other techniques that can be used to enhance your illustrations. The next section will deal with skills and techniques that can be applied to create your illustrations. Simple sketching and especially cartooning are not beyond your capabilities.

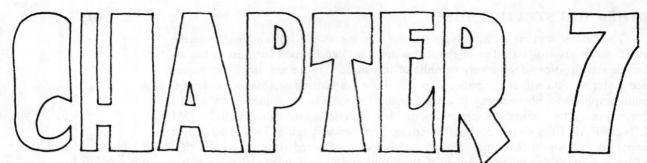

CHAPTER 7
CARTOONING TECHNIQUES AND APPLICATIONS:

For people who say,
"I can't draw a straight line."

NEXT!

CARTOONING TECHNIQUES AND APPLICATIONS

While there are many tearsheets available and also many techniques for copying, modifying, and manipulating these tearsheets, you are often faced with the problem of not being able to find exactly the visual you need to illustrate the concept you are trying to communicate. In this case you need to be able to create your own illustrations. While you can resort to photography, this is quite expensive and time consuming. It is probably easier, if you have the skills, to sketch or cartoon the visual that you want. If you are like most people, your first reaction is, "I can't draw a straight line, and he wants me to draw cartoons." Well, in the first place you can draw a straight line, and even if you can't, it is not a necessary prerequisite to cartooning. Actually, if you can print your name and address, you can draw almost anything you need. The same strokes used in cartooning are those that are used in printing your name and address. I do not have time here to go through the whole process, but I have included some examples from a pair of books that I have prepared to supplement the in-service workshops that I present to teachers. The first, CARTOONING FOR THE CLASSROOM, introduces you to the basic techniques for producing simple cartoons. Beginning with the techniques for drawing the head and expressions, it moves into the body, clothes, and eventually how to draw people places and things. The next two pages are examples from this book. The second book is CARTOONING: AN ANIMAL ALPHABET; it deals with the capital and lower case letters of the alphabet and the techniques necessary to transform them into animals whose names begin with that letter. The example that I have included is the lower case "a" and how it can be translated into an ant and an aardvark.

This brings us to the applications. First, the ability to render cartoons on the chalkboard quickly is an important skill that is almost guaranteed to grab the attention of your class. This ability to grab and hold the attention of an audience is a major reason for considering the skill of cartooning. However, cartooning can also be used to either illustrate or embellish instruction in almost all curriculum areas. In language arts we can provide cartoons as a vehicle for creative writing: see the last example in this section. We can draw science concepts, illustrate physics principles and otherwise utilize these cartooning skills to communicate instructional ideas. If you wish to acquire copies of these booklets, write to:

Les Satterthwaite
FLS, College of Education
Arizona State University
Tempe, Arizona 85287

THE BEGINNING!

Cartooning is a method of representing the elements you wish to present.

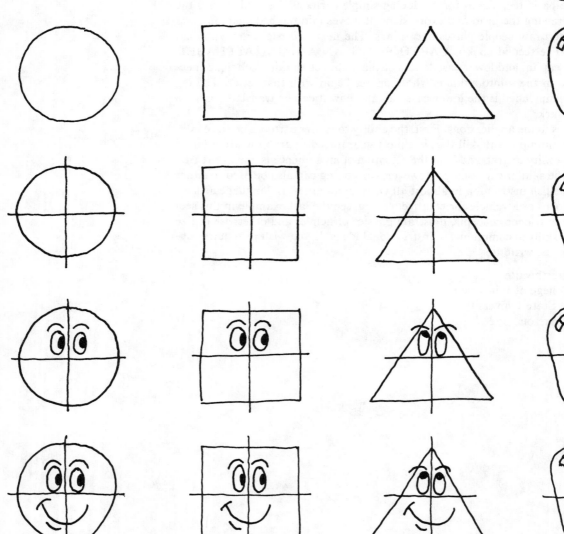

CLOTHING

THE ANIMAL ALPHABET

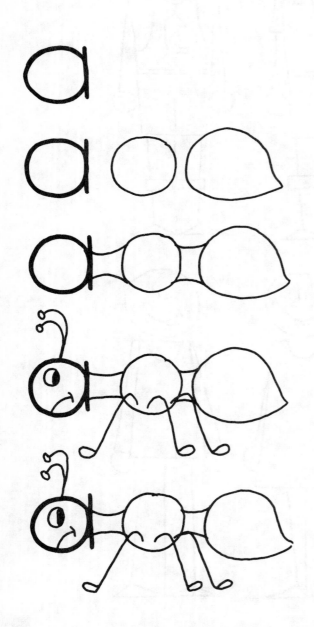

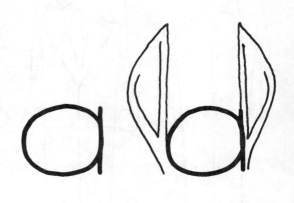

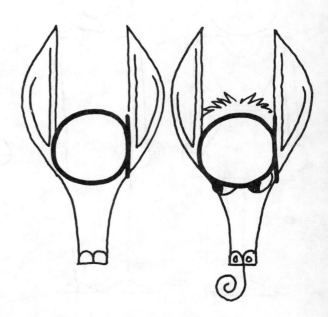

THE ANT AND   THE AARDVARK

APPLICATIONS

① WHAT IS BEING SAID?

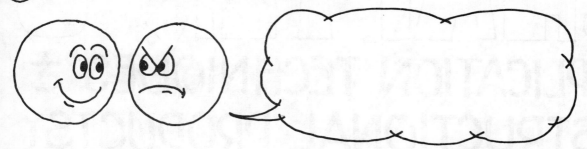

② WRITE THE DIALOGUE!

CHAPTER 8
DUPLICATION TECHNIQUES & INSTRUCTIONAL PRODUCTS:

DUPLICATING TECHNIQUES AND INSTRUCTIONAL PRODUCTS

Print materials are an important type of audiovisual media. In exploring these we will concentrate on those that are commonly found in the classroom, recognizing that there is a wide range of duplicated materials that can be used in instruction. We will look at four quite different print materials: 1) handouts, 2) seatwork, 3) booklets, and 4) reference materials. Handouts are items that are normally unique to your class. They announce assignments and field trips and generally keep students (and their parents) informed of special events that are related to your instructional system. Seatwork, on the other hand, is normally a drill and practice activity. It is a means of providing your students with the necessary practice to master skills that you consider to be important. While seatwork can also be a self-instructional activity (even programmed), it is more commonly a practice activity. Booklets are also a common type of print materials found in the classroom. There are literally thousands of booklets available both commercially and from free/inexpensive sources. I have noted an increase in local production of these booklets, and many times they are written and produced by the students in the classes. Reference materials are a fourth type of print materials. These are multiple copies of articles, or other materials that you deem appropriate to supplement the instruction of your students. The following chart may help you organize these print materials in terms of sources, utilization, and characteristics.

PRINT MATERIALS	sources			utilization				characteristics
	commercial sources	free/inexpensive	local production	presentation	interaction	independent study	drill/practice	General: these are printed materials that may contain visual elements. Normally they are multiple copies intended for student use.
handouts			X	X				primarily unique information
seatwork	X	X	X			X	X	normally drill and practice
booklets	X	X	X	X		X		large free/inexpensive selection
reference			X	X				copies of articles, etc.

Since all of these can be produced locally, we will concentrate on those local production techniques that are reasonably inexpensive and that are commonly available to the classroom teacher. We will look at: 1) the Hectograph system, 2) standard and thermal duplication, 3) standard and electronic stencil processes, and 4) a new process for making thermal silk screen products. These various techniques have certain advantages and disadvantages, and in the following pages we will share these with you. We will provide a variety of options so that you can select the process that is most appropriate to your situation and to your needs.

HECTOGRAPH DUPLICATION:

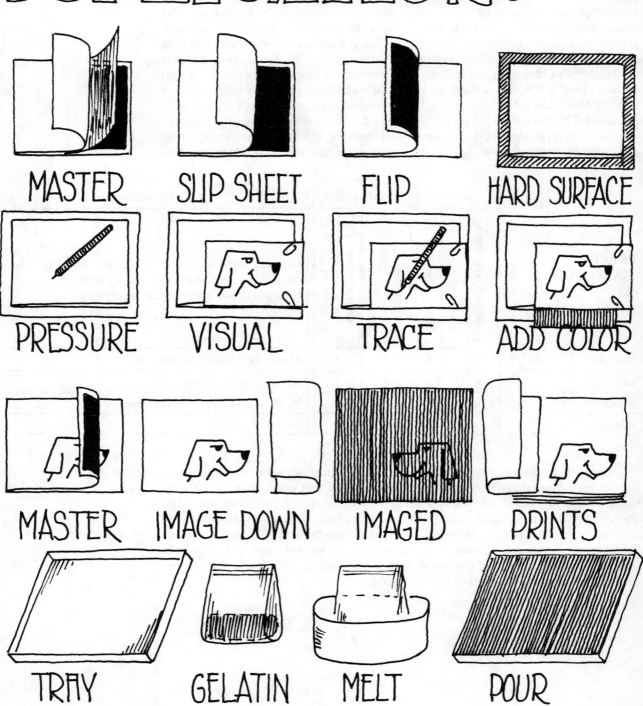

MASTER SLIP SHEET FLIP HARD SURFACE

PRESSURE VISUAL TRACE ADD COLOR

MASTER IMAGE DOWN IMAGED PRINTS

TRAY GELATIN MELT POUR

HECTOGRAPH DUPLICATION

The hectograph system is one of the oldest duplication systems that has been used in the public schools. The entire system, including the printer, is available for less than $15.00. Basically it is a spirit duplications system. Ditto (the purple process) is a spirit system, and the hectograph uses the same masters that are used for the ditto process. The spirit master comes in three parts: the paper master, a tissue paper slip sheet, and the analyne dye blanket. First remove the tissue slip sheet. It's only there to prevent any inadvertent marking of the master. With the slip sheet out, invert the master so that the analyne dye blanket is on the top and the paper master is on the bottom. Note that this is exactly the opposite of the way the master is used for "normal" spirit duplication. Now place the master on a hard surface. You are going to use pressure, probably a ball point pen, to create the image, and you need a good solid surface below the master. I prefer a clipboard since this will also allow me to clip the materials I am going to copy to the board and maintain registration.

Let's assume that you want to transfer a visual to the hectograph master. Since the visual will be damaged in the process, you may want to make a Xerox copy if it is one you want to save. Register the visual to the master and trace the visual with the ball point pen. Use a heavy pressure since you will be transferring the analyne dye from the blanket to the master. Check periodically to ensure that the tracing is going well. If you want colors other than the standard purple, just insert a different colored blanket into the sandwich and continue the process. These analyne dye blankets come in purple (standard), green, red, blue and black. You can also draw or letter directly onto the master, and, of course, you can roll it into a typewriter and type whatever information you desire.

Now you are ready for the printing process. The printer in the hectograph system is simply a tin tray that has been filled with a gelatin solution. The master is placed, face down, onto the surface of the gelatin. It has been moistened slightly, and the analyne dye image will transfer onto the gelatin surface. You will notice that the image on the gelatin surface is backwards; this is to be expected. Now all you have to do is to place the materials to be printed onto the surface, rub it lightly and peel it off. A part of the image will transfer to the surface, and you will have made your print.

One advantage of the hecto system is that you can print on a wide variety of surfaces (paper, construction paper, cardboard, cloth, even wood and sometimes metal). This process also allows you to print in up to five colors simultaneously, and, of course, it is very inexpensive. The disadvantages are the relatively few number of prints (30–75 is normal) and the fact that it is a hand operation. But all in all, you will find that the Hectograph is a printing system that is ideal for the local production of handouts, seatwork, and even booklets. Unfortunately, to print more than one page you need additional printing trays, and it takes about 24 hours for the image to completely disappear.

STANDARD SPIRIT DUPLICATION:

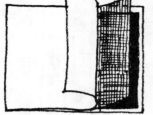
MASTER

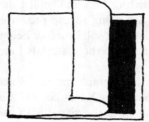
SLIP SHEET

HARD SURFACE

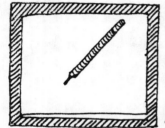
PRESSURE

VISUAL

TRACE

ADD COLOR

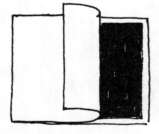
MASTER

IMAGE UP

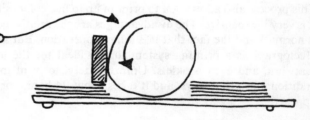
RUN YOUR COPIES

"SCRAPE"

ADJUST →

ADJUST ↓

OK

112

STANDARD SPIRIT DUPLICATION

Spirit duplication is the generic term for the process you may know as Ditto. However, Ditto is simply a brand name for one of the many companies that produce materials and equipment for the spirit duplication process. The process consists of two parts: 1) the preparation of the master and 2) the printing of the copies.

PREPARING THE MASTER

The standard spirit master is composed of three parts: 1) the paper master, 2) a slip sheet to protect from inadvertent marking, and 3) the analyne dye blanket (the color). The first step is to remove the slip sheet and prepare the master for imaging. It is best to place the master/blanket sandwich on a hard surface since you will be applying pressure with a ball point pen to create your images. I prefer to use a clipboard since this will hold the images you are tracing in register with the master during this process. Let's consider the problem of transferring a visual to the spirit master. First, select an appropriate visual, in this case one that is the right size and is preferably a line drawing. Clip it into place with paper clips or by using the clip on the clipboard. Now, trace directly on the visual with a ball point pen. The pressure will cause the analyne dye on the blanket to transfer to the paper master. The harder you press, the more dye will transfer. If you want a multicolored visual, it is only necessary to insert different colored analyne dye blankets under the master. These analyne dye blankets come in five colors: purple (standard), red, green, blue and black. In this process all of the colors can end up on the same master, and you can print multicolored visuals in a single pass through the spirit printer.

Of course, you can draw directly on the master, do hand lettering, or place the master/blanket sandwich in a typewriter and type in the information that you desire on the finished copy. When the imaging is completed, you will want to examine the master to ensure that it is ready for printing. If there are any extraneous marks on the master, just take a single-edged razor blade and scrape off the mistakes.

PRINTING THE MASTER

When the master is ready, it is time to print. First remove the analyne dye blanket from the master and discard the blanket. Then attach the master to the printer with the analyne dye image up. From this point on it is simply a matter of running a few test copies and adjusting the equipment for vertical and horizontal alignment and, when everything is ready, running your copies. Depending on the quality of masters you have produced, you should get 100–200 copies. A limitation of the standard spirit master is your ability to trace the images that you want to use. More complex visuals are easier to produce with the thermal spirit process. The advantage of the process is the relative ease and low cost of producing quality images. To enhance your printed materials you can also use a variety of colored spirit papers along with the multicolored images.

THERMAL SPIRIT DUPLICATION:

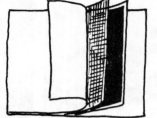
COMPONENTS

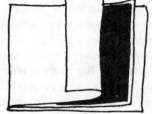
SLIP SHEET

LIFT BLANKET

ORIGINAL

"SANDWICH"

ACETATE COVER

MAKE THERMAL COPY

MASTER

IMAGE UP

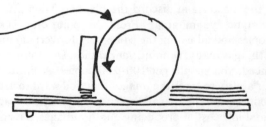
RUN YOUR COPIES

"SCRAPE"

ADJUST →

ADJUST ↓

OK

THERMAL SPIRIT DUPLICATION

The thermal spirit system is designed to transfer carbon based images to a spirit master by the judicious application of heat. Thus, it allows for the duplication of very complex line drawings that might be beyond the capabilities of tracing. There are three parts to this process: 1) creating the original, 2) imaging the master, and 3) running the prints.

CREATING THE ORIGINALS

The major requirement of the original for a thermal spirit master is that the original must be composed of carbon images. This means that you can either select existing materials that are carbon based (like most black printers ink), or you can create your own and make a Xerox copy. Xerox copying produces an excellent carbon based image. These originals can be a single unit, or they can be a paste-up. The term paste-up refers to originals that are created from a variety of sources such as visuals from newspapers, headlines from magazines, etc. Then these components are arranged onto an 8 1/2 × 11″ sheet of paper and fastened in place with scotch tape or rubber cement. Then it is best if the paste-up is copied by the Xerox process to ensure an equal degree of carbon for all images.

IMAGING THE MASTER

The master unit for thermal spirit duplication consists, normally, of four parts. The top part is a thin paper master, the next section is a tissue slip sheet, then there is the analyne dye blanket (purple) and, finally, a sheet of newsprint backing. Remove the slip sheet and insert the original between the backing and the analyne dye blanket. Make sure that the image side is toward the blanket. Now place the original/master sandwich in a special acetate cover and insert it into a thermal copier. You will probably need to try a number of settings until you find just the right speed to produce your masters. Once you have, make sure to mark the thermal copier so you can reuse the setting.

RUNNING THE COPIES

Once you have your master and have scraped off any mistakes, you are ready to run the prints. This will be a little more difficult than it was for the standard spirit master because the thermal spirit master is quite flimsy. If you remove the master from the sandwich, you will have difficulty inserting it into the printer without causing wrinkles that will give you less than quality copies. I have found that if I remove the analyne dye blanket and fold the master against the newsprint backing, it provides a stability that eliminates much of the problem. Naturally, you will want to run a few copies to check the vertical and horizontal alignment and adjust these as necessary. Then you can run your copies.

Unfortunately, the thermal spirit system will only run purple copies, but it can produce a remarkable amount of detail. Another disadvantage of this process is that it will normally produce only about 100 copies. However, since the original is not damaged it is quite simple to produce additional masters as necessary.

STANDARD STENCIL DUPLICATION:

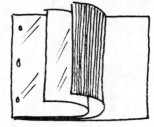

STENCIL

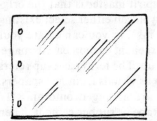

LIGHT BOX

ORIGINAL

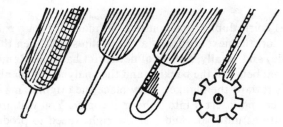

TRACE

TRACING TOOLS

TYPEWRITER

ACETATE

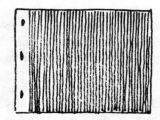

STENCIL/BACK

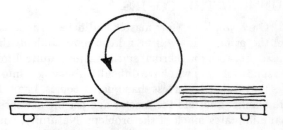

RUN YOUR COPIES

"FILL IN"

ADJUST →

ADJUST ↓

OK

STANDARD STENCIL DUPLICATION

The term stencil is the generic term for a duplication process that you may know as Mimeo. However, Mimeograph is a brand name of a stencil duplication process, and there are a number of other companies who manufacture and distribute these materials and equipment. In the process of standard stencil duplication there are two steps: 1) the preparation of the stencil and 2) the running of the copies.

PREPARATION OF THE STENCIL

The stencil is really a thin layer of wax that has been impregnated with linen fibers to hold the elements of the image together. This basic stencil is attached to two other elements. Above it is a thin plastic sheet that will increase your ability to draw and type images into the stencil itself. Below the stencil is a lightweight, translucent cardboard that provides the surface against which you will cut the stencil. There is no problem in typing onto the stencil; you simply roll it into the typewriter and type what you want with the machine at the stencil setting. When it comes to drawing on the stencil, things become a little more complicated. If you are drawing original images, it is best to draw or do your hand lettering on the stencil with the plastic sheet in place. When you are trying to trace existing visuals, it is necessary to utilize some sort of light box arrangement. The original visual is placed under the entire stencil, and since the cardboard backing is, at best, translucent, it is necessary to have a light source at the bottom. In this tracing or drawing process you will be using pressure to literally cut grooves in the stencil. This can be done with a ball point pen, or you can use a variety of tracing tools that are available for the stencil process. Some of these are for creating solid lines of varying widths, while some specialty tools have rotating heads that create dotted lines as they are run across the stencil.

It is vital that you purchase the stencil that is designed for your particular duplicating equipment. At the top edge of the stencil there are a series of perforations that are hooked onto the printing equipment. You must have the right ones for your system.

RUNNING THE COPIES

Once you have checked the stencil and made sure there are no errors, you are ready to print. If you should find mistakes, it is a simple matter to correct them. The stencil system has correction fluid, which is basically liquid wax. Just use this to fill in any lines that you do not want printed. Now, remove the plastic cover sheet. Next, attach the stencil to the duplicator. Just fasten the registration pins into the registration holes in the stencil. Make sure that the stencil is face down. Lock the stencil in place and remove the cardboard backing. Now you are ready to print. A good quality stencil will produce thousands of copies and, unfortunately, they will all be one color, normally black. Stencil duplication is an excellent system for producing large numbers of excellent copies.

ELECTRONIC STENCIL DUPLICATION:

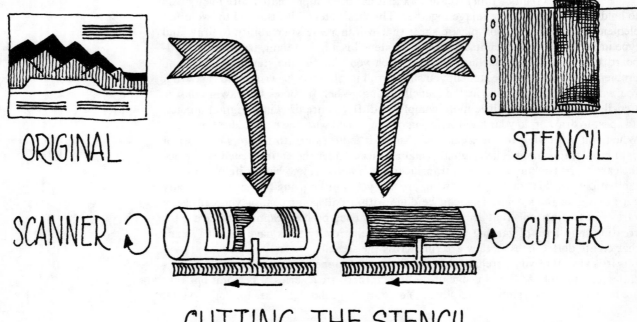

ORIGINAL

STENCIL

SCANNER

CUTTER

CUTTING THE STENCIL

CUT STENCIL

RUN YOUR COPIES

COPIES

COLOR STENCILS

RUN AND RERUN

FINAL COPIES

ELECTRONIC STENCIL DUPLICATION

The standard stencil duplication process is limited by your ability to trace and/ or draw. With the electronic stencil duplication process we can create much more complicated visual materials with much less effort. The process consists of three parts: 1) the creation and/or selection of an original, 2) the cutting of the electronic stencil, and 3) the running of the copies.

CREATING/SELECTING AN ORIGINAL

The original for electronic stencil duplication should be a black line image. These can be found in magazines and newspapers and copied directly, or you can produce a paste-up from a variety of sources. The paste-up is just that, the collection of visuals, headlines and copy from a variety of sources and the arrangement of these onto an 8 1/2 × 11″ sheet of paper. They can be adhered with rubber cement, MT-5, or simply fastened in place with scotch tape. Normally, it is best to make a Xerox copy of the paste-up. This will protect the original and make sure that the various elements have equal density black lines.

CUTTING THE ELECTRONIC STENCIL

This is the heart of the process. There are a number of different electronic stencil cutters on the market, and it is essential that you select the one that cuts stencils that are appropriate for your stencil duplicator. The electronic stencil cutter consists of two parts. One is the scanner that will read the original; the other is the cutter that will burn a corresponding image into the stencil. The original is placed onto the scanner, and a blank stencil is placed onto the stencil cutter. These two drums rotate in synchronization. As they rotate a scanning device (an electric eye) reads the original. Every time it sees a black line, it sends a signal to a cutting tool on the cutter drum, which burns a corresponding hole into the electronic stencil. This is an automatic process, and all you have to do is watch. It is also a very expensive process, with the unit costing thousands of dollars. Once the stencil is cut, you are ready to run your copies.

RUNNING THE COPIES

The electronic stencil is attached to the appropriate duplicator with the image side down. The cardboard backing is removed, and you are ready to run your copies. The electronic stencils will run hundreds of copies, but like the standard stencils, they are normally one color (usually black). However, some of the newer stencil cutters have the capability of producing multicolor stencils. Using a color original, various filters are placed in front of the scanning tool and then it cuts stencils for only that color. By cutting the appropriate stencils, it is possible to reproduce full color originals. However, since you have a separate stencil for each color, you must run the copies through the duplicator for new new color, and you must have the capability of exact registration. Like the standard stencil duplication process, the electronic stencil can produce high quality prints and even more complex visuals than you can produce by tracing or drawing.

THERMAL SCREEN DUPLICATION:

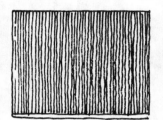

THERMAL SCREEN

ORIGINAL

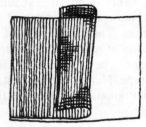

SEPARATE EDGE

INSERT ORIGINAL

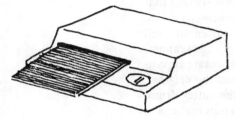

IMAGE WITH THERMAL UNIT

SCREEN

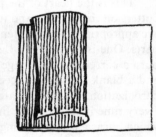

SEPARATE

PLASTIC FRAME

APPLY TAPE

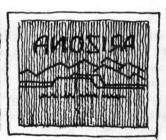

APPLY SCREEN

TURN OVER

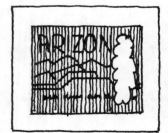

APPLY PAINT

SPREAD PAINT

PRINTS

THERMAL SCREEN DUPLICATION

Occasionally it is desirable to print multiple copies on wood, metal, cloth, or other surfaces than paper. Silk screen is an excellent process, but until now it has been difficult to cut the stencils that are used. Recently a new thermal silk screen process has been developed that shows great promise. The process has three parts: 1) creating the original, 2) imaging the silk screen, and 3) printing.

CREATING THE ORIGINAL

As with all thermal processes, the original must be a carbon based image. It can be a complete original torn from a magazine or newspaper, or it can be a paste-up with elements from a variety of sources. In either case it is essential that it be the right size and that it be a carbon image. The size is limited by the size of the printing frames that are available. To ensure that the final image is carbon based, you can Xerox a copy which will equalize the intensity of all of the carbon images.

IMAGING THE SILK SCREEN

Always run a test to find the proper setting on your particular thermal copier before going into production. Next, separate the bottom of the backing sheet from the speed screen. Place your original between the backing and the screen with the image facing the screen. Insert the sandwich into the thermal copier and make a copy. Correct any pin holes of errors in the screen with the correction fluid that is provided. Yes, it's just that simple.

PRINTING

Once the screen is imaged, we begin the printing process. First, we mount the screen to the plastic frame that is provided. To do this we have to separate the screen from the backing sheet. Place double-faced tape around the edge of the opening in the plastic frame. Now, position the top of the screen in place, working from the back of the screen. It is essential that it be tight, so keep the wrinkles out of the screen. Then adhere the rest of the screen, making sure that it is kept tight. It is essential that the smooth side of the screen (the film side) is down during this process. With the screen firmly and smoothly attached to the printing frame, you are ready to use it. Place the frame down on the surface you want to print and place a length of printing ink onto the screen. Then using a squeegee spread the ink across the image. The ink will be forced through the holes in the screen and onto the surface below. To make multiple copies just lift the screen and reposition it onto a new surface and repeat the process.

This system is available from the Welsh Products Co., 3100-G Kerner Blvd., P. O. Box 3116, San Rafael, Cal. 94902. A starter set is available for about $100.00, and it will allow you to produce a number of screens. Additional screens can be ordered at about $1.25 per screen. It is relatively expensive, but it is an exciting new process with some very interesting capabilities.

CHAPTER 9
SIMPLE INSTRUCTIONAL MEDIA AND MATERIALS:

SIMPLE INSTRUCTIONAL MEDIA AND MATERIALS

This section begins our examination of the various media and materials that are possible for use in the classroom. The term simple that is used in this section refers to media and materials that can be produced using the basic graphic skills of mounting, lettering, and illustration that were previously covered. Later we will explore the so-called complex media that utilize photographic, audio and/or electronic skills in their production. As we examine each of these media, there are certain facts that are desirable to retain. We want you to be able to answer the questions: 1) "Where can I get these media/materials combinations?", 2) "How can I best use these media/materials combinations?", 3) "What are the characteristics unique to these media/materials?", and 4) "If I have to produce them myself, what are appropriate production techniques?" To assist in the acquisition of this information, we will provide a chart for each media that suggests appropriate sources, uses, and characteristics. The charts will look like this:

PRINT MATERIALS	sources			utilization				characteristics
	commercial sources	free/inexpensive	local production	presentation	interaction	independent study	drill/practice	General: these are printed materials that may contain visual elements. Normally they are multiple copies intended for student use.
handouts			X	X				primarily unique information
seatwork	X	X	X			X	X	normally drill and practice
booklets	X	X	X	X		X		large free/inexpensive selection
reference			X	X				copies of articles, etc.

We will consider three possible sources for the materials for these various media: 1) the commercial sources where they can be purchased, 2) the free/inexpensive sources where they can be acquired or borrowed inexpensively, and 3) if you can't find it anyplace else, local production (making it yourself). In the utilization section we will consider how this particular media might be used most appropriately. While there are probably as many teaching/learning strategies as there are teachers and students, we have settled on four basic ones: 1) presentation of information, normally to large groups of learners, 2) interaction in which the media and/or the materials are intended to generate an interaction between learners, 3) independent study either with the student working independently or with actual programmed materials, and 4) drill and practice where the students will have the opportunity to master information delivered in other strategies. We will also try to identify any unique characteristics that make this media and its related materials different from the class of media and materials that they are grouped with.

OPAQUE STILL PICTURES:

TEACHING PICTURES

STUDY PRINTS

OPAQUE PROJECTION VISUALS

FLASH CARDS

OPAQUE STILL PICTURES

The term opaque still pictures is used to describe a group of instructional materials that emphasize still pictures that are opaque and thus viewed directly and not normally projected. There are literally hundreds of different types of opaque still pictures, and it is also obvious that we don't have time here to cover them all. Thus, we will concentrate on four of the more common types of opaque still pictures in this section. These opaque still pictures have been selected because they are relatively common to the classroom, they represent four quite different teaching/learning strategies, and because they are available from a variety of sources.

As with each group of media that we examine, we are interested in: 1) where we can find them (selection), 2) how we can use them (utilization), 3) their unique characteristics, and 4) techniques for their production and delivery to the intended audience. Since these are the important elements in examining these various materials, the following chart might be useful:

OPAQUE STILL PICTURES	sources			utilization				characteristics
	commercial sources	free/inexpensive sources	local production	presentation	interaction	independent study	drill/practice	General characteristics: Visual materials where the emphasis is on the pictures. They are normally viewed directly and thus should feature large, bold visuals and lettering.
teaching pictures	X	X	X		X			normally teachers guide on the back
study prints			X			X		presents information, requires a response and provides feedback
opaque projection visuals			X	X				special format and mounting requirements. $10 \times 10''$ or smaller
flash cards	X	X	X				X	small for small groups or large for large groups, many subjects.

As you can see, this class of instructional materials has the common characteristics of being, as their name indicates, opaque still pictures. This means they are normally viewed directly rather than through a transparency projector. Because they are normally viewed directly, they should feature large, bold visuals and lettering. However, each of these types of opaque still pictures is different in terms of its utilization. The teaching pictures are best for creating and interaction; the study prints are best for independent study; the opaque projection visual are best for presentation; and the flash cards are best for drill and practice.

It is hoped that when you are faced with media selection decisions, these charts may assist in picking the right media for the task at hand. Once you have decided on the media, you either find examples of free or commercial materials that are available in your content area, or, if it is necessary to be more specific, you produce the instructional materials to meet the needs of the specific audience or content.

TEACHING PICTURES:

A SET OF OPAQUE STILL PICTURES

USED BY THE TEACHER TO STIMULATE INTERACTION.

CHARACTERIZED BY BOLD VISUALS AND CAPTIONS.

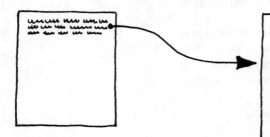

THIS IS A BEAGLE, A SMALL, SHORT-LEGGED, SMOOTH-COATED HOUND WITH PENDULOUS EARS.

NORMALLY WITH A TEACHERS GUIDE ON THE BACK.

TEACHING PICTURES, CHARACTERISTICS

Teaching pictures are a type of opaque still picture that are normally used to stimulate an interaction in a group of learners. These teaching pictures are used to present a visual concept to which the learners can react in terms of their particular background and experience. The role of the instructor changes from that of presenter of information to moderator. In utilizing teaching pictures, the instructor will generate questions related to the materials within the teaching pictures. These questions and the visual information will be designed to create a student discussion.

These teaching pictures usually come in sets, and the number of elements within a set is a function of the content that is being delivered. Some sets of teaching pictures may include only two visuals while others may contain twenty-two. However, no matter how many elements there are, they are all oriented toward a common theme or content. In the example on the opposite page the common theme is obviously dogs. It could just as easily be emotions, plants, occupations, or any other curriculum area where student interaction is appropriate.

Since these teaching pictures are intended to be viewed directly by groups of learners, it is essential that they feature large, bold visual elements and, where necessary, large, readable lettering. The term bold implies that the essential elements in the visuals are emphasized. These teaching pictures are commonly used at the elementary level, and in these situations it is possible to cluster the group of learners closer to the instructor and the teaching pictures. Since it is the responsibility of the instructor to encourage and direct the group discussion evolving from the presentation of these teaching pictures, there is often a teachers guide printed on or attached to the back of the visuals. It is visible to the instructor but invisible to the students and contains questions that can be used to instigate the group discussion. While the teachers guide normally contains these questions, it is also possible that it may contain information, games, or other suggestions to assist in beginning or directing the discussion.

There are a number of commercial sources that specialize in the production of these teaching pictures. However, since it is difficult to acquire catalogues for all of these producers, you can go to a major source such as the NICEM Indexes for listings of commercial teaching pictures. In additional to the commercial collections there are also large numbers of free/inexpensive teaching pictures available for use in the classroom. Listings of these are available in the various publications of the Educator's Progress Service such as the "Educator's Guide to Free Science Materials" or the "Educator's Guide to Free Elementary Materials." And in those instances where neither the commercial nor the free/inexpensive teaching pictures meets your specific needs or objectives, you may always turn to local production. Using the basic graphic skills of mounting, lettering and illustration, it is possible to design and produce, locally, excellent teaching pictures in the particular subject matter area that you want to cover.

TEACHING PICTURES:

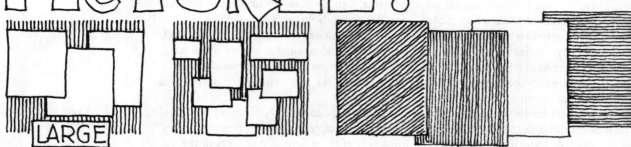

SELECT APPROPRIATE VISUALS AND BACKING (SIZE).

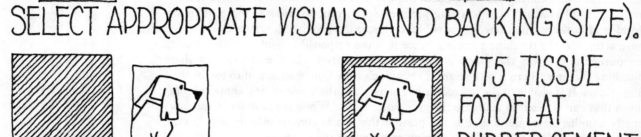

SELECT COLOR

MT5 TISSUE
FOTOFLAT
RUBBER CEMENT

MOUNT

DON'T LAMINATE

HAND LETTERING
WRICO LETTERING
CUTOUT LETTERING

LETTER THE CAPTION

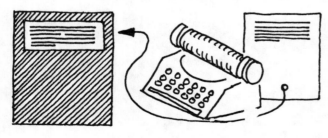

TYPE TEACHERS GUIDE

ASSEMBLE / UTILIZE

TEACHING PICTURES, PRODUCTION

The preparation of teaching pictures can employ all of the basic graphic skills of mounting, lettering, and illustration. But before we begin these processes we begin with the idea and the objectives and find a series of related visuals that effectively communicate the concept. If the visuals are not the right size, it may be necessary to enlarge them through projection or grid square, or to modify existing visuals through picture manipulation. Once we have the necessary visuals, we determine the appropriate size for the backing to which these visuals will be mounted.

While this is normally 11 × 14″ (a standard size), it may be any size that the instructor can conveniently hold. Not only do you have to select the size but also the appropriate color. The proper color of backing can emphasize the important elements in the picture. While there are some advantages to having all of the visuals in a particular set a common color, it may be more appropriate to mix the colors to pull out the visual elements you want to emphasize in each picture. Now, the visuals have been selected, the size determined and the appropriate colors picked, and you are ready to assemble these elements into the final product.

You may use any mounting technique to adhere the visual to the backing. The determining factors are the cost, the availability, your skills, and the nature of the visuals. Actually, in terms of the end product you can use rubber cement, MT-5, or Fotoflat as the adhesive and end up with a product that is quite satisfactory. You may want to review the various standard mounting techniques and their requirements before you make the final decision as to which to use.

Once the visuals are mounted, you may have to consider the addition of captions or headlines. Often it is desirable to use simple captions to direct the way the audience should read the visuals to which they are attached. Again, you can use almost any of the lettering techniques from hand lettering to Wrico. The final decision as to the best system to use is dependent upon your skills, the availability of the lettering system, and, perhaps most importantly, the size of lettering that is required. Remember the size readability rule (32:1) and pick the system that is most appropriate. There is also the teachers guide to consider. In this case it will be viewed at less than arm's length by the instructor, so you can easily use small lettering. It can be hand lettered, but for a more professional look you may want to type the information and then mount the typewritten materials onto the back of the teaching picture. It is normally a good idea to number the set of teaching pictures on this teachers guide so that you can always put them back into the proper order and sequence.

There is one thing you should definitely avoid in the preparation of these teaching pictures, and that is lamination. While lamination will serve to protect the visuals, it will also set up a potential glare problem. The reflection from the overhead lights may make it difficult to see the detail that you want learners to see. While matte lamination film can be used (it does not have a glare problem), the standard Seal-lamination film should be avoided for this media.

STUDY PRINTS:

OPAQUE STILL PICTURES

DESIGNED BY THE TEACHER BUT USED BY STUDENTS OPERATING INDEPENDENTLY. CHARACTERIZED BY:

1) THE PRESENT-ATION OF VISUAL AND/OR VERBAL INFORMATION,

2) A REQUIRED RESPONSE--- FROM THE LEARNER, AND

3) FEEDBACK--- TO THE LEARNER (WITHOUT THE TEACHER).

STUDY PRINTS, CHARACTERISTICS

Study prints are another type of opaque still picture. These sets of visuals that we call study prints are designed by the instructor to be used by the individual learners operating in an independent mode. There are a number of commercial and free materials that go by the name of study prints, but the majority of them lack the essential characteristics of what we mean by study prints. The real study print is a set of materials that is used independently by the individual learner and: 1) presents visual and written information, 2) requires that the learner make a response to this information, and 3) provides the learner with feedback as to the accuracy of his responses.

These study prints are intended primarily as self-instructional tools for individual learner use. While they can be appropriate for any learner in a particular class, they appear to be exceptionally useful for learners who are behind or learners who are ahead of the rest of the class. Used for remediation purposes, these study prints allow the student who has fallen behind to catch up without requiring an excessive amount of instructor time. Likewise, there are always students who have mastered the content quickly or even before the content was explored by the class. Without any productive activity these bright students can become behavior problems. Through the use of study prints for an enrichment activity, these students can be kept productively occupied as the rest of the class covers the normal content. In short, the study print is a means of meeting the individual needs of the students.

While there may be some commercial items that meet these vital characteristics, they are few and far between. I have not, personally, seen any study prints in the listings of free and inexpensive materials, so it basically means that study prints are normally available through local production. In this case the role of the instructor is not so much to deliver instruction but rather to design instruction that will be delivered independently through this particular media.

When designed for enrichment these study prints normally present large amounts of information with relatively few required responses and feedback systems. When they are designed for remediation, it is more common to present smaller amounts of information and to have more frequent requests for responses and more feedback sections. At first glance these may appear to fit the presentation of teaching/learning strategy, but they are more than this. They may appear to fit the drill and practice strategies, but, again, they are more than this. They seem to fit best into the self-instructional teaching/learning strategy and are a type of programmed instruction. Now, the self-instructional strategies may be programmed types of materials, or they may be materials like the text, in which the students are simply assigned a reading in a resource that is related to the content to be mastered.

Since the study prints are primarily locally produced, it is important that we explore the techniques related to the production of these important instructional materials.

STUDY PRINTS:

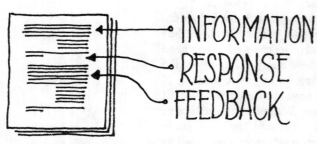

PLAN THE PROGRAM.

- INFORMATION
- RESPONSE
- FEEDBACK

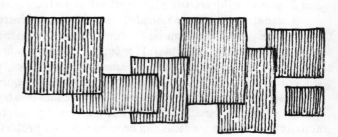

COLLECT/PREPARE VISUALS

PREPARE WRITTEN COPY

  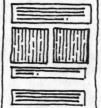 

ORGANIZE ELEMENTS

{ MT-5 TISSUE
FOTOFLAT
RUBBER CEMENT

 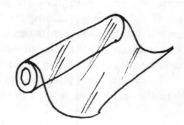

MOUNT THE ELEMENTS

LAMINATE

SEQUENCE AND NUMBER

ASSEMBLE/UTILIZE

STUDY PRINTS, PRODUCTION

Because of their nature, the production of study prints must begin with some solid production planning. First, determine the objectives that you want the learners to attain. Then determine the type of instruction that is necessary (in small bits for remediation and large bits for enrichment) and develop appropriate questions and feedback. Note that in this case the written material precedes the visualization. It is only after the verbal content is developed that you begin to locate visuals that will supplement or illustrate this written content.

Produce the final written copy. Because the materials are to be hand-held by an individual student (one at a time), the lettering can be done with a typewriter and the typewritten sections cut apart and mounted with their corresponding visual embellishments. Now you need to organize the elements. Remember there is going to be a "bit" of information (combinations of written and visual information) that is followed by a question that is followed by appropriate feedback. Then the process of information, response and feedback is repeated until you have covered all of the objectives and content that you need to have covered. At this point you are concerned with both the organization of the information and the arrangement of it on a series of panels or pages. Normally these panels are $11 \times 14''$ and made from railroad board. There are valid reasons for making sure that there is an overall color coordination and that the individual panels are either numbered in the proper sequence or taped together in an accordion fold format (see the accordion fold display later in this section).

Once the materials, visuals and copy have been produced and the backing selected, it is time to mount them into their desired positions. You may use any mounting technique (rubber cement, MT-5, or Fotoflat). However, since you *will* want to laminate these materials, you must use MT-5 if you are going to use Sealamin laminating film, or you can use any mounting adhesive if you are going to laminate them with pressure sensitive lamination film. Mount both the copy and the related visuals, making sure that the panels have been numbered in the proper sequence; then laminate the materials and they are ready for use.

We should spend a few moments talking about the types of responses that might be used for these study prints. First, these responses can be either overt or covert. The learners can just "think" the answers (covert), or they can actually write the answers. In addition to writing answers to the questions, the learners can be expected to draw, construct, recognize, and do other types of behavioral activities. If you do want the learners to make an overt response, you either need to provide them with a response sheet to accompany these materials or, since you have laminated them, you can give them a grease pencil and have them indicate their responses directly on the materials. With a damp rag the grease pencil responses can be wiped off, preparing the materials for the next student who needs to utilize them.

OPAQUE PROJECTION VISUALS:

A SET OF OPAQUE STILL PICTURES

PRESENTED THROUGH THE OPAQUE PROJECTOR,

HAVING A SPECIAL FORMAT AND SPECIAL MOUNTING TECHNIQUES.

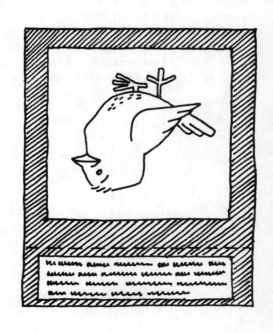

OPAQUE PROJECTION VISUALS, CHARACTERISTICS

Opaque projection visuals are a type of opaque still picture that is designed primarily for presentation through the opaque projector. This is one of the few types of opaque still pictures that are used in conjunction with a projection system, and because these are *opaque* still pictures, it is necessary to use an opaque projector. Obviously, it is necessary to understand the delivery system, the projector, if we are to understand the characteristics of the media, the opaque projection visuals.

The opaque projector is, first, the only projection system that we have that will project original materials that are opaque. Quite literally anything that is placed in the opaque projector will be delivered to the screen in full color. Basically the system works through reflected light. A high wattage bulb reflects light off of the item in the projector and first bounces it off a mirror inside the projector, then through a lens and onto the screen. Because of the way this system works, there are certain disadvantages. First, the projector develops a great deal of heat due to the high wattage bulb. This means that: 1) the visual will be exposed to a great deal of heat and can be damaged if left in too long (these projectors have been known to literally melt the binding of a book) and 2) a heavy duty fan is required to keep the equipment and materials even relatively cool (and the fans are usually quite noisy). In addition to the problems created by heat, there is also the problem of light. Even with the high wattage lamp the opaque projector requires almost complete room darkening to be an effective presentation device. Last but not least, there is a size problem. The aperture of the opaque projector measures $10 \times 10''$. This means that only visuals that are $10 \times 10''$ or smaller can be delivered effectively through this system.

Because of all of these disadvantages and limitations, one of the major characteristics of the opaque projection visuals is the fact that they require a special mounting format and treatment. Thus, the opaque projection visual must have a backing that measures $11 \times 14''$ but a visual area of $10 \times 10''$ or less. The visual must be mounted in an apparently upside down position because it will be bounced off the mirror inside the projector and reversed in this process. The visual cannot be laminated because it is delivered through reflected light, and the laminating film may provide a shiny surface that will distort the visual. The adhesives that are used in the mounting process must be able to resist the high temperatures generated inside the projector and maintain their integrity and adhesion.

But even with all of these problems and constraints, the opaque projection visual is a welcome addition to our collection of opaque still pictures. It is the only way we can present opaque still pictures to a large audience. Because of all of these limitations we are forced into local production. While commercial and even free/inexpensive materials can be inserted into the projector, items designed specifically for the opaque projector—what we choose to call opaque projection visuals—must be locally produced.

OPAQUE PROJECTION VISUALS:

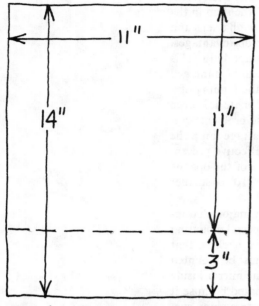

11"

14"

11"

3"

STANDARD SIZE

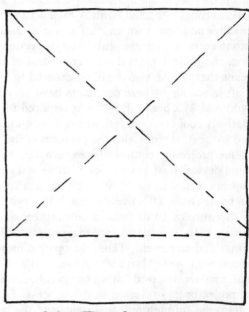

LOCATE CENTER

MOUNT VISUAL

ADD TEACHERS GUIDE

OPAQUE PROJECTION VISUALS, PRODUCTION

Since opaque projection visuals can only be produced through local production efforts, this page is vital if this is the delivery system that you desire to employ. As usual, we begin with the selection of an appropriate visual. In this case we can utilize visuals that are a little more detailed since they, and the details, will be enlarged in projection. In addition, the visual must be 10 × 10″ or smaller since the aperture of the opaque projector measures only 10 × 10″. Once the visual is selected, the next step is the selection of the backing. I have found that 11 × 14″ railroad board works best. Note that if the visuals you are using measure less than 10 × 10″, a portion of the backing will show around the visual as it is projected. In this case you need to pay particular attention to the relationship of the color of the background to the elements in the visual that you want to emphasize. Personally, I prefer to use black railroad board as this seems to direct the viewers attention to the visual, but if you want a different color, make sure that it works.

To prepare this backing you need to divide it into two sections: first, an 11 × 11″ portion that will contain the visual and second, a smaller section measuring 3 × 11″ that will contain the teachers script or guide that will accompany the particular visuals. The 11 × 11″ part will go into the projector itself, and the 3 × 11″ section will extend out the back of the projector and be visible to the operator during its utilization.

Next, it is necessary to identify the center of the 11 × 11″ part of the backing material. To do this simply draw light lines from the diagonally opposite corners; where they cross is the center of this portion of the area. The visual is to be mounted as close to the center as possible. The diagonal lines will be useful in positioning the visual.

MT-5 dry mounting tissue is the only adhesive you should use for preparing these opaque projection visuals; the other adhesives will deteriorate under the heat of the opaque projector. Turn the visual over, and tack the tissue in place. Then trim the tissue/visual sandwich to the desired size and/or format. Position the visual in the 11 × 11″ area of the backing board, tack it in place, and adhere it with a dry mount press set at 225 degrees. Note that the visual is mounted with the top of the visual toward the 3 × 11″ portion of the backing.

All that is left is to type up the teachers guide and adhere it to the 3 × 11″ section that will extend outside of the projector. The opaque projection visual should never be laminated, as the lamination will adversely affect the ability to project a quality image. Now the visuals are ready to use. They are inserted into the rear of the opaque projector and the projector turned on. The image will be faithfully reproduced on the screen and enlarged so that the audience can see all of the detail that you desire to communicate. However, even with the MT-5 it will be advisable to limit the amount of time that the visual is left in the projector.

FLASH CARDS:

A SET OF OPAQUE STILL PICTURES (OF VARIOUS SIZES)

DESIGNED FOR DRILL AND PRACTICE IN A WIDE RANGE OF CURRICULUM AREAS.

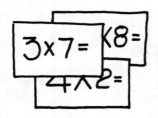

SMALLER SIZES FOR SMALLER GROUPS.

LARGER SIZES FOR LARGER GROUPS.

FLASH CARDS, CHARACTERISTICS AND PRODUCTION

Flash cards are the last type of opaque still picture that we will consider. These are sets of opaque still pictures of various sizes that are intended for drill and practice activities in a wide range of curriculum areas. Probably you are all familiar with the media that we call flash cards, but it is equally certain that when you think of flash cards, you think of small cards that are used to practice math skills. The first thing that you must recognize is the fact that math is only one of the subject matter areas in which flash cards can be used. I have seen commercial flash cards for color recognition, road signs and symbols, map symbols, beginning consonants, and a number of other areas of the curriculum. There are even a number of free and inexpensive sources that produce flash cards for concepts such as the four basic food groups, steps in making steel, and other curriculum areas. In addition to flash cards being suitable for a number of different curriculum areas, they are also available in a variety of sizes. Most people think of flash cards as a one-on-one drill and practice activity. There are commercial flash cards that measure 11 × 14″ and can be used quite effectively to drill an entire class. Probably the only size limitation on flash cards is the ability of an individual to hold them up in front of an audience.

In addition to commercial and free/inexpensive flash cards, it is quite possible to make your own through local production techniques. Obviously, those that deal with math and language arts skills will probably contain only letters or numbers. In developing flash cards for practicing visual concepts such as road signs, map symbols, etc., you will need to use your illustration techniques to get all of the visuals the same size. It is essential that they all be the same size to enhance your ability to show them to the learners. Any mounting technique can be used to mount these visual elements to a rigid backing, but they should never be laminated. The lamination film will set up a glare that will interfere with the practice activity. In addition, you will want the correct response on the opposite side so that whoever is presenting them will be able to either correct or approve the response of the learners.

Flash cards are a type of opaque still picture that is used for drill and practice activities. They are available from commercial sources, free/inexpensive sources, and also from local production activities. They can be used in any area of the curriculum and for groups of almost any size.

DEMONSTRATION BOARDS:

- CHALKBOARDS

- FELTBOARDS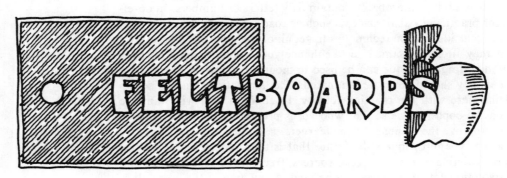

- HOOK 'N LOOP BOARD

- MAGNETIC BOARD

DEMONSTRATION BOARDS, CHARACTERISTICS

Demonstration boards are a class of simple media and are quite useful when it is desirable to manipulate concepts and ideas. With the materials appropriate for these various demonstration boards we can add and/or subtract information during our presentation. There are a number of different media that fall under the general classification of demonstration boards. We have selected four for this section: first, the chalkboard, because it is the most common of all demonstration boards; second, the feltboard, because it is also common and, perhaps more importantly, because it is easy to acquire or produce instructional materials for this media; third, the hook 'n loop board, because it has the ability to display and present extremely heavy items; and last, the magnetic board, because it can be combined with the chalkboard to provide a wider range of applications. The sources, utilization, and characteristics of these media and their materials are illustrated in this chart.

Demonstration Board Materials	sources			utilization				characteristics
	commercial sources	free/inexpensive sources	local production	presentation	interaction	independent study	drill/practice	General characteristics: Demonstration boards and their instructional materials are primarily used to manipulate ideas and concepts; these tools and their materials give you the ability to add and/or subtract information as desired.
chalkboard materials			X	X	X		X	images can be created using a variety of tools and techniques
feltboard materials	X	X	X	X	X		X	available in many subject areas, easy to produce locally
hook 'n loop materials			X	X	X		X	supports very heavy materials, excellent for real objects
magnetic board materials	X	X	X	X	X		X	supports moderately heavy items, chalkboard/ magnetic board combo

You will note that while some of these demonstration board materials are available from commercial, free/inexpensive and local production sources (feltboard materials and magnetic board materials), the others are only available through local production efforts. In all cases these materials can be effectively used for presentation to large groups, to develop an interaction within a group, and for drill and practice activities. About the only teaching/learning strategy that is not appropriate for demonstration board materials is independent study. We should point out that when a presentation is combined with the general manipulation characteristic of demonstration boards, it can really increase your communication capabilities. For in an interaction activity learners can not only interact verbally, they can also physically interact with the materials displayed on these demonstration boards. While drill and practice is probably the least important teaching/learning strategy for these media, we can all remember the work at the front of the room using the chalkboard. The other demonstration boards and their materials can be used in a similar fashion.

THE CHALKBOARD

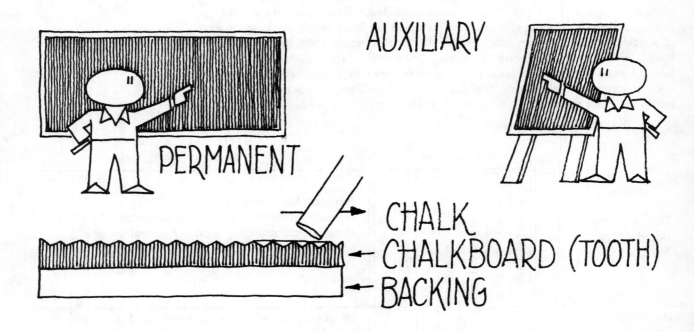

AUXILIARY

PERMANENT

CHALK
CHALKBOARD (TOOTH)
BACKING

❋ PREPARING THE CHALKBOARD

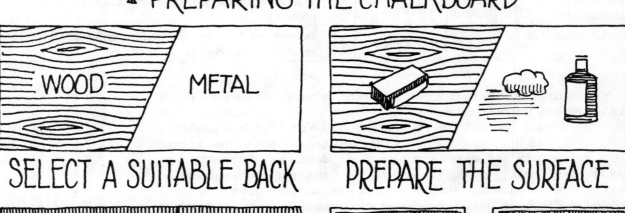

WOOD   METAL

SELECT A SUITABLE BACK

PREPARE THE SURFACE

APPLY CHALKBOARD PAINT   PERM. IMAGE   PRIME

THE CHALKBOARD, CHARACTERISTICS

The chalkboard is probably the most common type of demonstration board. No self-respecting classroom space would be without it, yet it is probably the most misused instructional media that we have. Part of the reason for this misuse is the simple fact that we do not understand how the chalkboard itself works. First, a good chalkboard surface must have what is called "tooth." Basically, this means that the surface must be rough—not rough to the touch but rough enough so that as the chalk is drawn across it, particles of the chalk will be scraped off and deposited on the board. Second, for a chalkboard surface to work well, to be easily imaged and erased, it needs a thin layer of chalk dust to serve as a lubricant. Perhaps you have noticed that on Monday morning the chalkboard in your room does not work as well as it did on Friday. If this is the case, it is probably because the good-hearted custodian has washed your chalkboard over the weekend. In washing away the thin layer of chalk dust, he has made it more difficult to produce images and to erase them. A simple solution to this problem is to keep a dirty, dust-filled eraser in your desk, and before class on Monday just go all over the board.

These chalkboards come in two basic formats, those that are permanently attached to the walls of your room and those that are movable, either on wheels or supported on easels. These auxiliary chalkboards are excellent for class interaction activities and for drill and practice. The permanent chalkboards work well for presentation as well as interaction and drill and practice. The images on a chalkboard are normally transitory. They are put on the board and then erased. Thus, they are really only available through local production activities. However, there are tools that can be purchased that will assist you in the construction of these images, or it is even possible to put permanent images on the chalkboard. With tape or paint, a musical staff, street map, map of the state or nation, or an outline of the human body can become a permanent image to which you add or subtract the information that you desire the learners to react to. Even when the added images are erased, the permanent lines will remain to be used over and over again.

It is a relatively simple task to produce your own chalkboard. First, select a suitable backing material. It can be either wood or metal backed with wood. Next, the surface must be prepared to accept the chalkboard paint that will be applied. For the wood surfaces this means that they must be sanded smooth and possibly painted with a primer paint. For the metal surfaces you will probably want to etch the surface with acid. Use standard household vinegar to avoid acid burns. Just apply, let it set for 3–5 minutes, and then wash and dry the surface. To paint the surface you will want to use chalkboard paint. This is a special paint with a "tooth" built in. This paint comes in either a brush-on type paint or a spray paint. Follow directions on the container to apply it properly. You may then prepare the permanent images you desire, prime the board with chalk dust, and you will have a demonstration board to which you can add or subtract information.

THE CHALKBOARD
CREATING IMAGES:

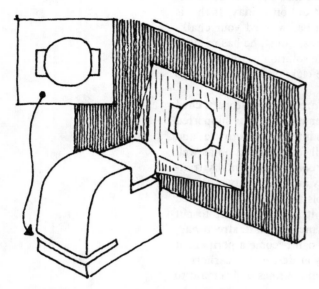

PROJECTION ENLARGEMENT

DRAWING/WRITING

POUNCE

STENCILS

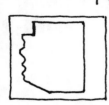

ORIGINAL

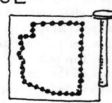

PUNCH HOLES

POSITION

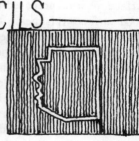

TRACE

CHALK DUST

CONNECT DOTS

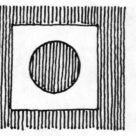

POSITION

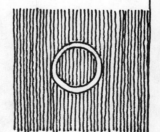

TRACE

THE CHALKBOARD, CREATING THE IMAGES

A chalkboard without images is just a black wall, so our obvious concern will be with the techniques that you can utilize to create the instructional images for your chalkboard. Remember that to both draw and erase these images easily you will need to have a thin layer of chalkdust on the surface of the board.

The chalk is the material we will use to create these images, so a brief comment about chalk is in order. There are different qualities of chalk, and the best quality is only slightly more expensive than the cheapest quality. The slight extra money will make the use of high quality chalk very worthwhile. Also, chalk comes in a variety of colors. However, there is chalk designed for paper and chalk designed for the chalkboard. The chalk designed for paper is usually more brilliant and available in a wider range of colors, but if it is used on the chalkboard, you will have a great deal of difficulty erasing the images. Normally, these images must be washed off and then the board primed all over again. The chalk designed for chalkboards is less brilliant in color, but it will be easier to use and especially to erase.

The obvious way to create images on the chalkboard is through drawing and lettering, but there are other techniques that will allow you to create exciting visuals without any real artistic ability. The opaque projector can be used to project images directly onto the chalkboard surface, and after the images are traced, the projector can be put away. The result will be professional looking illustrations and the feeling by your class that they have an artist for a teacher. Later you can introduce them to the opaque projector, and they can help in the creation of instructional materials for your chalkboard. If your original is transparent, you can use the overhead projector in the same manner.

The pounce pattern is a little different. An image is created on a piece of railroad board using any illustration technique that is appropriate. Then, using a blunt nail or a punch, holes are punched along the lines. Holding the pounce pattern against the chalkboard surface, you can dust it with a dirty eraser, and the chalkdust will go through the holes and onto the chalkboard. Then remove the pounce pattern and simply connect the dots. One teacher I know of makes her pounce patterns on old window blinds that are attached to the top of her chalkboard. When needed they are rolled down and dusted. When not in use they are rolled up for storage. Obviously, these are for often-used images.

Stencils can also be used to transfer images to the chalkboard. Commonly used shapes like geometric forms or map outlines can be cut from cardboard or light plywood and placed against the chalkboard. Then, using chalk, simply draw around or inside the stencil, and you will have transferred the desired image to the chalkboard. If possible, you will want to attach a handle to these stencils to hold them in place during the tracing process. You will also want to recognize that the tracing will be slightly larger than the stencil.

THE FELTBOARD:

THE VISUAL

 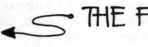 THE FELTBOARD

✳ PREPARING THE FELTBOARD

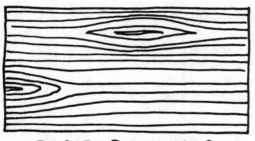

RIGID BACKING

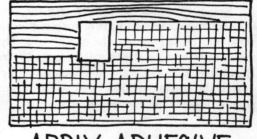

APPLY ADHESIVE

APPLY FELT

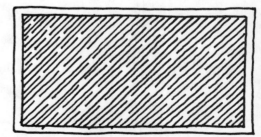

FRAME THE EDGES

THE FELTBOARD, CHARACTERISTICS

The feltboard is a type of demonstration board that operates on the principle that fuzzy things stick to fuzzy things. In this case, the feltboard itself is a fuzzy surface made from felt, flannel or any cloth with a texture. The instructional materials, the feltboard pieces, are backed with materials having a texture that will adhere to these surfaces. Like other demonstration boards, the feltboard gives you the ability to manipulate these elements, to add and/or subtract information as part of the presentation.

But the feltboard is useful for teaching/learning strategies other than presentation. It can be used quite effectively to generate an interaction within a group: not only a verbal interaction but also a physical interaction as students actually manipulate the pieces that are arranged on the feltboard. This type of demonstration board is also useful for drill and practice. In this teaching/learning strategy the feltboard can either display materials the entire class can react to, or students can manipulate the materials on the feltboard.

Feltboards are the type of demonstration board for which there are the most instructional materials. Numbers of companies produce commercial instructional materials for use on the feltboard. These are available in a surprising number of curriculum areas and for a wide range of grade levels. In addition, perhaps because of their low cost, felt board materials are available from a number of free/inexpensive sources such as the American Dairy Association. While many of these free/inexpensive feltboard pieces are biased, it is quite easy to modify and manipulate them to meet your needs or objectives. And, last but not least, it is a simple matter to use the basic graphic skills of mounting, lettering and illustration to produce feltboard materials that are specific to your subject, audience or objective.

There are commercial feltboards available for purchase, but it is also quite easy to produce your own. Begin with a rigid backing such as wood or heavy cardboard. Apply an adhesive such as Elmers glue to the backing and then cover it with a material that has a good texture. Felt is best, but flannel is almost as good and not quite as expensive. Once the felt or flannel is adhered to the backing, you may want to trim the edges of the board. This can be done either with tape or by putting a wood frame on the board.

There are some disadvantages with the feltboard. First, the materials are not very well adhered to the board. It is advisable to use the feltboard at less than a vertical angle, as shown on the opposite page. This way the adhesion will be increased as gravity pulls the feltboard materials against the feltboard. Even so, bumping the board may cause the pieces to be dislodged. But even with these disadvantages, the feltboard can become a valuable addition to the array of instructional media that can be used to increase your ability to communicate effectively.

THE FELTBOARD
CREATING IMAGES:

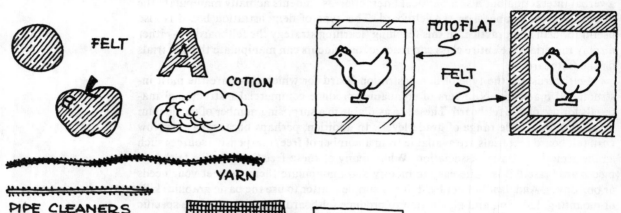

FELT

COTTON

FOTOFLAT

FELT

YARN

PIPE CLEANERS

FOAM RUBBER

SAND PAPER

VARIOUS BACKING

FELT BACKED VISUALS

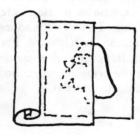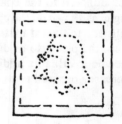

SANDPAPER BACKED VISUALS

PELLON TRACED VISUALS

THE FELTBOARD, CREATING IMAGES

As we indicated, one of the advantages of the feltboard system is the fact that there are a number of commercial and free/inexpensive instructional materials available to feed this system. However, it is not always possible to find exactly what you want, and this leads us directly to the local production of materials for the feltboard.

First, there are many materials that can be used directly on the feltboard. Shapes and letters cut from felt will adhere nicely to the feltboard. It is even possible to produce a "build-up" of felt cutouts. For example, a map of the United States could have the original thirteen states placed on top of it and even a special state or battle placed on top of this. Don't try to build up too many layers, but you can achieve some interesting applications. Cotton fluffs will also adhere to the feltboard. If you are discussing weather, these can represent the cloud patterns that would accompany a frontal system. Pipe cleaners will also adhere to the feltboard, and these can be bent into shapes for a number of different purposes. Sandpaper and even foam rubber will also adhere to a feltboard surface, but these are more commonly used to back other instructional materials.

Perhaps the most common technique to produce materials for the feltboard is to back them with felt. The process begins with the selection of the visual. It may be one that will eventually end up in a rectangular format or one that will end up as a cutout. In either case you should use Fotoflat as the adhesive. Tack the Fotoflat to the back of the visual, then trim the visual to the desired format if it is to end up rectangular, or rough trim it if it is to end up as a cutout. Position the visual onto a piece of felt and adhere it by cooking it in a dry mount press at 180 degrees or ironing it on with a home iron set at the rayon setting. Then trim the visual into the desired size and format, and you have produced a visual suitable for use on the feltboard.

You can also back the visual with sandpaper. This will cut the cost, and sandpaper is almost as good a backing as felt. The process is a little different. Here, the first step is to mount the visual to a rigid backing such as railroad board. For this part of the process you can use any adhesive. Once the visual is mounted and trimmed to the desired size and format, you then adhere trips of sandpaper to the back. Here, the adhesive to use is rubber cement. Heat may melt the glue that holds the sand to the paper. Now this visual is ready for display.

Another material that will work well on the feltboard is pellon. This dress lining material is translucent, and you can simply lay it over the desired visual and trace the image onto the pellon. It can then be colored and cut out and used directly on the feltboard.

These represent just a few of the ways that you can prepare materials for display on the feltboard. As long as you follow the basic principle and back your visuals with a fuzzy material that will adhere to the fuzzy feltboard, you can easily produce instructional materials.

HOOK 'N LOOP BOARD

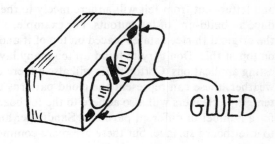

GLUED

LOOP MATERIAL/BACKING

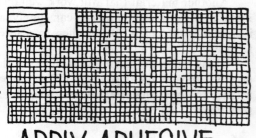

HOOK MATERIAL/VISUAL

❈ PREPARING THE HOOK 'N LOOP BOARD

RIGID BACKING

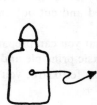

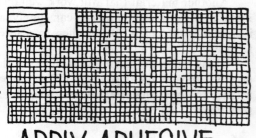

APPLY ADHESIVE

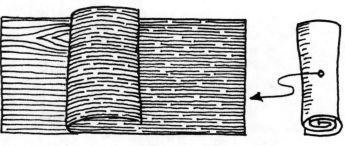

APPLY LOOP MATERIAL

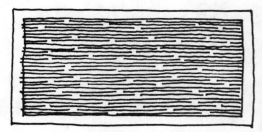

FRAME THE EDGES

HOOK 'N LOOP BOARD

The hook 'n loop board is one of the more unusual demonstration boards. This is primarily because the hook 'n loop board will support very heavy instructional materials. The board is made of a nylon loop material, and the visuals are backed with a nylon hook material. When these two surfaces come together, it is said that one square inch of the hook material will support up to 15 pounds. This means that we can display, present, or manipulate real objects that would be too heavy for other demonstration boards.

The hook 'n loop board, like other demonstration boards, can be used to present information to large groups of learners or to develop either a verbal or physical interaction with the materials. It can also be used for drill and practice activities. Because of the nature of the materials, there are few, if any, commercial materials produced for this system. You can purchase the nylon hook material and attach it to almost anything, but there are few instructional materials that can be purchased with the material already attached. This is also true for free/inexpensive sources. If there are any free/inexpensive instructional materials available with the hook material already attached, I am not familiar with them. This leaves only local production as a source for visuals that can be used on the hook 'n loop board.

Local production is quite simple. For substantial items all you have to do is clip off a piece of the nylon hook material and either fasten it in place with the adhesive on the back or glue it in place if the object is really heavy. For lightweight materials such as tearsheet visuals, it is important to mount them first to cardboard to provide a solid backing. Then the hook materials are attached to the back, and they can be used on the board surface. This process is needed because it takes some effort to remove the visuals from the board, and if they do not have a solid backing they are likely to tear.

While the hook 'n loop boards are available commercially, they are also quite expensive. You can purchase the materials and easily produce your own. Because this is used to support heavy materials, it is essential that a heavy backing be provided for the board. I have found that a good quality plywood works well. To this backing you need to apply a high quality adhesive. The company that sells the materials provides such an adhesive, or you can use white Elmers glue. With the glue spread completely over the board surface, place the nylon loop material onto the board and apply weights until it is solidly adhered. The board can be edged with tape or wood, but it is even more important that it be firmly attached to the wall. If it is supported by an easel, the heavy materials that you might display will have a tendency to topple the entire board. This hook 'n loop board and the locally produced materials can work well for special uses where it is important to display and manipulate real objects or materials that weigh a lot.

THE MAGNETIC BOARD

MAGNETIC BOARD

MAGNETIC CHALK BD

ENAMEL PAINT

CHALKBOARD PAINT

RIGID BACK — METAL

RIGID BACK — METAL

PREPARING THE CHALKBOARD

METAL TO RIGID BACK

COAT WITH ACID (VINEGAR)

APPLY CHALKBOARD PAINT

FRAME THE EDGES

THE MAGNETIC BOARD, CHARACTERISTICS

The magnetic board is the last of the five instructional media that we will look at under the classification of demonstration boards. While the magnetic board, like all other demonstration boards, can be effectively used to manipulate concepts and ideas, it has some different characteristics that make it unique. This is especially true when we begin to modify the magnetic board and turn it into a magnetic chalkboard—a combination board.

Materials for these magnetic boards are available from all three of our sources. There are commercial magnetic board materials listed in the NICEM Indexes, and there are free/inexpensive magnetic board materials available through sources listed in the various Educator's Progress Service publication. And it is also perfectly possible to create your own materials for the magnetic board by using the various mounting, lettering and illustration techniques covered earlier in the text. While there are not as many magnetic board materials available as there are feltboard materials, they are usually available in many curriculum areas and for a range of grade levels.

These magnetic board materials and the magnetic boards that they are manipulated on can be used for a variety of teaching/learning strategies. They can be used to present information to large groups of learners. Obviously, the larger the group, the larger the materials and lettering need to be. They can, like other demonstration boards, be used to develop an interaction situation in the class. This means both a verbal interaction and a physical interaction. The learners can both discuss the information and actually manipulate the magnetic board materials. In addition to using these materials for presentation and to generate an interaction, we can also effectively use them for drill and practice activities. While there may be less expensive media that can be used for drill and practice, the magnetic board works, and works effectively, perhaps because it is different.

In addition to the production of magnetic instructional materials, it is also possible to manufacture your own magnetic board. The process is quite simple. First, you begin with a metal backing to which magnets will adhere. If this is coated with a galvanized coating, you may have to remove it and treat the surface for painting. This can be done using a household acid such as vinegar. Coat the metal surface with this vinegar and let it set for three to five minutes. Then wash it off and dry the surface. If you want a simple magnetic board, you can then paint the surface with any good quality enamel paint. However, if you want a combination board, you can paint the metal surface with chalkboard paint. When painting metal, it is preferable to use the spray type of chalkboard paint. Simply follow the instructions on the aerosol canister. If the metal surface is rigid, you are ready to use the magnetic board. If the metal surface is the least flexible, you will want to back the metal sheet up with a rigid backing of wood. Then, of course, you can tape the edges of the board or put a wooden frame around it to finish it off. The resulting magnetic board can be used mounted to the wall or even on an easel.

MAGNETIC BOARD VISUALS:

TEARSHEET

TISSUE

BACKING

TRIM

OR CUTOUT

REVERSE

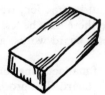
BAR MAGNET

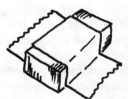
APPLY

TEARSHEET

TISSUE

BACKING

TRIM

OR CUTOUT

REVERSE

STRIP MAGNET

APPLY

MAGNETIC BOARD MATERIALS, PRODUCTION

Like most instructional materials, those for the magnetic board begin with tear-sheets. These tearsheets can be used directly if they are the proper size and cover the appropriate content, but if not they can be manipulated to change their meaning or enlarged to change their size through various illustration techniques. Once we have the visual that communicates and is the right size and format, our only problem is to make it suitable for display on the magnetic board. Basically, this means that we must attach magnets to the back so that they will adhere to the board surface.

The visual should first be mounted to a rigid backing such as railroad board. You can use any adhesive and mounting technique that you want to for this part of the process. These visuals can end up as standard illustrations in a rectangular format, or they can be cut out so that there is no distracting background. The last step in the process is to adhere the magnets to the visual. Standard magnets are called bar magnets, and they come in many sizes. Utilizing small bar magnets, we can glue them directly to the back of the visuals. However, even the small bar magnets are expensive, and visuals with magnets attached are difficult to store. A simple and more inexpensive technique is to simply tape the bar magnets to the back of the visual. This will cut the magnetic quality slightly, but when you are through with the visuals for this unit, you can peel off the magnets, put them in a box and store the visuals flat. Then reuse the magnets for the next set of visuals that you want to adhere to the magnetic board.

However, there have been new technological developments in magnets. They are used for a wide range of purposes. Have you ever wondered what keeps your refrigerator door closed? Yes, there is a strip magnet that runs around the inside of the door. This new type of magnet is really just a strip of rubber that has been impregnated with steel filings and then magnetized. The advantage is expense and flexibility. It is possible to cut these magnets into different lengths with scissors and glue them to the back of the magnetic board visuals. In many instances these strip magnets come with an adhesive back. Just peel away the paper exposing the adhesive and attach the magnet to the visual. The process again begins with the visual. Once it has been selected and/or modified, it should be mounted to a rigid backing. This is necessary since the paper that the visuals are printed on is too flimsy to stand up for very long. Then the visual can be trimmed into the standard rectangular format, or it can be presented as a cutout. This cutout process is difficult with a visual that has been backed with railroad board but worth the effort when completed. The strip magnet is then attached to the back, either by gluing it in place or by using the pressure adhesive backing that often comes with the strip magnet.

Either the bar magnet or the strip magnet will allow the visuals to be adhered, manipulated and displayed on the magnetic board. The ability to manipulate these items is common to all demonstration boards.

DISPLAYS:

- BULLETIN BOARDS
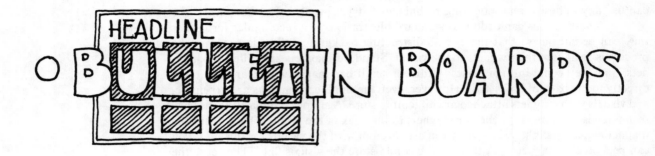

- POSTERS

- EXHIBITS
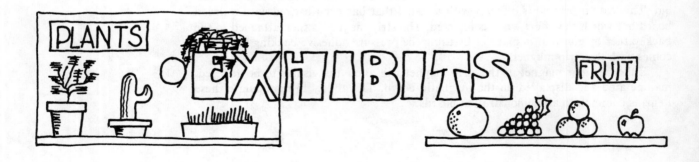

- MODELS

DISPLAYS, GENERAL CHARACTERISTICS

There is a class of instructional materials that falls under the name "displays." Materials such as bulletin board displays, posters, accordion fold displays, exhibits, models and dioramas are but a few of the instructional materials that can be listed under this general category of displays. These instructional materials are available from a variety of sources and are useful for a variety of teaching/learning strategies, as the following chart will show.

Display systems	sources			utilization				characteristics
	commercial sources	free/inexpensive sources	local production	presentation	interaction	independent study	drill/practice	General characteristics: Display systems are primarily used to present information. While they can be used for other teaching/learning strategies, their most vital role is the presentation of information. To do this they must be designed so that they attract and hold the attention of the learners and deliver the information clearly and quickly.
Bulletin boards	X	X	X	X	X	X	X	Primarily used to display two dimensional materials
Posters	X	X	X	X	X			Can also be used as reference materials for the learners
Accordion fold displays			X	X		X		Can also be used successfully for independent study activities
Exhibits			X	X	X			Primarily used to display three dimensional realia, hands on
Models	X	X	X	X				Simulating real objects to enhance a demonstration/presentation
Dioramas			X	X				Simulating a real environment event or activity

These various display systems have a flexibility that allows the different displays to be used effectively for different purposes as well as for the common purpose of all displays—presentation. If a special need arises, perhaps one of these systems will fit your unique needs. Some of these materials, such as the bulletin board, are a combination of media and materials, the media being the display surface itself, the bulletin board and the materials being the elements that are displayed on that surface. Other display systems such as the poster and the diorama are both media and materials, and it is almost impossible to separate the one from the other.

As we examine these systems, pay particular attention to the unique characteristics of each: which is primarily a presentation of two dimensional materials and which is best for presenting three dimensional materials. When it is desirable to bring realia into the classroom, is the exhibit best, or will the model allow the learners to see elements of the real thing that would be invisible even if the real thing were present? If you want to develop a self-instructional unit utilizing a display media, would a bulletin board or an accordion fold display do the best job for you? Remember one of the most important considerations in mediated communications is the selection of the right media to do the job that you want done.

BULLETIN BOARD DISPLAYS:

A SYSTEM FOR PRESENTATION, INTERACTION, INDEPENDENT STUDY, AND EVEN

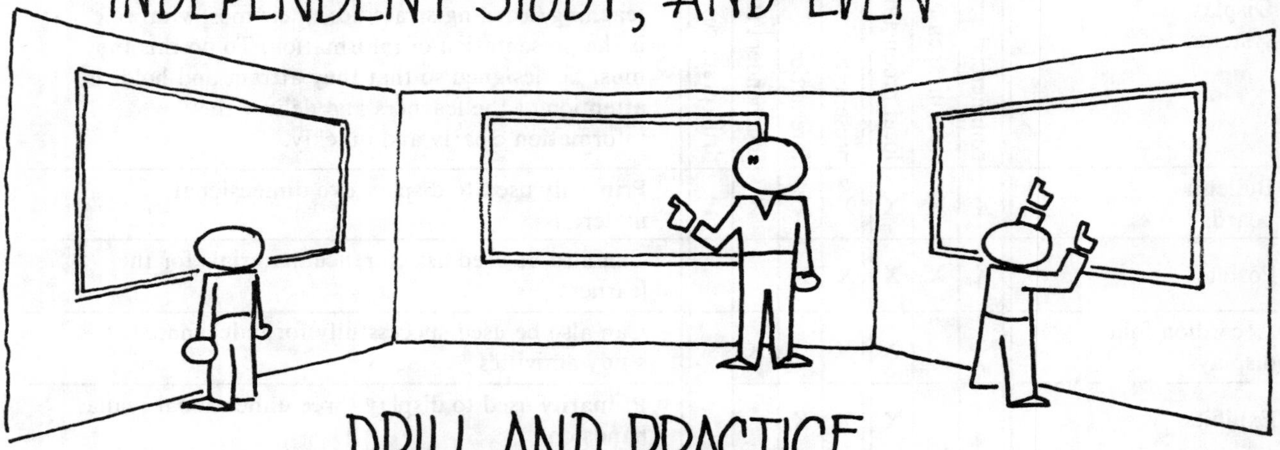

DRILL AND PRACTICE.

PREPARING THE BULLETIN BOARD.

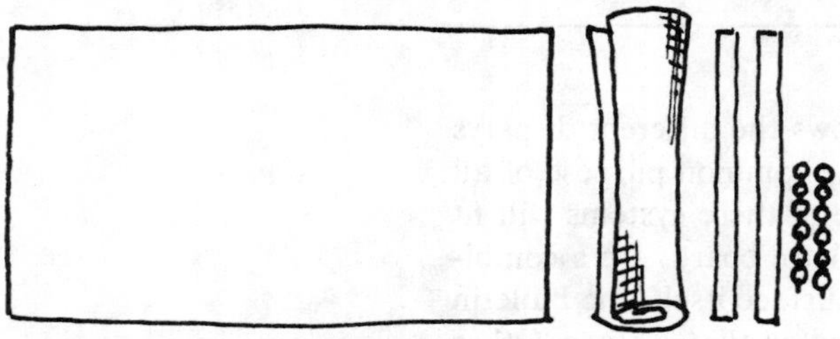

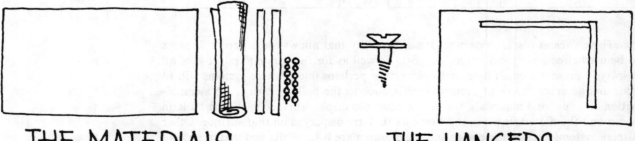

THE MATERIALS

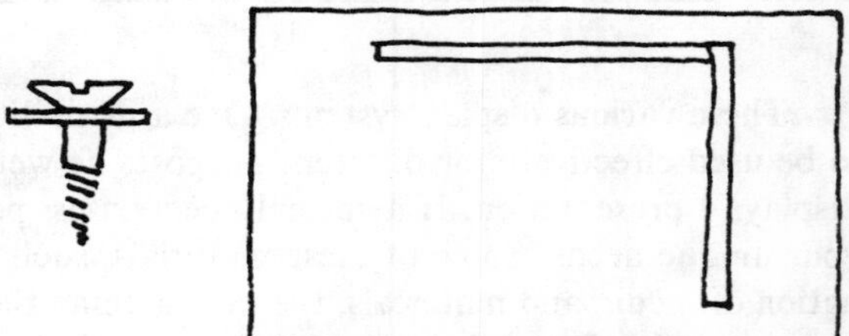

THE HANGERS

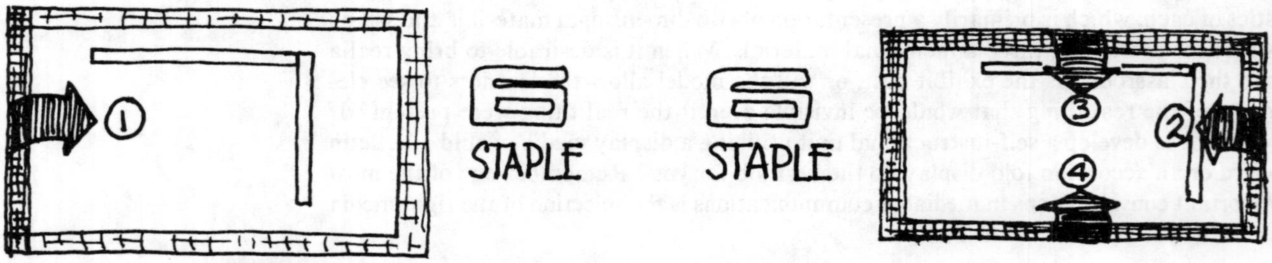

COVER WITH CLOTH AND STAPLE

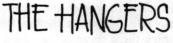

BULLETIN BOARD DISPLAYS, CHARACTERISTICS

The bulletin board is probably the most common display system that is found in an instructional setting. Basically, the bulletin board is a surface to which an assortment of two dimensional visuals can be attached. Depending upon the design of the board and the layout of the elements, bulletin boards can be used for presentation to large groups, as stimulus for interaction, and even for independent study and drill and practice. While the most common application is as a display that is intended to attract attention and transmit information, this very versatile display system can fit into almost any teaching/learning strategy.

The bulletin board that is designed to assist in a presentation to a large group needs to have large, bold visual and captions. Often it is used to assist the presenter and then remains up as a reference for the students as they work through a unit of study. The bulletin board that is designed to generate an interaction often has a headline that asks a question, and the other elements continue with the question rather than providing answers. The display that is intended for independent study must have the basic characteristics of any self-instructional media. It must present information, require a response and provide feedback without the physical presence of the instructor. The bulletin board that is designed for drill and practice may be nothing more than a large electric board (see the section on electric boards) that will allow the learners to master information they have already learned. Even though the bulletin board is versatile, its main function is the transmission of information in a presentation mode.

Materials that are designed for display on a bulletin board can be acquired from commercial, free/inexpensive and local production sources. There are packages of commercial bulletin board materials for most of the standard topics. There are also many free/inexpensive sources that provide not only the materials for a bulletin board but also the ideas for layouts to attract, hold and direct the attention of the learners. Of course, it is entirely possible to produce materials for the display locally, using basic skills of mounting, lettering and illustration. In short, there are a number of different sources for the headlines, visuals and copy that comprise the information elements of a bulletin board.

The bulletin board itself can be purchased commercially, or you can make them locally. Basically, what you want is a surface that will allow you to fasten materials to it and will not distract from the message. To produce a simple bulletin board, begin with a backing. I suggest a material called Celotex. Attach wooden strips to the back of this material; these will be used to hang the board against the wall. Then cover the Celotex with a material. I prefer burlap since this comes in a wide range of colors and will not show pin holes where the materials are attached. Pull the burlap tight around the Celotex and staple it in place. Then you can attach cup hooks to the wood braces and use chain to support the board from the wall or ceiling.

BULLETIN BOARD MATERIALS:

  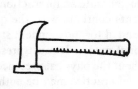 

MT'D PICTURES   TEARSHEETS   CUTOUTS   OBJECTS

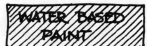

CAN YOU PAINT?

HARDWARE

CAPTIONS   HEADLINES

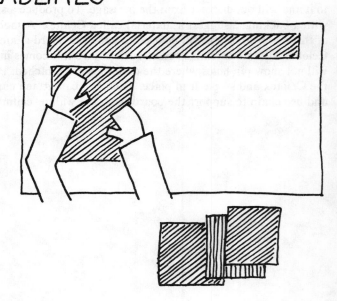

THUMBNAILS   MANIPULATION

BULLETIN BOARD MATERIALS, PRODUCTION

Basically, there are three types of elements that go into any layout, including that for a bulletin board. These are the visuals, the headlines, and the captions or copy. Before you begin the actual production of these elements, you will want to determine how they will be arranged in the visual field called the bulletin board. This process of arriving at an appropriate layout should, if possible, utilize the necessary design principles to attract, hold, and direct the attention of the audience. See the chapter on layout and design for some of these principles. To determine the actual arrangement, you will want to prepare a series of thumbnails or manipulate some blank paper forms to determine the final layout. The thumbnails are a series of small-scale sketches that show the various possible arrangements. When you find the one that seems to work best, this becomes the blueprint for the arrangement of these elements. The manipulation of blank paper forms is another technique for arriving at the final layout. Here, the forms are normally the substitutes for the elements, and they are just manipulated on the bulletin board surface until you are satisfied. Either this arrangement of elements or the acceptable thumbnail sketch shows what elements you need to include and how they should be arranged.

The actual production of these elements really poses no problems if you have mastered the basic graphic skills of mounting, lettering and illustration. Let's look at the visual elements first. Their size and complexity is a function of the determined use of the board. For presentation they should be large and bold enough to be seen by all members of the class. For interaction they might be more detailed and smaller since the learners will probably walk to the board to view the display. Similarly, for self-instruction and drill and practice we can assume that the learners will come to the board and that the visual elements will be viewed from quite close up. These pictures should be mounted to a rigid backing such as railroad board to keep them protected and to aid in the presentation. In some cases you will want the railroad to form a border around the visuals, and in others you will not want the railroad board seen. Illustration and manipulation techniques can be used to make the visuals more specific to your needs.

Headlines and captions are the other elements that will be part of the display. Both of these are produced with lettering techniques, but they require different systems. The headline needs to be large and thus will require a lettering system that produces large letters. Stencil systems, cutout letters and even Wrico will produce lettering that is large enough to use. On the other hand, the captions (or body copy if it is required) should be done with lettering systems that produce smaller letters. Smaller Wrico stencils or even Leroy will produce very professional lettering of appropriate sizes.

While bulletin boards normally feature two dimensional visuals, it is not unusual to have real objects or even an indication of three dimensionality in effective displays. Large illustrations and pictures that are larger than life can also be effectively used.

POSTERS AND WALL CHARTS:
MATERIALS INTENDED TO INFORM, REMIND AND/OR CAUSE ACTION.

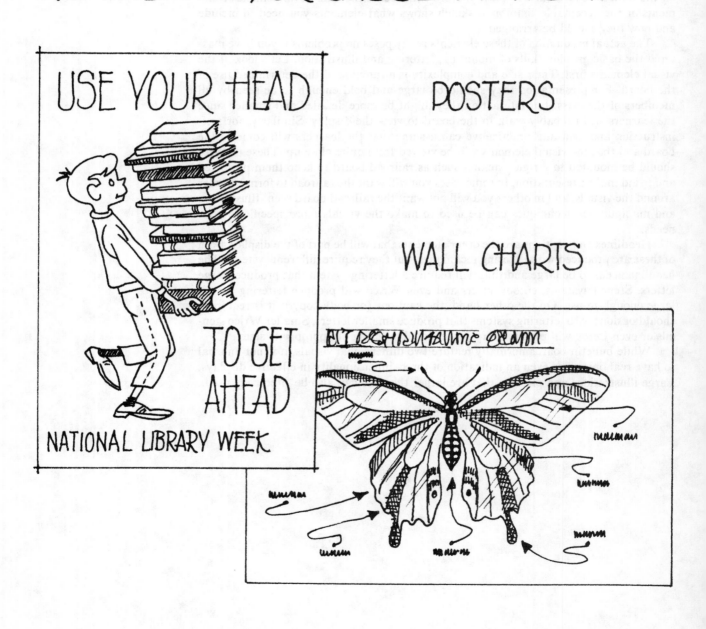

USE YOUR HEAD

POSTERS

TO GET AHEAD

NATIONAL LIBRARY WEEK

WALL CHARTS

POSTERS AND WALL CHARTS, CHARACTERISTICS

Posters and wall charts are similar in appearance. Both utilize very large, bold visuals and are in a format suitable for viewing from a distance. This means that they are normally 11 × 14″ or larger. It is not uncommon for posters and wall charts to be 22 × 28″. Both posters and wall charts contain the same basic elements as the bulletin board. They have a major visual, a headline, and captions or body copy that elaborate on the concept they are trying to communicate. But posters and wall charts have major differences that do not appear on the surface.

The poster is normally used to announce an event or point out rules, like the example on the opposite page. Here the emphasis is on National Library Week, and the poster is simply to call attention to this event. However, it also shows a relationship between the event and the viewer, implying that the library is a place that will help you get ahead. Now, posters can also just be decoration. Travel posters of France can brighten up a classroom where French is being taught. The information is presented quickly and clearly—you just don't have time for reading lots of copy. It might be said that the message that a poster is designed to communicate should be transmitted in just a few seconds. Thus the poster must quickly attract the attention of the viewer and quickly deliver the message to the audience.

The wall chart, on the other hand, may have the appearance of a poster, at least physically, but it is more concerned with information transmission of a more detailed nature. The wall chart on the opposite page deals with the nomenclature of a butterfly. It would be used during a unit of study dealing with insects, and while the teacher might refer to it during a presentation, it is more likely to be used as a referent for the learners who need to utilize this nomenclature to master the subject matter. Here it is not so essential that it attract the attention of the audience since they will be highly motivated to use the information. It is quite possible that learners will look at the wall chart time and time again to utilize the information it contains. Other wall charts might contain symbols used in map reading, a diagram of an engine or a process, or similar information.

Both posters and wall charts are available from a wide variety of sources. Commercial manufacturers produce posters and wall charts for classroom use. There are even posters and wall charts available from free and inexpensive sources that can also be adapted for instruction. And with mounting, lettering and illustration techniques it is not difficult to produce your own.

These media are primarily presentation media, though they can also be used to stimulate an interaction in classes. However, the poster is primarily an information source, while the wall chart is primarily a resource. Small bits of information are presented quickly via the poster, but the information in the wall chart is more detailed and may be utilized over a much longer period of time.

POSTER/CHART PRODUCTION:

SINGLE COPIES ▶

OBJECTIVE   THUMBNAIL

ENLARGE OR MOUNT VISUALS   LETTER   FINISH

MULTIPLE COPIES ▶

OBJECTIVES   SKETCH

CUT STENCIL   ADHERE   APPLY PAINT   DRY

POSTERS AND WALL CHARTS, PRODUCTION

The local production of posters and wall charts will allow you to have materials that are more specific to your audience, content and objectives. And objectives are where you begin. Normally, these media will be only part of the instructional materials related to a particular objective, but they may be a very important part.

As with most display systems, the next task is the development of an appropriate layout, utilizing design principles in the sketching of a series of thumbnails. These small-scale sketches help you arrive at an appropriate arrangement of the headline, visual and captions or copy. With the selected thumbnail as the blueprint you will then select and/or modify the desired visual elements. Since most posters and wall charts are large, this often means using illustration skills to develop illustrations that are the proper size and will provide the proper impact. The headlines need to be visible from a distance, and this requires large lettering. Make sure that you select a lettering technique that will produce letters of the appropriate size. On the other hand, the captions or body copy are normally read closer up, and they may not need to be as large as the headlines. The transfer of these elements from the thumbnail sketch to the finished poster or wall chart will provide you with single copies. However, it is not unusual to want multiple copies, especially for posters.

The process of producing multiple copies begins the same way but quickly deviates from the process used to produce single originals. You begin with the objectives—what do you want the learners to do? With this as the blueprint you produce a series of thumbnails until you arrive at the desired layout. Then you transfer this small-scale thumbnail to the size that you want the finished materials. This is normally called a comprehensive. At this point in time you need to make some production decisions. You can utilize silk screen to reproduce multiple copies of the entire poster, or you can use other techniques to produce multiple copies of the elements and make the posters by mounting these elements in sort of an assembly line operation. The silk screen process is the easiest if you already have the materials and know the process of silk screen duplication, but if you are limited to the techniques described in this manual, you may want to use the thermal silk screen system to reproduce the visuals (this is a small visual process) or the various duplication techniques to produce paper copies. Then use the appropriate mounting techniques to assemble these into multiple copies.

Posters and wall charts are more easily produced as single units, but it is possible, even with limited graphic skills, to produce multiple copies. The time and effort expended will be worth the effort you put into the process if you have done the preproduction planning and design that will result in a predictable instructional product.

ACCORDION FOLD DISPLAY:

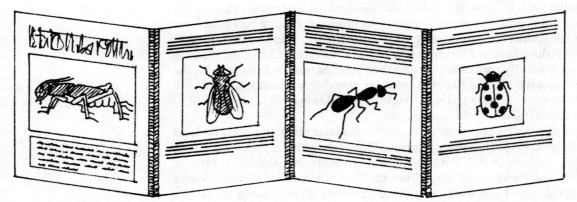

PRESENTATION — RESPONSE — FEEDBACK

PRESENTATION

ACCORDION FOLD DISPLAY, CHARACTERISTICS

Display systems are normally used for presentation activities, and the accordion fold display is no exception. However, because of the rather unusual format of the accordion fold display, it is also quite useful for self-instructional activities. While most displays are flat surfaces, the accordion fold is a collection of flat surfaces that are normally hinged together with tape. This arrangement allows the accordion fold display to be set on a table top and viewed in this fashion, or it can be attached to a vertical surface in either a flat mode or with some of the panels extended to form a three dimensional display. This accordion fold can also be used like a book. With the panels folded together the learner can literally read the accordion fold in the same way that he would read a book. Because of the physical arrangement of the accordion fold, it has a versatility that the other display systems lack.

As we indicated earlier, the accordion fold can be used for the presentation mode. However, it is normally smaller than other display systems, and here the learners must approach it more closely. This means that while it works for presentation, the number of learners who can utilize it at one time is rather limited. However, this seeming disadvantage provides increased options for the unit. Since the visuals and lettered information are viewed from a reasonably close distance, the visual can be more detailed and the lettering smaller. It also sets up an excellent format for self-instruction: individual learners can either use this as an information source, as they would a textbook, or they can use it for self-instruction in the programmed mode if the display presents information, requires a response, and provides feedback without the physical presence of the instructor. In this latter configuration the information can be delivered through the visual elements or the written elements or a combination of the two. The responses can be overt or covert and the feedback provided visually or pictorially.

Accordion fold displays are not normally available through commercial sources. While I have seen one or two, they were all of the straight presentation type, and their numbers were so small as to make commercial sources an unlikely location for accordion fold displays. Likewise, there are few if any accordion fold displays available from free/inexpensive sources. This leaves only local production as a means of acquiring the accordion fold display. If you are looking for a good system for developing self-instruction or even presentation to individuals, you must rely on the basic graphic skills of mounting, lettering and illustration to produce your own. Since local production is the only available source for the accordion fold display, the next few pages will explore the techniques for designing and producing these versatile display systems.

ACCORDION FOLD PRODUCTION:

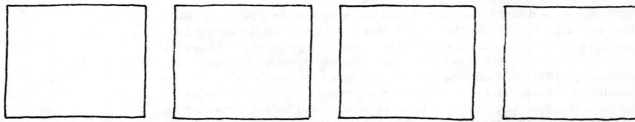

SELECT THE PANEL SIZE/FORMAT

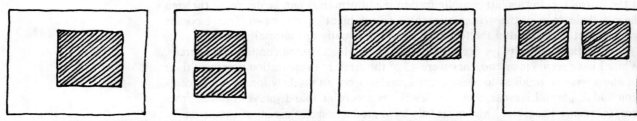

SELECT AND MOUNT THE VISUALS

PREPARE AND MOUNT LETTERING

POSITION AND TAPE THE PANELS

ACCORDION FOLD DISPLAYS, PRODUCTION

The production of an accordion fold display begins with an objective, a clear, concise statement of what you want your learners to be able to do. With this as a blueprint and the knowledge of the content and audience as materials, you simply apply the tools of mounting, lettering, and illustration to the construction of a predictable set of instructional materials. From the objectives and a knowledge of the content you determine what visuals need to be used. From a knowledge of the audience and the principles of perception you develop a series of thumbnail sketches of what arrangement you want for these elements. Then preparing the copy to guide the instruction and the visual to supplement it, you can develop a guide as to what you want the finished product to look like.

After the planning the actual production begins with a determination of what size you want the finished product to be. Basically, this means determining the size of the panels for the display. Not only do the panels need to be the same size, they need to be the same format so that they will easily fold together. With the thumbnail as a guide, select the arrangement of visuals and lettering and then find the visuals that will supplement the instruction. You may have to use illustration techniques to make the visuals appropriate to your needs and space, but when you have, they should be mounted to the backing units—the panels. Since we will want to laminate these, it is best if you use MT-5 dry mount tissue for the mounting. Prepare the lettering next. Since this will be viewed at an arm's length, you can do your lettering with a typewriter quite successfully. With the lettering complete, trim the paper to the appropriate size and format and mount it to the appropriate spaces on the panels. Again, MT-5 is probably the best adhesive to use. With the visuals and the lettering mounted in place, you are almost half way through the process. The next step would be to laminate the individual panels. This lamination is not necessary, but it will add protection to the panels, and it will also allow the learners to indicate their responses directly on the display. If they use grease pencils, the marks can be erased with a damp rag and the accordion fold is ready for the next learner.

The last step in the process of producing an accordion fold display is the assembling of the individual panels into their final arrangement. These panels may be attached with tape or even with Chartex, but I have found that using colored library tapes provides a substantial hinge and often adds a needed spot of color. In preparing these hinges it is necessary to make sure that the panels will fold together. To do this it is necessary to make sure the vertical edges of the panels are at least as far apart as twice the thickness of the backing material for the panels. If the panel is 1/8" thick, then the space between the adjacent panels should 1/4". Make sure the bottom edges are straight and then simply apply the tape. Flip the accordion fold over and apply a second layer of tape to the back. These hinges will allow the display to be folded and unfolded easily.

INSTRUCTIONAL EXHIBITS:

USUALLY AN INTERACTIVE DISPLAY

MAY CONTAIN INFORMATIONAL ELEMENTS.

MAY UTILIZE A VERTICAL DISPLAY.

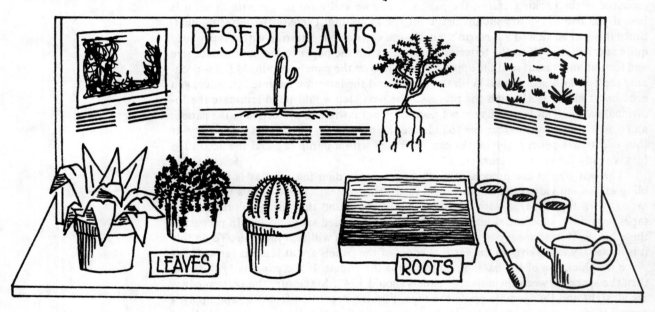

DESERT PLANTS

LEAVES

ROOTS

NORMALLY CONTAINS REAL OBJECTS THAT CAN BE EXAMINED AND MANIPULATED BY THE STUDENTS.

OFTEN CONTAINS THE TOOLS THAT ALLOW THE STUDENTS TO WORK WITH THE ELEMENTS THAT ARE ON DISPLAY.

BEGINS WITH OBJECTIVES.

INSTRUCTIONAL EXHIBITS, CHARACTERISTICS

Instructional exhibits also fall into the class of media that we call displays. While bulletin board displays are primarily of two dimensional materials, the exhibits generally feature three dimensional materials. The bulletin board is normally a vertical display, and the exhibit is normally a horizontal display on a table top. While most displays are used for presentation, the emphasis of the exhibits is on interaction. They can be used to assist in a presentation or as part of a demonstration; their primary function is to provide real items (called realia) which the learners may interact with. In the example on the opposite page the exhibit on desert plants goes beyond just letting the learners see the real plants. They can cut off samples of the leaves and examine the plants' ability to hold water. In the other section there might be small transparent pots that would show the various root systems, but there is also a cactus bed that can be dug into to examine the root systems in more detail. Thus, the instructional exhibit displays real three dimensional objects, and it also provides the audience with the tools and opportunity to examine the hidden details of these items.

Like any good instructional materials, the exhibit begins with an objective. Using the example on the other page again, the objective might be that the learners will describe the leaf and root structure of specific desert plants. After the opportunity to actually manipulate these items, it is quite likely the students will be able to attain this objective.

We should also point out that there are other types of exhibits: for instance, an exhibit of the materials that can be produced by a specific process or an exhibit of materials produced by a particular artist. These are valuable additions to the classroom, but we will concentrate on exhibits that are instructional in nature and that guide the learners toward the attainment of a specific objective.

Instructional exhibits are almost always locally produced. While there are many organizations that develop traveling exhibits, these are usually very general in nature and not aimed specifically at a given unit of instruction. They are enrichment rather than instruction with a specific purpose. Here in Arizona we have the famous Sonora Desert Museum. This organization has a traveling exhibit that brings real animals into the classroom and allows the students to actually handle them. Even so, the goal of this activity is quite general, and it is not normally a part of the school curriculum. Worthwhile? There is no question about this; it works, and it works well. But it does not have a set of objectives or a teaching purpose that is directly related to the curriculum.

Thus, the instructional exhibit is almost always locally produced. It may be used simply to present information or to support an instructor's demonstration, but it seems most appropriate when it is desirable to develop a class interaction, especially an interaction with the actual items that are being studied.

INSTRUCTIONAL MODELS:

THREE-DIMENSIONAL REPRESENTATIONS OF UNAVAILABLE REALIA. THEY CAN BE SCALED UP, SCALED DOWN, OR THE SAME SIZE AS THE ORIGINAL.

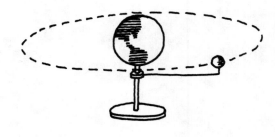

CROSS SECTIONAL MODEL   WORKING MODELS

INSTRUCTIONAL MODELS

Instructional models are normally three-dimensional representations of items that are difficult or impossible to bring into the classroom. While it might be difficult to arrange transportation to a live volcano and impossible to bring a live volcano into the classroom, it is quite reasonable to acquire or construct a model that will let the class experience what happens when a volcano erupts.

These models can be scaled up or scaled down or the same scale as the object or process that they represent. The volcano is an example of a scaled down model. The model is smaller than the original. The thermometer on the opposite page is also a model. However, it is a scaled up model that is larger than the real thing. The owl that the teacher is holding is an example of a "to scale" model, meaning that it is the same size as the original. In addition to the different scales that models are available in, you can also get models that are cross sectional and working models. The model of the volcano allows you to see inside by either removing a covering part or as just showing a simple cross section. The model of our solar system in the lower right corner is an example of a working model. It does what the real object does. In this case the moon rotates around the earth just as it does in real life, and the students can see an event that otherwise would be invisible to them. As you can see, models can take many shapes and forms, but, basically, the model is intended to provide the learner with a look at something that would not easily be seen in real life.

Models are available from a wide variety of sources. They are listed in major commercial sources such as the NICEM Index, or you can rely on the producers' catalogues. There are relatively few producers of models, and it is not difficult to collect their catalogues. It is also possible to purchase models from unusual commercial sources such as the local toy and hobby store. Here they may range from the visible man which shows the interior of the human body to models of cars, boats, prehistoric animals, etc. Many of these toy store models come unassembled, and if you are not a proficient model builder, it is always possible to identify a student who can assemble and paint these for you. There are also many free/inexpensive sources that have models available. And, of course, it is possible to construct your own models through local production.

Models are part of the instructional media that fall under the general category of display systems, and in this case they are really only appropriate for presentation types of activities. It is true that students can manipulate models, but the primary application is to support or enhance the instructor's presentation or demonstration. It makes the invisible, visible; it makes the difficult to understand simpler to comprehend. It supports the instruction and illustrates the concept in a way that other instructional media do not.

INSTRUCTIONAL DIORAMAS:

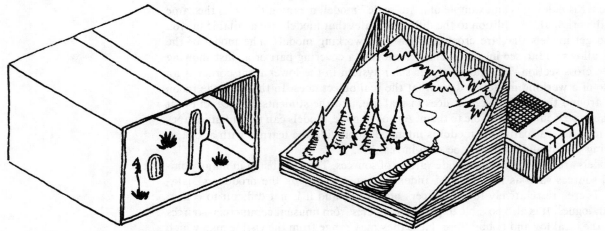

REALISTIC RECREATIONS IN MINATURE.

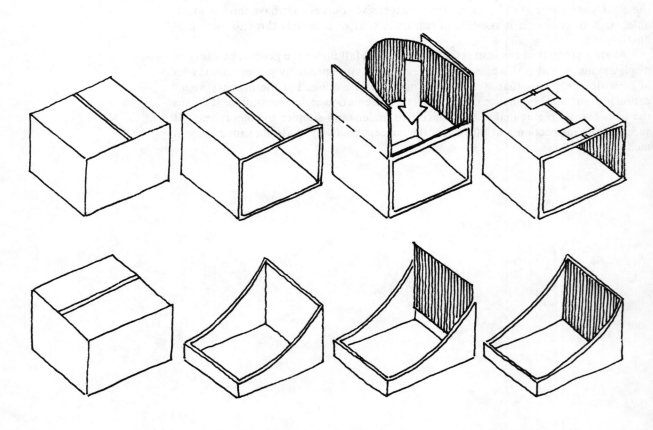

INSTRUCTIONAL DIORAMAS

The instructional diorama is probably one of the most "different" display systems that we will discuss. The diorama is basically a realistic re-creation of an environment or an event in miniature. It may stand on its own, or it may be accompanied by some sort of audio display system such as a tape recorder. Instructional dioramas are usually quite small and are often referred to as shoe box displays. In the museums the diorama may depict a slice of prehistoric life with full sized dinosaurs, or it may show the life that exists under the Arctic ice caps. The audience stands in front of a window that appears to open into a world that they are not likely to see. In many situations the dioramas will have lighting effects that simulate the actual conditions of the situation or environment, and they may even have an audio hook-up that will allow you to push a button and have a narrator describe the place or event that you are watching. Dioramas in the classroom are usually less elaborate. First, as we said, they are normally quite small. Also, it is probably too expensive for fancy lighting effects. However, it is not unusual for these classroom exhibits to have a tape recorder attached that will describe the purpose of the place or event that is being depicted.

These dioramas are normally not available from either commercial or free/inexpensive sources. There just isn't that much call for them. This leaves local production and the problems related to that production. As with all good instructional materials, we begin with a reason, and the reason is an objective—what we want our learners to be able to do as a result of exposure to this particular message. In the case of dioramas, they may be best used to motivate students to explore a topic in more detail. Once we have the objective and the content, it is a matter of collecting the materials and constructing the display. First, the environment: this may be a closed box with a cyclorama in the background or an open box with a sliding background. Then it is simply a matter of arranging the materials to create a realistic, small scale world. Often the best place to get materials for these dioramas is the local hobby shop. Model railroads sell trees, buildings, plants and other items built to a small scale.

You can add impact with an audio tape recorder that will deliver a narration concerning the content. Probably this would be best fed into earphones so that it would not disturb the rest of the class. And this brings us to utilization. Like all display systems, the dioramas are quite effective as presentation devices. For that matter, this is about the only teaching/learning strategy that is appropriate for this type of display. We can make presentations, but because of the small format of the dioramas, the presentation is normally to one or two students at a time. This is an unusual display system and not practical for all purposes. However, when it is appropriate, when it fits the instructional objective, the diorama can be a valuable addition to the instructional media at your disposal.

MISCELLANEOUS SIMPLE MEDIA:

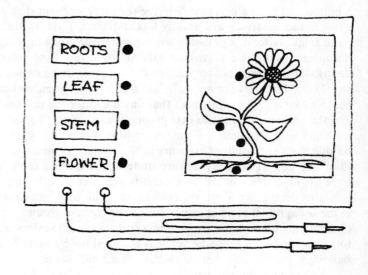

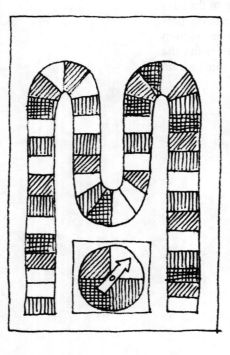

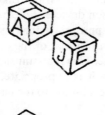

MISCELLANEOUS SIMPLE MEDIA

The previous simple media that we have looked at tended to fit into nice, neat classifications. Now we are faced with other simple media that don't appear to fit any of these classifications; nor do they fit any grouping strategy other than miscellaneous. However, these are sufficiently valuable to be worthy; of your consideration, and so the title of this section—miscellaneous. These range from the electric board, which is an idea for drill and practice, to the field trip, which is primarily an interaction media. Some are available from commercial sources, like games and simulation activities, while others, like the flip chart, are more normally local production activities. The following chart will show the differences in sources and utilization strategies of these various media better than we can in a written dialogue.

Miscellaneous Simple Media	sources			utilization				characteristics
	commercial sources	free/inexpensive sources	local production	presentation	interaction	independent study	drill/practice	General characteristics: There are a number of valuable simple media that just do not easily fit into a classification system. In this case, these miscellaneous simple media do not have a general characteristic other than the fact that they don't fit into other groupings.
Electric board			X				X	An effective media for the disguise of drill/practice activities
The flip chart			X	X	X	X		Large format for presentation and small format for independent study
Games/simulation	X	X	X		X		X	Games for drill/practice and simulation activities for interaction
Learning Centers	X	X	X	X		X	X	Interest centers for presentation, learning centers for drill/practice
Field Trips			X		X			Controlled exposure to the real world

ELECTRIC BOARDS:
DISGUISED DRILL AND PRACTICE.

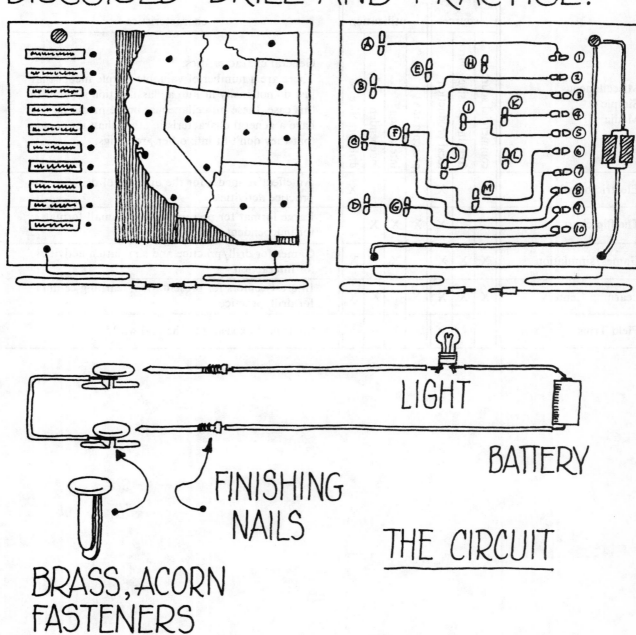

LIGHT

BATTERY

FINISHING NAILS

BRASS, ACORN FASTENERS

THE CIRCUIT

ELECTRIC BOARDS

The electric board is a locally produced drill and practice media that disguises this drill in a manner that makes it quite acceptable to the learners. The student takes one probe and puts it on the information or question source, and the other probe and places it on what he considers to be an appropriate response source. If he makes the right match, a light will light or a buzzer will buzz, providing him with an indication that he has made the correct selection. In the example on the opposite page we have a map of the western United States as the information/question source. On the left we have a list of names of cities or states as the response source. The student who touches Arizona and then touches either the response Phoenix or Arizona will be rewarded by a light signal or a buzzer. The diagram to the right shows the back of the board and a seemingly complicated array of wires and batteries. Actually, it is quite simple. Wires connect the information with the proper response. The two probes have the battery and light or buzzer between them. When the circuit is completed by touching both ends of the information response wire, the light will light.

You see the basic system illustrated just below the diagrams of the front and back of the electric boards: the partial circuit of probe, battery, light and probe and the partial circuit from response to information. When these are connected, that makes a complete circuit, allowing the electricity to flow and the feedback response to be given. Standard light weight wiring is suitable for connecting the elements. The information and response points are usually brass acorn fasteners that will pass the electricity from the front of the electric board, where the information and responses are, to the back of the electric board, where the wiring is.

The production of the electric board is sufficiently complicated that it should be adaptable to different applications. To do this we have to solve two problems. First, we must be able to easily change both the information and the responses on the front of the board. This will allow us to use the same electric board for drill and practice in a variety of curriculum areas. Second, we need to be able to change the wiring pattern on the back so that students will respond to the information and answers and not to the configuration of acorn fasteners. In the example on the opposite page this would be difficult to do. The information pattern is unique to the map. However, with a parallel set of information panels and response panels it would be much easier to change these panels. Changing the wiring to a new information and response pattern is simply a matter of disconnecting one end and connecting it to another acorn fastener. In other words, it is quite possible to design these electric boards so that you can easily change them when you want to make drill and practice activities available in a new subject matter area.

THE FLIPCHART:

FASTENERS

FLEXIBLE PAGES

HOW TO TRAIN YOUR DOG

RIGID BACK

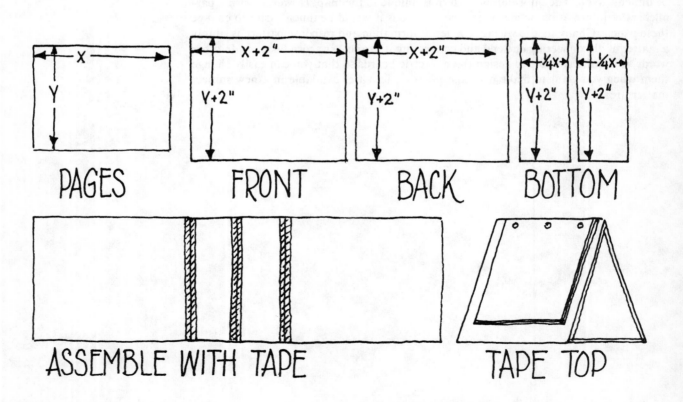

PAGES

X

Y

FRONT

X + 2"

Y + 2"

BACK

X + 2"

Y + 2"

BOTTOM

¼X

Y + 2"

¼X

Y + 2"

ASSEMBLE WITH TAPE

TAPE TOP

THE FLIP CHART, CHARACTERISTICS

The flip chart is a media for the sequential presentation of information to large groups or for the delivery of self-instruction to individuals. The different uses are a function of the size of the flip chart. Large flip charts can be viewed by large audiences and are excellent media to supplement or support the live presentation of the instructor. The small flip charts are normally viewed by individual learners, and it is relatively easy to design them into an information, response, feedback mode that is ideal for self-instruction. In addition to the more normal presentation and self-instructional modes, it is also possible to design a flip chart to stimulate the interaction that you might desire in a classroom situation.

The word sequential was used in the original description, and that is important. If you remember, the exhibits were ideal where the manipulation of information was a requirement. Here, the flip chart is ideal when you are concerned with the sequential presentation of information. This is simply because the pages of the flip chart are in a sequential order and are difficult to use other than in a sequence.

There are few if any commercial flip charts available, perhaps because they are relatively expensive to produce, but probably because they are more normally used for instruction or information transmission that is content specific, audience specific or even instructor specific. The same is true for the free/inexpensive sources. While there may be some flip charts available from free/inexpensive sources, they are so few and far between that for all practical purposes the flip chart is only available from local production activities.

The flip chart is another media where there is a good distinction between the media (delivery system) and the materials (the information system). The flip chart pages are the instructional materials that carry the instruction to the audience, and to support these pages you require a flip chart stand that can be used for any flip chart materials. On the opposite page you will see the diagram for the construction of a simple flip chart stand. This stand has the advantage of being collapsible in the sense that it will fold flat for storage when the flip chart stand is not in use.

Since this is designed to support flip chart pages for a variety of subjects, it is essential to begin with a standardized size for the flip chart itself. If it is to be used for presentation and/or interaction it should be large, if for independent study it should be small. Cut a series of panels as shown on the opposite page.These should be cut from heavy cardboard or light weight wood. Then the panels are assembled with tape. Duct tape is good to use, or also colored cloth library tapes. Put holes at the top of the stand where the flip chart pages can be attached, using the brass acorn fasteners. Because of the way the bottom is constructed, it will hinge up, thus the entire unit will fold into a flat package for storage. If this is to be used outside of the classroom, you may want to make the top a little higher and fashion a carrying handle there.

THE FLIPCHART, PRODUCTION:

THUMBNAILS

GUIDELINES

CARTOONS:

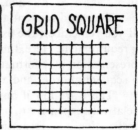

GRID SQUARE

LETTERING
- ALL CAPS BEST.
- USE COLORS
- ERASE DRAFT
- RIGHT SIZE
- SEQUENCING

LEAVE SPACE FOR FASTENING.

LETTERING

PROJECTION:

VISUALS

ACETATE OVERLAY

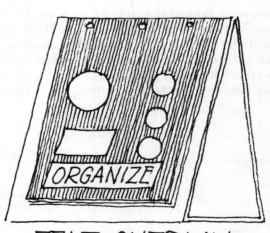

FELT OVERLAY
AND
FELTBOARD PIECES

THE FLIP CHART, PRODUCTION

As with any locally produced media, the production process begins with planning: the development of the content outline, the audience description, and the objectives. The translation of these into thumbnail sketches of what each page will look like and then the final layout on the actual pages of the flip chart itself.

In the actual production we begin by either acquiring pages of a common size or by cutting pages to the common size that is required by the flip chart stand. These pages should be a fairly good quality paper. Newsprint can be used, but generally it is so light weight that the images from the second page show through the first page. This can be eliminated by doubling the pages, but this means you have increased the cost and would have probably been better off using heavier paper in the first place. Once the pages are selected and cut to the right size we are faced with the problems of creating the visuals and written information they will contain. Obviously, the thumbnail sketches will provide the guide for the layout and content, but there are some concerns with the actual imaging.

Lettering requires guidelines to ensure that the lines of lettering will be parallel and that the letters will be of a uniform height. While you can put the guidelines directly on the paper, this means that you will need to erase them later. If you are using light weight paper, you can draw the guide lines on a template and overlay the pages, which will eliminate the need for guidelines directly on the paper. Make sure that you consider the readability factors as you produce the lettering. Also remember that it is essential that you not only leave space for the fastening of the pages to the flip chart stand, but also for the roll of paper that will build up at the top as you turn each page over. Using the appropriate lettering techniques and appropriate colors to attract attention or provide color coding cues, letter the information.

Now you are ready to add the visual elements. These may be plain tearsheets, but normally these are limited to the flip charts that are used for independent study. For the flip charts that are used for presentation or interaction, it will probably be necessary to apply the illustration techniques that will allow you to enlarge existing visuals. Both projection enlargement and grid square are appropriate techniques. If you have the skills, it is possible to create your own illustrations through cartooning techniques. It has quite an impact if you can actually draw these cartoons into the flip chart during the presentation. And this brings us to variations in the flip chart.

Paper is not the only material that is suitable for the pages in a flip chart. Obviously, materials such as sign cloth will make excellent flip chart pages. You can also use acetate pages quite successfully. These can be used in self-instructional flip charts for the learners responses or as areas to add information for presentation. You can also insert pages made from felt. These can actually be used as feltboards and are especially useful when, in your sequential presentation, you hit a point where you want to manipulate an idea or concept.

GAMES AND SIMULATION:

COMMERCIAL GAMES

CARDS   DICE

HOME MADE GAMES

ACTION CARDS

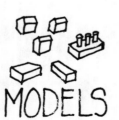

MODELS

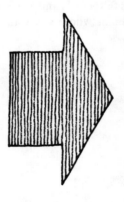

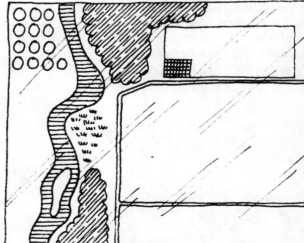

SIMULATION ACTIVITIES

GAMES AND SIMULATION ACTIVITIES

Games are activities that are designed to disguise drill and practice activities; simulation activities are designed for interaction and to simulate a real world experience that is unavailable to the learners. Games are available from commercial sources, free/inexpensive sources and local production. These games may be designed for pure entertainment, but it is relatively easy to adapt them to appropriate drill and practice activities. Consider the simple game of checkers. By placing letters in the squares on the board, you can add an appropriate drill or practice aspect to the game. The game is played normally, except that now the player must give a word beginning or ending with the letter on the space that they want to move to. This is an example of a simple modification. It is also quite easy to make your own gaming activities. On the opposite page is Sammy the Snake. The "game" is quite simple—how many words did Sammy swallow? Obviously "cam" is one, then "came," then "am," then "camel," etc. These homemade games can use dice, spinners, or action cards that will allow the learners to move their various pieces and complete the game. Obviously, there are some commercial games that do not require modification. These already have elements that are appropriate to practice activities in counting, addition and subtraction, vocabulary, etc. Just find the game that meets your needs or modify an existing game to be more specific to your requirements.

Simulation activities are a little more complicated, and while they are available in limited numbers from commercial and free/inexpensive sources, it is more common to produce your own locally. The concept here is to create an environment in which the learners will react as they would in a real world situation so that they can see the results of their actions without physical or emotional damage. An example of this was a simulation activity I saw used in a classroom not too long ago. The game board almost covered the entire floor. It was a series of sheets onto which an environment had been drawn, similar to the one on the opposite page. The directions are quite simple. The students are to build a community. A series of action cards show them how to proceed. First they build houses; then they need to develop a sewer system, find employment, and build factories; soon they are enmeshed in the same problems that any expanding community faces. There is a commercial simulation activity that pits the English traders against the Colonial merchants, and as the simulation evolves, the students get a feeling for the events that created the Revolutionary War. These simulation activities allow the learners to experience a situation or even an event that might not normally be available to them. These simulation activities are normally an interaction activity, with the learners participating as a group. Both gaming and simulation are media that can be effectively used in the classroom in a wide variety of curriculum areas.

LEARNING CENTERS:

VARIOUS LEARNING AND/OR PRACTICE UNITS FOR REMEDIATION OR ENRICHMENT.

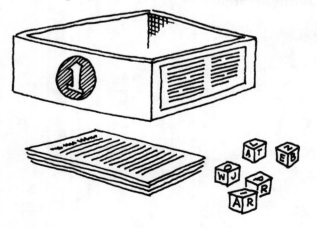

PACKAGED ACTIVITY UNITS

RECORD KEEPING

LEARNING CENTERS AND INTEREST CENTERS

Learning centers and interest centers are two media that can be used to separate the students in your class into more productive groups. It is easier to work with 15 students than it is to work with 30 students. The development of learning centers for drill and practice or interest centers for enrichment will allow you to keep half of the class productively occupied with appropriate self-instructional activities while you can deal with the remainder on a more personal basis. Though these two types of centers serve to group students, they serve quite different teaching/learning strategies. The learning center is normally a media designed for a drill and practice activity, providing the students the opportunity to master a concept in which they have already been instructed. The interest centers are more normally designed to present information that is enrichment in nature, information that goes beyond the content of the curriculum and that keeps students who have mastered the necessary information productively occupied.

There are basically two parts to any well designed center. First is the vertical display that is intended to attract and hold the attention of the students. This backdrop also normally contains the instructions on how to use the center, and any record keeping system necessary. The second part of the center is the horizontal surface. This contains the various activities that are designed for the center. Note in the sketch on the opposite page the backdrop indicates that this center is aimed at a creative writing activity. This vertical surface contains a list of what can be done in the center: the activities, an illustration, some sort of system for monitoring the use of the center, and an inventory of what is in the center. The inventory is necessary to ensure that when you assign students to the center, they will have everything they need. The horizontal surface contains what seems to be a supply of boxes and cans. In actuality, these are the various activities in which students can be involved in the center. By placing them in containers, you can more easily make sure that they are there when the students need them. These are the packaged activity units that are the heart of the center. Note that the containers are attractively colored and that they also have the specific instructions for that unit taped or mounted to the sides. In addition to the containers that hold the activities there will also need to be containers for record keeping. This is especially important for the learning centers where you need to be able to analyze the learners' performance. These records are normally forms that are filled out by the learner as he completes the activity. They can then be added to the student's file folder and evaluated to determine the next stage that is appropriate for a particular learner.

The activities in a learning or interest center may involve a single learner, or they may involve a small group. A game, for example, may be played against the clock by an individual or against other students in a small group activity. Thus, a center may have one to fifteen different activities and may serve one to thirty students at a time.

INSTRUCTIONAL FIELD TRIPS:

INSIDE THE SCHOOL

SCHOOL GROUNDS

LOCAL COMMUNITY

THE EXTENDED WORLD

INSTRUCTIONAL FIELD TRIPS

Field trips are normally locally produced (designed) opportunities for the student to interact with the real world under controlled circumstances. Field trips are controlled experiences outside of the classroom. This means that planned experiences inside the school, on the school grounds, in the local community and in the extended world are all reasonable for field trips.

Consider the school cafeteria as a site for a class field trip. Beginning with how the meals are prepared, you can guide students to an exploration of the sources of foods (Where does a hamburger really come from?), or explore the world of nutrition, or examine the waste of food and the cost effectiveness of school lunches. I had one set of students that actually sorted the garbage left over from a lunch, weighed it, and determined that there were classes of foods that it was a waste of time to prepare for school lunches.

Even the school grounds are possible sites for field trips. You might want to stake out an area for each student and provide them with the necessary tools to classify all of the different plants and animals that exist in a cubic yard of playground. I remember one teacher who had her students explore a tree that was growing in the playground. By the time the students had finished, they had developed a notebook that was two inches thick concerning all aspects of that particular tree.

The immediate community is also a prime source for field trips. Many times, within walking distance of the school, there are fire stations, stores, fast food restaurants and other exciting places to explore. Finding the person who can bring these areas to life is not as easy as it sounds, but once you identify a good person to explain the activities in the location you are visiting, you have a place that you can return to again and again.

And, of course, there are the extended trips where you pile the kids onto a school bus and take them to the zoo or museum or someplace that requires more than foot transportation. This transportation should be a major concern with field trips. If it is necessary to transport your students to an off-campus location, avoid private automobiles. Even if the owners sign releases, the use of private automobiles can still make you liable for accidents. School buses, public transportation and foot travel limit this liability.

A good field trip begins with an objective: not only a reason for going, but a behavior that you want the learners to achieve through this experience. Once you have the objective and the location, the next step is to get permission. First, get permission from the principal who has to release the school transportation or approve your absence from the classroom. Second, get permission from the learners' parents if the learners are under age. Then prepare the students by giving them the objective, doing research or discussing what they are going to experience. Then after the field trip, bring things to closure through discussion or other activities that will ensure that the learners got out of the field trip what you had set forth in your objectives.

CHAPTER 10
OVERHEAD TRANSPARENCY AND PROJECTION IDEAS:

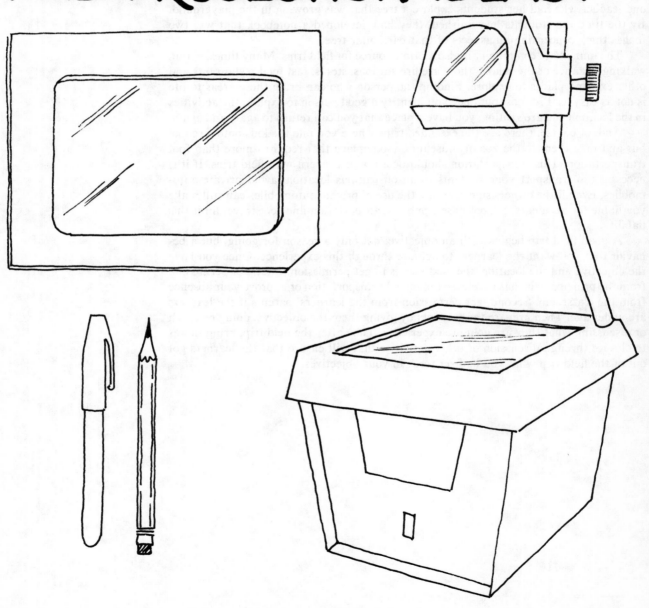

OVERHEAD TRANSPARENCY AND PROJECTION IDEAS

The overhead system is a logical transition between the simple media we have been discussing and the more complex media that we have yet to explore. The overhead system consists of hardware, the projector, and software, the transparencies. This combination of media and materials is extremely popular for a number of reasons:

1. The overhead is a delivery system used from the front of the room. You can maintain eye contact with your learners.
2. The overhead is a delivery system that does not require room darkening, though some transparencies are enhanced by this.
3. The overhead is relatively inexpensive and commonly found in schools and training programs.
4. There are many overhead transparencies available from commercial and free/inexpensive sources.
5. There are many local production techniques for making transparencies that are specific to your particular needs.

This chapter will explore the media and the materials for this system. We will look at the capabilities and limitations of the hardware, the overhead projector, and we will explore the techniques for the local production of transparencies. Yes, the local production of transparencies to serve this media is quite possible, but these are also available from commercial and free/inexpensive sources. The following chart will tell us a little about the system.

	sources			utilization				characteristics
	commercial sources	free/inexpensive sources	local production	presentation	interaction	independent study	drill/practice	
Overhead Transparencies								General characteristics: The overhead transparency is a combination of opaque images on a transparent backing. When the materials are projected, the opaque images will show up as black and the transparent areas as white. Color is created by the use of transparent colors on the transparency.
Transparencies	X	X	X	X	X		X	There are many techniques for producing your own transparencies

As you can see from the chart, the overhead and its transparencies are suitable for presentation, interaction, and even drill and practice. Perhaps the most common and best use is for presentation of information to large groups of learners. Because of the advantages of the system, such as working with the room lights on and facing the audience, this presentation mode is enhanced. While presentation to large groups may be the best utilization, we can also use these transparencies to stimulate an interaction in the class. Delivering visuals that are open-ended in terms of their interpretation should cause students to bring their own experiences to the interpretation. Last but not least, we could also use the overhead system for delivering drill and practice information. However, there are probably less expensive systems that would do just as good a job in this teaching/learning mode.

THE OVERHEAD PROJECTOR:

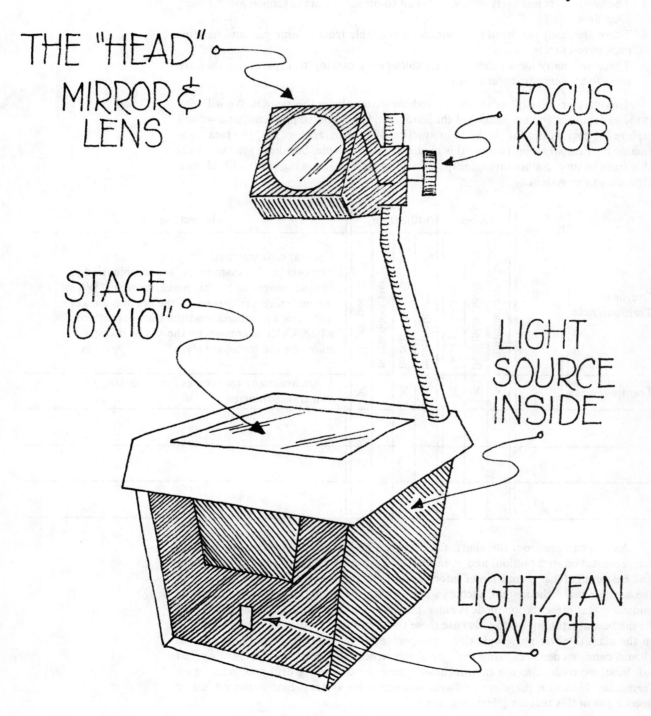

THE "HEAD"
MIRROR &
LENS

FOCUS
KNOB

STAGE
10 X 10"

LIGHT
SOURCE
INSIDE

LIGHT/FAN
SWITCH

THE OVERHEAD PROJECTOR

The overhead projector is the hardware portion of the overhead system. It is designed to deliver the transparencies to the intended audience. Basically it is a simple machine, and perhaps this accounts for its relatively low cost. Beginning at the base, we have a box that contains the light, light switch and fan. The light is intended to go through the top of the box, and to increase the amount of the light there is usually some sort of a mirror in the base of the box. When the switch turns the light source on, it usually activates a fan to keep the lamp and the projector cooler. The light passes through the top of the base structure through a fresnel lens and the glass or plastic stage of the projector. The fresnel lens serves to direct the light to the head of the projector, and the stage is where the images to be projected are placed. The stage area of the projector is normally $10 \times 10''$; this means that you can only project an image where the original is $10 \times 10''$ or smaller. At the stage area the light is blocked by the opaque portions of the visual creating the image that will eventually be delivered to the screen. The light continues up and enters the head of the projector. There are two elements in the head, 1) a mirror and 2) the objective or focusing lens. The mirror bends the angle of the light from vertical to horizontal, thus the name overhead for projecting the image over the head of the presenter. The image is directed to the screen by the mirror but focused by the objective lens. Raising and lowering the head of the projector will ensure that the image on the screen is in fine focus.

If the screen on which the image is displayed is vertical, you will probably notice that the image has a slight distortion. The vertical edges of the projected image will not be parallel. Instead they will look like the main stone in the arch of a bridge. This is called key-stoning. It is a result of the light from the projector striking the screen at less than a ninety degree angle. To compensate for this key-stoning of the image you will need to change the angle of the screen. This is why many screens for overhead projection are mounted on the ceiling away from the wall. When they are pulled down and attached to the chalkboard tray, they form a ninety degree angle to the light. However, this type of compensation is really only necessary where parallel vertical lines are essential for the correct reading of the visuals, as in a unit on geometry. In most cases this distortion will not inhibit your ability to communicate effectively with the overhead system.

The overhead system will project real objects as well as transparencies designed for this system. If the real objects are opaque, they will project on the screen as silhouettes, providing only peripheral cues for recognition. You can even project items such as ants or other small insects to show their movements enlarged on the screen. The versatility of this system, as well as the large number of visuals that it can deliver, goes a long way toward making it one of the most popular systems for large group presentations.

THE OVERHEAD TRANSPARENCY

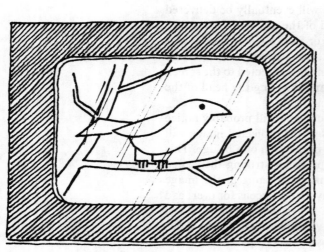

STANDARD

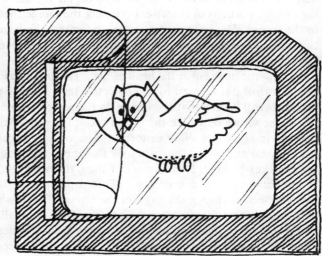

OVERLAY

SELECT AN IDEA.
PREPARE A SKETCH.
REGISTER ACETATE.
SELECT TRACING MEDIUM.
TRACE THE LINE DETAIL.

REVELATION

MASKS

THE OVERHEAD TRANSPARENCY

Before we explore the specific tehniques and materials used to produce transparencies for the overhead system, it might be wise to consider them in a more general context. There are many formats that the transparency can take, and each of them has certain applications that make it a valuable addition to the tools of the communicator.

The standard transparency is one that is simply a single sheet of acetate that is often mounted into a cardboard mask and placed directly on the stage of the overhead. The mask may be a commercial mask or one that is prepared to emphasize some element in the visual. In many cases it is not even necessary to use a mask. The acetate transparency is just placed on the stage and projected as is. Where the transparency is transparent, the corresponding area on the screen will be white. Where the transparency is opaque, the corresponding area on the screen will be black. When transparent colors are used on the transparency, they will change the wave length of the white light, and the corresponding areas on the screen will be in the same color.

The overlay is applied where you want to add or subtract information from a base visual. The base visual is a standard transparency, and the overlay is hinged to the top of one of the four edges of the cardboard mask. If the information is to be added or subtracted in a sequential fashion, then the overlays will be attached to the same edge of the mask. If you may want to change the order and sequence of this manipulation, they would be attached to different edges of the mask. The base transparency is always attached to the bottom of the mask and the overlays hinged to the top. In deciding how many overlays to use, remember that acetate is not totally transparent, and as you add more layers you will cut down on the amount of light that is delivered to the screen.

The revelation technique is the term for a system for revealing information at a speed that you desire to present it to your audience. It is not uncommon to have a list of items or a series of procedures on the base transparency. If you just place this on the overhead, all of the items or steps will be visible. While you are talking about item one, your audience may well be reading item two or five or twenty-seven. To control this delivery you can place a sheet of opaque material over the information and reveal it only as you want the audience to react to it. Using a sheet of notebook paper will allow you to block the projection and still see the next item through the notebook paper.

Opaque masks can also be used to either add or subtract information. In the example on the opposite page the opaque masks can be flipped out to reveal the visuals underneath. The audience is asked to name, from a description, a particular bird. As they do, the appropriate mask is flipped up and the bird revealed, providing feedback to the audience. This is just one application of the use of opaque masks on the overhead transparencies. There are other applications and techniques that you will discover to make the presentation of your overhead transparencies more effective for the content you are delivering.

TRANSPARENCIES, CUTOUTS:

SELECT APPROPRIATE VISUALS.

ORIGINAL

TRACE

CUTOUT

POS/NEG.

CELLOPHANE FOR COLOR

TAPE TO ACETATE

TRANSPARENCIES, CUTOUTS

Since opaque materials will project as black silhouettes, it is possible to use cutouts as the images on your transparencies. However, since they are decoded using only peripheral cues, you must begin with an image that has strong edges. Look at the examples on the top of the opposite page. There are five separate images there. Do you have difficulty interpreting any of these? Many people cannot decode numbers one and four. Number two is rather obviously a baseball player, and number three is a cowboy, and the last visual is a boy pushing another boy in a car. But did you "read" number one as a boy and his dog or number four as a boy singing? If not, it was probably because these images do not have very strong peripheral cues.

In selecting an original image that will end up as a cutout, look for strong cues. It is even possible to get stencil books from many of the same publishers that present coloring books. These have been designed with this recognition factor in mind, and they work quite well as cutout transparencies.

Once you have the visual, transfer it to an opaque surface, using the tracing techniques described in the illustration section. If the visual is not the right size, that same section will suggest techniques for enlarging or reducing the size of the original. Once the original has been transferred to an opaque surface, it is then simply cut out. In this process you end up, if you are careful, with a positive and a negative cutout. These names refer to the way the image will be projected. The positive cutout has the image cut from an opaque surrounding, and when projected the cutout will appear white on the screen. The negative cutout is the opaque piece that was cut out, and when it is projected it will provide a black silhouette on the screen. Pick the format that is appropriate to your needs. For example, if you want to point to the city of Phoenix in a cutout of Arizona, you should use a positive cutout so your pointer will show. If you want to point to the location of California, Nevada, etc., then it would be more logical to use a negative cutout.

These cutouts can be used as they are, or they can be modified. In the first example on the bottom of the opposite page, a positive cutout of a fish has color added to it by simply taping colored acetate or cellophane to the back of the visual. Now the fish will project in the color that was applied, rather than white. In the example next to it the cutout (negative) of the umbrella is attached to a clear sheet of acetate taped to a standard overhead mask. In this case double-faced tape was used to hold the visual in place. While it could have been used without a mask, the mask makes it much easier to store and utilize.

These cutouts are a simple and effective way to prepare simple overhead transparencies. They have a special impact because they do not usually contain a large number of cues and the audience has to become involved to read the message you are presenting.

TRANSPARENCIES, TRACING:

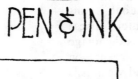 GREASE PENCIL

PEN & INK   FELT PENS    MONGOL

→ LINE DRAWING

KEEP FINGERPRINTS
OFF THE ACETATE →

THE ORIGINAL   COVER WITH ACETATE

↗ CLIP BOARD

PICK THE
RIGHT MEDIUM ←

REGISTER   TRACE

↗ ON THE BACK

ADD COLOR

MOUNT

TRANSPARENCIES, TRACING

If it is desirable to get more details into your transparencies, you might consider the tracing techniques that were introduced in the illustration section. In this case, the tracing of images directly onto sheets of acetate is a simple way to produce transparencies. Of course, our first concern is to identify those tracing materials that will work on the smooth acetate surface.

Among the appropriate media we find grease pencils which are easily erased with a damp cloth, pen and India ink that will produce black, crisp lines, felt pens of various colors and degrees of fineness, and Mongol colored pencils that are used on matte or frosted acetate. Each of these various media will produce line images of different degrees of color, opacity and fineness. Pick the right medium for the images that you are working with and for the effect that you are trying to create.

Obviously, part of this decision will be influenced by the nature of the original that you are planning to transfer onto the acetate surface. It is suggested that you begin this process with an original that is a line drawing. The process of translating an original half-tone or photograph into a line drawing is usually beyond the capability of people not trained in art skills. Once you have selected the line drawing, your next concern is with its complexity. How much detail is there, and how much will you need to translate to the acetate? Now you have the original and the medium that you intend to use and are ready to begin the actual tracing process.

Place the acetate over the original, making sure that you keep the original free of fingerprints. Fingerprints are grease, and the medium that will work on acetate will not work on grease. Clip the original and acetate sandwich together to maintain registration during the tracing process. While you can use paper clips or other materials, I have found that the clip board is best. It not only holds the elements in register, it provides a smooth surface to work on and the ability to move the materials into different positions during tracing.

Now simply trace the image onto the acetate surface. Make sure you use a scrap of newsprint or other material to keep your hand and fingers off the acetate during the tracing. I have found it quite useful to keep a slip of paper on hand that I can periodically slip between the acetate and the original to see how the tracing is progressing. The image is normally traced in a line format, and these lines may be either black lines using the India ink or black felt pens, or they may be colored lines from the felt pens.

With the lines completed and the line drawing reproduced, you may want to add color. It is advisable to add color to the opposite side of the transparency to avoid damaging the line image that you have created. None of these medium, with the possible exception of the Mongol pencils, will produce good, solid colored areas. You may have to resort to line or stipple shading to indicate the color you desire. Mount your transparency, and it is ready for projection.

TRANSPARENCIES, THERMAL:

CARBON IMAGES

OWL

TEARSHEET ORIGINALS

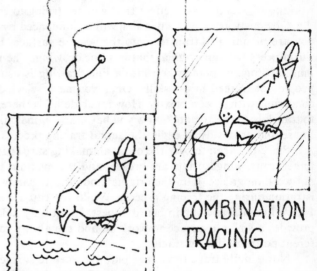

COMBINATION TRACING

TRACED ORIGINALS

BIRDS

BIRDS

TRANSPARENT TAPE

PASTE-UPS

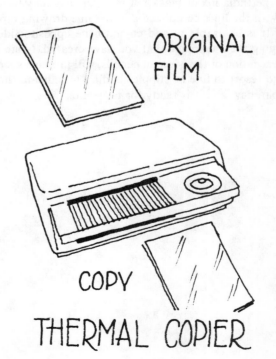

ORIGINAL FILM

COPY

THERMAL COPIER

TRANSPARENCIES, THERMAL

Many times the line drawing original is too complex for your abilities to trace it. In this case, there is a more costly system that is quite simple—the thermal transparency system. For use of this the physical nature of the original must meet certain specifications—it must be a carbon image. Most black printers ink is carbon, pencil and India ink drawings are carbon, typewritten material is carbon, and, perhaps most importantly, Xerox copies are carbon. So if you find an image you want to produce thermally and it is not carbon, just make a Xerox copy and use it.

The original must not only be a carbon image, it must represent the concept you desire to communicate. Perhaps you can find just the right visual in a magazine or newspaper with just the right lettering of just the right size. However, it is more likely that you will need to modify and manipulate materials from a variety of sources to create the instructional materials that meet the needs of your audience, content and objectives. This can be done either through tracing or through the paste-up process.

Tracing is simply the process of tracing an element from one source and then adding a second (or third) traced element from another source. The example at the top left side of the opposite page shows this process. Notice that in this process you must make allowances for where the second visual will overlap the first visual. If you trace both the pail and the seagull completely, the lines of the pail will show through the feet of the seagull. Since this is to be a thermal transparency, you will do the tracing in either ink or pencil (carbon) onto tracing paper.

The paste-ups are a second way to produce manipulated masters for the thermal process. In this case, you select elements from a variety of sources and cut them out. Note that you do not cut them out along the lines of the image but rather simply to eliminate other elements in the original that are undesirable. These can be visual or lettering as shown in the example at the bottom left of the opposite page. The elements are mounted to a sheet of paper with rubber cement(best) or by simply taping them in place. Often these can be used directly as masters for the thermal process, but it is usually better to make a Xerox copy of the paste-up and use this as the master. This will ensure that all of the images are equally well-carboned, and you can eliminate any unwanted marks with white liquid paper. Once the master is ready, the thermal printing process can begin.

Begin with the selection of the right film. You can use black line on clear or colored line on clear. You can also use black line on a colored background, or even reversal films which will produce a negative image. Once you have selected the film, place it over the master with the notch in the upper right hand corner. Now simply insert the film/master sandwich into a thermal copier that is at the right setting, and a few seconds later the copy will come out imprinted onto the acetate with the original undamaged.

TRANSPARENCIES, DIAZO:

MATERIALS

COVER ORIG.

LINE MASTER

AREA MASTER

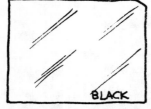
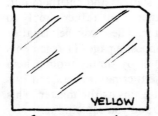
SELECT FILM (COLORS)

GLASS
ORIG.
FILM
BOARD

PREPARE "SANDWICH"

EXPOSE TO ULTRA-VIOLET

DEVELOP THE FILM

BLACK LINE
YELLOW AREA

ASSEMBLE THE FILMS

MOUNT

TRANSPARENCIES, DIAZO

The diazo system is also used to produce transparencies. It is not a common system, but it produces such professional results, especially in the areas of solid colors, that it is worth describing. As with the thermal system, we will first produce a master and then make the print from the master. However, the master in the diazo process is quite different from the thermal master. Here we are not concerned with carbon images but rather with opaque images on a transparent or translucent base.

Here it is also advisable to begin with a line drawing. In the example on the opposite page we have a line drawing of a cat. Cover the original with tracing paper and register it with a clip board to hold the elements in register during the tracing process. It is best to use India ink (as black as you can get) to transfer the image onto the tracing paper. However, we want the end product to have yellow eyes and a yellow tie, so for the second color we must produce a second master. Still using India ink, we color in the areas that we want to be yellow. Make sure that the area is completely opaque, or the print will be speckled. Now the two masters are matched with the appropriate colors of diazo film. Diazo film has a much wider range of colors than the thermal films, and each sheet of film will produce only one color. In the case of our example we are going to print the lines black and the solid-colored areas yellow.

We place the master into the sandwich shown on the opposite page with some sort of a board on the bottom to support the materials. Then the proper color of diazo film is placed with the notch in the upper right corner. The next element is the master with the image side down. Last, a sheet of glass goes on to hold everything in place. The sandwich is only needed when you are making an exposure without an exposing unit. If you have one of these, just follow their directions. But with our sandwich we now expose the materials to ultraviolet light. Either the sun or a special lamp will do. You will need to run a test sheet to determine the proper exposure time. When the exposure is made, you are ready for the next step in the process, developing the image.

The exposed film is then placed into an ammonia atmosphere. This can either be a professional developing unit or simply a large jar that has a few drops of ammonia in a sponge at the bottom. In either case the image will slowly begin to appear after it has been introduced into the ammonia atmosphere. When it reaches the proper color intensity, remove it, and you have made your print. Continue this process until all of the masters have been reproduced onto diazo film.

Our last problem is to place these various prints in register and mount them into a transparency mask. The result will be a truly professional looking transparency that has the capability of producing excellent solid-colored areas. However, the process is relatively expensive since each color will cost 25–35¢. This means that a transparency with three colors will cost 75¢ for the film and another 15¢ for the mask.

TRANSPARENCIES, LIFTING:

ORIGINAL

CLAY TEST

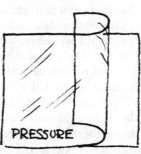 
SELECT LAMINATION FILM

LAMINATE

 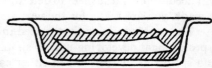
SOAK THE VISUAL

SEPARATE

INK SIDE UP

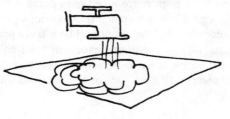
WASH OFF EXCESS CLAY

SPRAY

OR LAMINATE

PREPARE MASK & MOUNT

204

TRANSPARENCIES, LIFTING

In all of the previous techniques for producing transparencies, one of the limitations has been the accurate reproduction of halftones (photographs printed in magazines and newspapers), both black and white and color. With this process, lifting, we can literally lift the ink from the page of a magazine and transfer it to a sheet of acetate to produce a full color image.

The lifting process begins with the selection of the visual. Here we are interested in identifying visuals that are printed on clay-based paper. Since this is not obvious, we need to apply a simple test to the materials we want to lift. Simply spit on the end of your finger and rub lightly in a white area of the visual (in the margin). If this leaves a small deposit of clay on your finger tip, it is clay-based paper and the visual can be lifted.

Next you select the type of lamination film that you want to use. There is the heat sensitive type like Sealamin laminating film and the pressure sensitive type like Contact. The heat sensitive lamination film is a little easier to use, but it requires a $400 dry mount press. Once you have selected the type of laminating film, you laminate the visual. With the pressure sensitive film, peel away the backing and apply it to the face of the visual you want to lift. Make sure that you burnish it carefully to insure that it is entirely laminated. If you are using the heat sensitive laminating film, place it and the visual in the dry mount press set at 225 degrees. Make sure that the dull side of the lamination film is toward the surface of the visual you want to lift. Once the visuals are laminated, the next step is the same for both types of lamination materials.

Place the laminated visuals into a pan of water. To speed the process you may want to add a few drops of detergent to allow the water to penetrate the visual and melt the clay layer more quickly. This process should only take 3–5 minutes if your visual is printed on a paper with a good clay coating. If it takes longer than that, it means that either it isn't a good clay coating or there is none at all and you really can't lift the visual successfully. When the paper separates from the acetate, there will still be deposits of clay on the acetate. Using cotton and running water, wash off the excess clay. Then allow the lifted visual to dry. When it is dry, check to see how well it projects on the overhead; if you are satisfied, you are ready for mounting. If it seems a little dull, you will want to make it a little more transparent. With the heat sensitive lamination film, this may mean spraying it with a clear plastic spray such as Krylon. If it is a pressure sensitive lamination film, you may want to simply apply another layer of the film to the ink side of the lift.

Now you are ready to mount. Since the lifted visuals are never an appropriate size to fit a standard mask, you will probably have to make your own by trimming railroad board to the outside dimensions of the standard mask and then cutting a "window" slightly smaller than the lifted visual. The results will be a full-color visual.

TRANSPARENCIES, MISC. TECH.∴

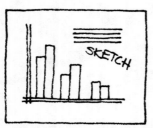 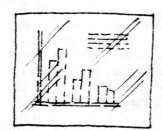  

TRANSPARENT TAPE TRACING.

 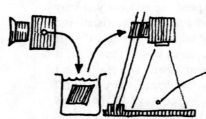  

HIGH CONTRAST PHOTOGRAPHY.

MONGOL PENCIL TRACING.

✳ AND COMBINATIONS

TRANSPARENCIES, MISCELLANEOUS TECHNIQUES

While we have examined using cutouts, tracing, thermal, diazo, and lifting as ways to produce transparencies, there are still many other ways that we can create appropriate materials for the overhead system.

TRANSPARENT TAPES

There are colored transparent tapes available that can be used to produce professional looking charts and graphs. These tapes come in a wide range of colors, widths and even patterns. Simply sketch the desired chart or graph on a sheet of paper and cover it with acetate. On the acetate you can apply the tapes in almost any configuration that you desire. Some of the tapes are so thin that you can actually draw with them, but this system is best for the production of professional looking charts and graphs.

HIGH CONTRAST PHOTOGRAPHY

Often we are faced with a limitation in the size of the visuals we find in magazines and newspapers. The process called high contrast photography will allow you to take small visuals and reproduce them exactly in almost any size that you desire. First, we photograph the original with high contrast film. The film is developed to produce a negative. The negative is then placed in an enlarger and brought up to the desired size. At this point, things begin to depart from normal. Rather than printing the copy onto photographic paper, we print it on film. It will be the opposite of the negative, which means that it will look like the original except that it will now be the size you want it to be. The result will be an opaque photographic image on a transparent base—an overhead transparency. Simply mount it into a mask and you are ready to deliver it to the audience.

MONGOL COLORED PENCIL TRACING

This system was alluded to in the tracing section, but it is different from the other tracing medium in that it requires a different type of acetate. In this case, a matte or frosted acetate is used. The Mongol colored pencils will image on the frosted surface, and small particles of the lead will be deposited in the hills and valleys formed by the matte surface. You can outline the visual with either black lead pencil or India ink and then add the desired color with the Mongol colored pencils. When the tracing and coloring is completed, apply a coat of plastic spray (Krylon) to the imaged side of the acetate. This will flatten out the irregularities of the matte surface and make the transparency truly transparent. This system will provide fairly good solid colors, but they will be a little more pastel than the diazo or thermal processes.

COMBINATIONS

These and all of the other transparency production systems can be used separately, or they can be used in conjunction with each other. For example, it is easy to add information to a diazo transparency by tracing or lettering in India ink. Felt pen lettering can be added to thermal transparencies, etc. Pick the combination that meets your particular needs.

CHAPTER 11
COMPLEX INSTRUCTIONAL MEDIA AND MATERIALS:

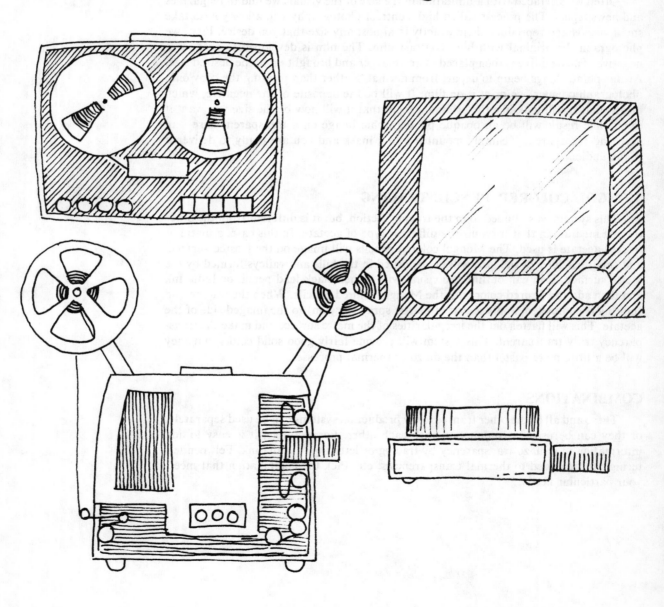

COMPLEX INSTRUCTIONAL MEDIA AND MATERIALS

As you can see by the chart below, there is a wide range of what we are calling complex media and their related materials. They are normally available from a wider range of sources than the simpler instructional media and materials, and they generally have a wider range of teaching/learning strategies.

Complex media and their related materials	sources			utilization				characteristics
	commercial sources	free/inexpensive sources	local production	presentation	interaction	independent study	drill/practice	General characteristics: Complex media and their materials generally have a wide range of sources and utilization. They also require more complex skills for local production as well as more preproduction planning than simple media.
Silent 2 × 2 slides	X	X	X	2	1	3	4	Best suited for interaction since they are instructor controlled.
Slide/tape programs	X	X	X	1	3	2	4	Best for canned presentations. The media controls the pacing.
Silent filmstrips	X	X	X	2	1	3	4	Best suited for interaction. Not easily modified or updated.
Sound filmstrips	X	X		1	3	2	4	Best for canned presentations.
Sequential multimedia	X	X	X	1	1	1	1	Media used in a sequence to deal with a common topic or concept.
Simultaneous multimedia			X	1				Two or more media used simultaneously. Best suited for motivation.
Motion pictures	X	X	X	1	2	3	4	Fixed pacing. Excellent to introduce or review a topic.
Audio tape and radio	X	X	X	1	1	1	1	Can be used to support many other media or used alone.
Disc recordings	X	X		1		3		Can be used to support many other media or used alone.
Broadcast television	X			1				Presented on a fixed time schedule which may not meet your needs.
Video tape and cable	X	X	X	1	2			Presenter has more control over the information delivery system.
Computers	X		X			1	2	Perhaps the fastest growing media at the present time, great potential.
Interactive video			X			1		Combines video and computers into a fantastic system, great potential.

One of the major differences between the simple and the complex media is the amount of preproduction planning that is required for their local production. While a series of thumbnail sketches may be all that is necessary for the simple media, the complex media require the production of a complete set of planning documents. They begin with the development of the content outline, audience analysis, media selection and of course the preparation of the instructional objectives. These are used to produce the scripts and storyboards that become the blueprints for the actual production. Only then are the production skills in photography, audio and electronics applied to create the products that will deliver the instruction to the intended audience. This production process is necessary because of the cost and time that is normally involved in the local production of these complex instructional materials.

PHOTO MEDIA, GENERAL:

PHOTOGRAPHIC MEDIA AND PRODUCTION SKILLS

There are a number of complex instructional materials that use photographic skills. Slides and filmstrips and even motion pictures and television production require knowledge of the nature of basic photographic processes and how they work. In this short section we will look at just a few of the characteristics of the photographic system. First, photography is a system. The system consists of: 1) the camera, 2) the film, and 3) the end product. Cameras can be either simple or complex. The simple cameras have a fixed lens system, a fixed shutter, and a fixed aperture. In the more complex system these elements can be varied to achieve the desired effect under a variety of light situations. Perhaps this is better understood if we look at how the camera works. Light is reflected from the subject and passes through the lens of the camera. In the simpler cameras the fixed lens means that you must be a certain distance from the subject for it to be in focus. In the more complex cameras not only can you change lenses to fit particular needs, you can also adjust the focus of the camera for almost any distance. Once the light passes through the lens, it encounters the aperture or iris. This is basically a hole that lets a specific amount of light into the camera. In the simpler cameras this aperture is fixed, and this means you can shoot only under a certain set of light and subject conditions. In the more complex cameras this aperture can be opened or closed to meet the needs of the conditions, providing you with a greater flexibility. Once past the aperture, the light is interrupted by the shutter. This shutter controls the duration of the light—the amount of time that the light will strike the film. In the simple cameras this is normally fixed at 1/30th of a second. In the complex cameras it can be varied to meet the needs of the circumstances. And finally the light strikes the film, making the desired exposure.

Film is the second component of the photographic system, and there are a wide range of films available. Here we will concentrate on only two color films, those that end in the suffix chrome and those that end in the suffix color. For example, Ektacolor film will result in a photographic print on paper, while Ektachrome will result in a 2 × 2 slide. You will want to pick the right film for the end product that you want. Once you have exposed the right type of film, you have what is called a latent image. To make this image visible you have to develop the film. While it is possible for you to develop your own film, we will simplify and send the film out for development. With the film ending in the suffix color, the development will result in a negative which is put into an enlarger and printed on paper to the size you desire. With the film ending in the suffix chrome, the film will be developed directly into a 2 × 2 slide format without an intervening negative.

This photographic process can be used to produce prints or slides of people, places and things. You can photograph anything, and if you can't afford a trip to France, it is quite simple to photograph pictures of France using a process called copy photography. In short, through photography we eliminate many of the visual restrictions that existed with the simple media, where we were relying only on existing visuals.

THE 2×2 SLIDES GENERAL:

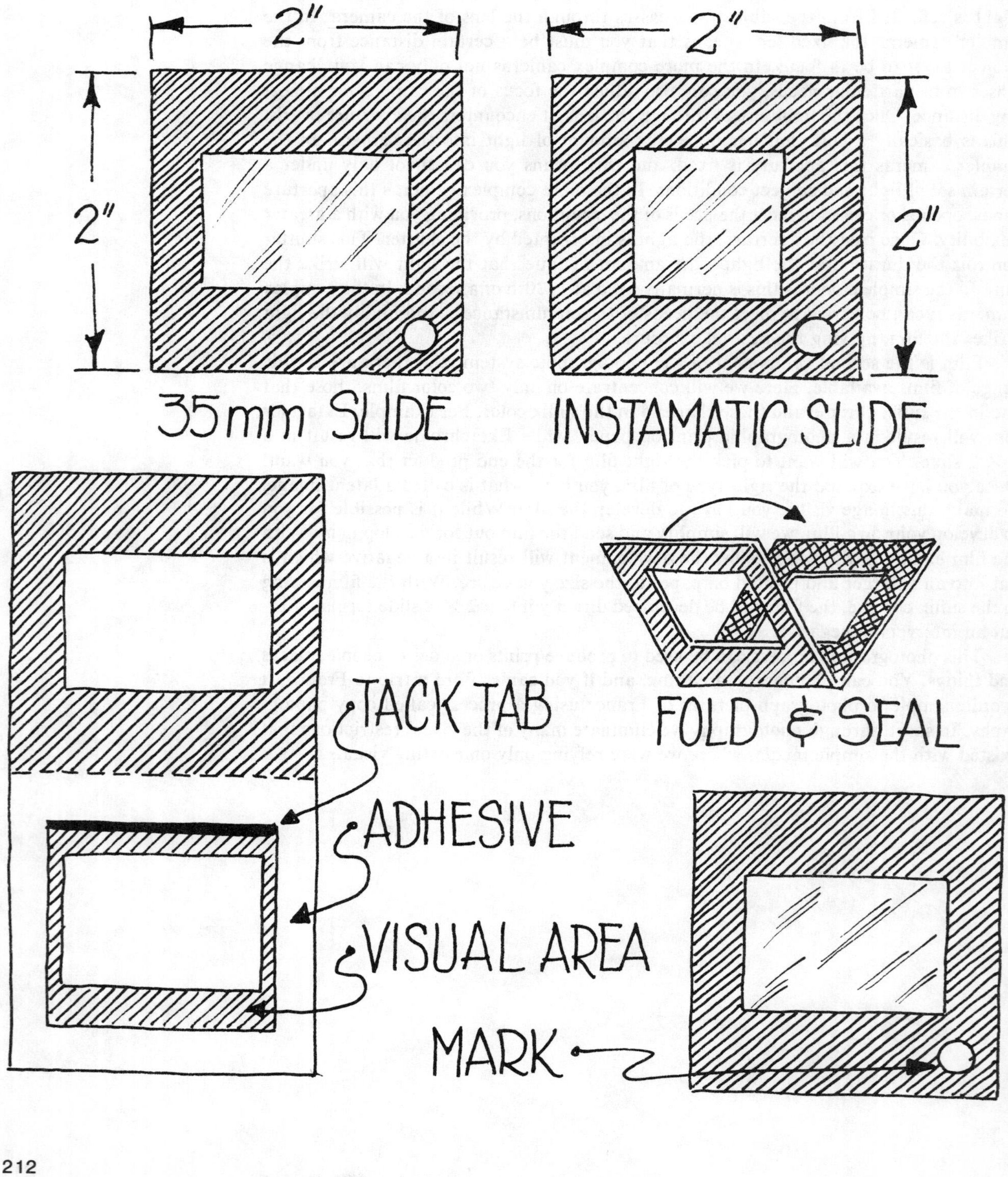

2"

2"

35mm SLIDE

2"

2"

INSTAMATIC SLIDE

TACK TAB

ADHESIVE

VISUAL AREA

FOLD & SEAL

MARK

THE 2 × 2 SLIDES, GENERAL

The photographic process can result in either photographic prints on paper or transparent photographic images that are designed to be presented in a slide projector. Since almost everyone has a collection of photographic prints in an album, we will concentrate on the 2 × 2 slides. These 2 × 2 slides are quite popular as instructional materials, and they are normally used in two quite different formats. The slides can be used in a silent mode. Basically, this means that the slides are presented and the instructor provides a live narration or discussion of the content. This system is ideal for developing an interaction within the class. The instructor can control the pacing and can insert the pauses where it is appropriate for learner interaction. These slides that are accompanied by the instructor's live narration can also be used for a straight presentation, and with the appropriate lettered slides they could even be used for self-instruction and drill and practice. However, these latter applications are perhaps better done through other media.

When slides are used with an audio tape or disc recording, it is usually referred to as a slide-tape program. In this case the sync between the slides and the audio can be achieved by: 1) the instructor memorizing or having a written copy of the script and advancing the slides on cue, 2) having an audible signal on the tape such as a tone or chime to signal when the slides are to be changed, or 3) the audio tape having an inaudible signal that will actually control the slide projector and change slides on electronic command. The slide-tape programs are best suited to the presentation of information to a large group. While they can also be used for the other teaching/learning strategies, they are not really appropriate.

Both silent and slide-tape programs are not only available from commercial and free/inexpensive sources, they are also capable of being locally produced. The slides can be shot with either a complex or a simple camera and sent out for development. While it is quite possible to develop your own 2 × 2 slides, it takes time and equipment that might not be available. When they are returned, they will be in the 2 × 2 format. This simply refers to the outside dimension of the slides. This is standardized to allow slides with different visual formats to be projected in a variety of 2 × 2 slide projectors.

In some cases you may even want to mount your own slides. There are cardboard masks available that will allow you to do this. They will allow you to mount either 35mm slides or the Instamatic slides into the 2 × 2 format. There are even masks that will allow you to cut apart the filmstrip frames and remount them as 2 × 2 slides. These cardboard masks are adhered by a material similar to MT-5 and thus can be mounted with either a professional slide mounter or with a tacking iron used in dry mounting. There are even slide mounts that are circular or shaped like hearts. These can be used when a special effect is desired. Using these masks, it is even possible to sandwich two visuals into a single slide for superimposing titles or other information.

THE 2×2 SLIDE PROJECTOR:

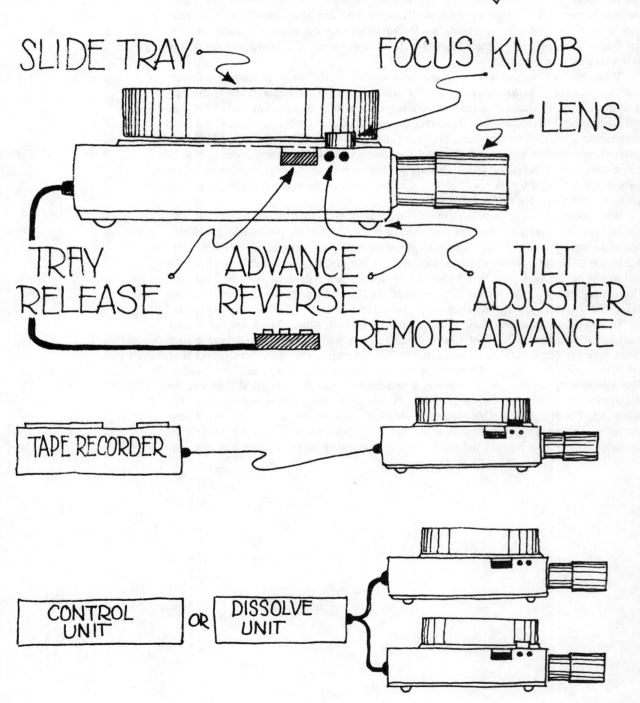

SLIDE TRAY

FOCUS KNOB

LENS

TRAY RELEASE

ADVANCE REVERSE

TILT ADJUSTER

REMOTE ADVANCE

TAPE RECORDER

CONTROL UNIT OR DISSOLVE UNIT

THE 2 × 2 SLIDE PROJECTOR

The 2 × 2 slides are only part of the system. They are the information source, the materials, but to get them to the audience we need a delivery system, a media that will accommodate these 2 × 2 slides. There are many brands and models of 2 × 2 slide projectors on the market, but all will successfully present the slides to the intended audience. Basically, these projectors consist of a projection system and a slide delivery system. In the diagram on the opposite page the slides are delivered to the projection system via the tray on the top. This circular tray rotates, and when it reaches the appropriate spot, the slides are dropped into the projection system. The slides are loaded into the tray upside down since they will be inverted as part of the projection process. The standard tray will carry about 80 slides, but there are trays that will accommodate more.

The projection system will vary depending on the brand and model you purchase and how much you want to spend. The advance/reverse buttons on the side of the projector will allow you to advance or reverse the slides during the projection. However, this is operated from the projector, and the projector is normally used in the back of the room. If you want to work from the front of the room during projection, you will need to get a remote advance unit that plugs into the rear of the projector; the cord can run to the front of the room allowing you to operate the projection system from there. Also on the side of the projector you will find some sort of tray release. This is used when you load the tray into the projector or want to remove it from the projector. By depressing it, you can rotate the tray to the number of the slide you desire to project.

The standard lens on the projector is a fixed focus lens. While it can focus the image, you must move the projector closer to or further from the screen to make the image larger or smaller. Focusing is done by rotating the focus knob on the front of the projector. This fixed focus lens can be replaced with a zoom lens that will allow you to increase or decrease the size of the projected image by simply rotating the lens. To move the image vertically on the screen there is a set of tilt adjustments that will angle the projector properly.

At the rear of the projector there are the on/off controls and also a control that will allow the projector to deliver its slides at intervals of five seconds or more. There is also an attachment that will allow the slide projector to be operated by the inaudible signal from the tape recording that is designed to accompany the slides.

This system is so popular that there are quite a number of auxiliary units that can be attached to it. For example, you can use two slide projectors interconnected with a dissolve unit and dissolve from the slide on one projector to the slide on the other, thus eliminating the often undesirable black screen that occurs with single projector operation.

PHOTO SLIDE PRODUCTION:

*PLANNING - DESIGN:

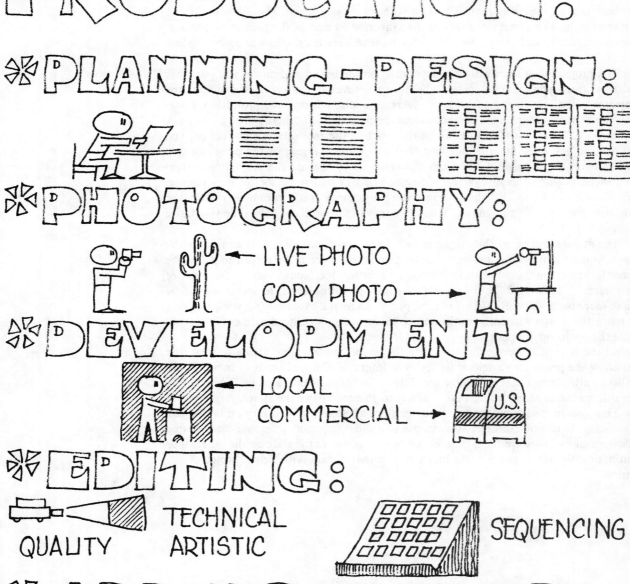

*PHOTOGRAPHY:

LIVE PHOTO

COPY PHOTO →

*DEVELOPMENT:

LOCAL

COMMERCIAL →

U.S.

*EDITING:

QUALITY   TECHNICAL   SEQUENCING
           ARTISTIC

*ADDING SOUND:

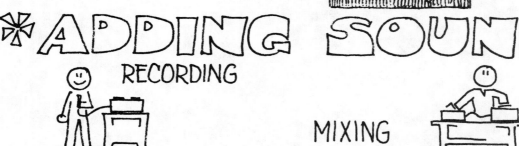

RECORDING

MIXING

PHOTOGRAPHIC SLIDE PRODUCTION

As we indicated earlier, it is quite easy to produce slides for the 2×2 slide system. However, if you are interested in a predictable instructional product, photography is only part of the process. The process begins with objectives and ends with a product that will assist the learners to attain the objective.

PLANNING AND DESIGN

In this phase you are preparing the blueprint for your production. Without it you may end up with a product, but the product may not do what you want it to do. Begin with the objective, a clear concise statement of what you want the learners to be able to do as a result of the instruction. Develop a content outline that specifies the content and the order and sequence in which it should be presented. Also prepare a description of the audience that specifies the characteristics of the audience that will influence the way in which the program is designed, produced, and delivered. With these as a guide you then prepare a storyboard visualizing the product and indicating the concepts that are to be covered in the audio portion. Last, write the script that contains the narration and music or sound effect to complete the program. Only after these documents are produced and checked are you ready to move into actual production.

PHOTOGRAPHY

There are basically two photo techniques that can be used in the production of your slide-tape program: 1) live photography and 2) copy photograph. Live photography simply refers to the photography of the people, places, and things that you can get in front of your camera. Copy photography means the photography of existing visual materials. These may be pictures from magazines and newspapers, illustrations that you create or manipulate, and lettering or titles that you prepare. Copy photography does raise a problem, that of copyright. Many of the photographs that are printed in magazines and newspapers are owned, and it is normally illegal to photograph or copy them. However, if you do not cause the owner to lose money and/or you do not make money, it falls under the fair use doctrine for teachers.

DEVELOPMENT AND EDITING

I recommend that you let the commerical sources take care of the development of your slides unless you are interested in photography as a hobby. But once you get your finished slides, it is time for editing. This is the process of evaluating the photographs and arranging them in the sequence suggested by your storyboard. This is the stage where the professional takes a great deal of time and energy, and it is what makes the difference between a professional and an amateur production.

ADDING SOUND

The last step is to create the sound track that will accompany your slides. Creating the narration and mixing it with the necessary music and sound effects is just the beginning. You also need to add either the audible signals to advance the slides or the inaudible sync that will control the slide projector.

GRAPHIC SLIDES: 2x2

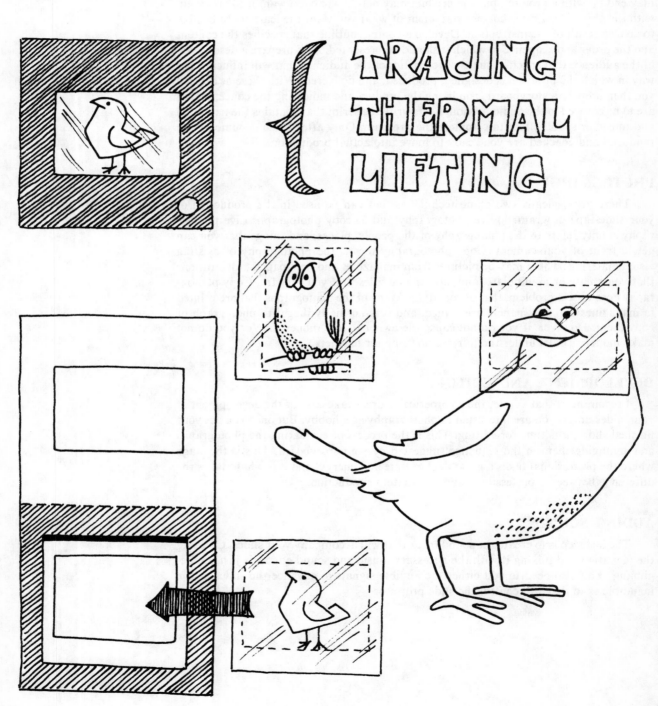

{ TRACING
THERMAL
LIFTING

GRAPHIC 2 × 2 SLIDES

Up to this point we have emphasized the photographic production of 2 × 2 slides, but it is possible to produce slides without ever using a camera or photographic film. The 2 × 2 slide is simply a transparent image in a cardboard frame—if you stop to think about it, that's what an overhead transparency is, a transparent image in a cardboard frame. Since they are so similar, it means that they can be produced with the same techniques. This means that all of the techniques we used to produce overhead transparencies can also be used to produce 2 × 2 slides. The difference is simply the image size. The image size for an overhead is roughly 8 × 10″, while the image area in a 2 × 2 slide is approximately 1 1/4″ × 7/8″. You can see just how small the image area is on the scale drawings on the opposite page.

However, if you can find visuals of the appropriate size (and they are all around us), it is possible to produce 2 × 2 slides graphically. Note in the example on the opposite page that the owl is a visual that does fit inside the visual area of the slide mask, while the larger bird requires using only a portion of the existing visual. Some visuals that are too big may be reduced successfully through the Xerox system.

Some of the tracing medium may not be too appropriate. For example, the grease pencils will not produce a line small enough to trace visuals of the appropriate size. However, they can be used to color in the areas of visuals traced with other medium. Even the standard felt pens may produce lines that are too wide, but many companies are now producing felt pens with fine and superfine tips that will work quite well for this technique. Perhaps the pen and ink tracing technique is the best if you use the fine tipped crowquill pens.

Even the thermal systems can be used. However, rather than copying one small visual on an 8 × 11 sheet of thermal film, it is best to paste-up a variety of visuals and copy them all at the same time. Obviously, you will need to work with originals that are small, but they should also have as thin lines as possible. Use the 2 × 2 mask to identify the visual that would be appropriate for this process.

Even lifts are possible. Unfortunately, when they are enlarged they often show the dots of color that they are composed of. Even so, these lifts give an added impact to the graphic slide presentations. You can use either the pressure sensitive of the heat sensitive lifting process to produce these graphic 2 × 2 slides.

There is one real problem that can cause some difficulty. Look at the picture of the owl on the opposite page. Note that there is a visual area and a mounting area that is required. When you are preparing the graphic slides, only a portion of the acetate will actually be projected. The remaining area is used to attach the visual to the cardboard mask. Again on the opposite page you will notice a diagram of the mask in the lower left corner. The cover on top shows the visual area of the slide. On the bottom half you can see a duplicate of this area plus the area that is necessary to mount the slide into the cardboard mask.

FILMSTRIPS IN EDUCATION:

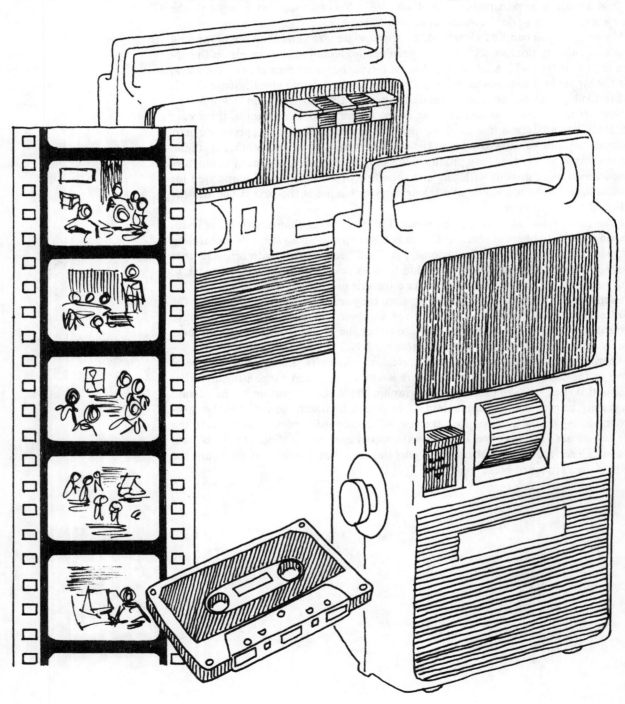

FILMSTRIPS IN EDUCATION

The filmstrip is, as the name implies, a strip of 35mm film with the images (or frames) arranged in a sequential order. Since they are a fixed sequencing of visuals, these filmstrips are normally used where a fixed sequence is desirable in the presentation. Filmstrips come in two basic types: 1) the silent filmstrip and 2) the sound filmstrip. The silent filmstrip is easily identified because it does not have a tape or disc recording to accompany it. However, it also normally has a caption or written materials on each frame. These captions can be read by the instructor, but more normally they are read by the learners in the class, generating a productive interaction situation. On the other hand, the sound filmstrips do not normally have these captions, though they may have some written materials. Here the narration is supplied by the tape or disc recording that accompanies the tape.

Both sound and silent filmstrips are available from commercial and free/inexpensive sources. However, they are not normally available through local production. The image or frame on a filmstrip is half the size of the image that a standard 35mm camera produces. Thus, to produce your own filmstrip you would need to have a half frame camera. Also, since the filmstrip is a series of images on a single strip of film, that means that if we make a mistake on frame thirteen, we must begin the process again at the beginning. Thus, local production of filmstrips is not normally a reasonable activity. However, you can produce your own filmstrips designed to fit your needs. You simply shoot a series of slides, then ship them off to the laboratory and have the lab translate them into the filmstrip format.

Filmstrips can be used for all of the teaching/learning strategies. The silent filmstrip appears to be best where an interaction is desired during the filmstrip, since the instructor retains pacing control. The sound filmstrip seems best for a presentation since the media begins to control the pacing in this situation. The other applications are possible but not the best uses for filmstrips.

A disadvantage of the filmstrip is that it cannot be easily up-dated or modified. It is difficult to cut out a single frame and splice in another frame. Basically, you are stuck with the design if you want to retain the format. However, it is possible to change a filmstrip into another format and in this new format make the adjustments you desire to make. Let's consider this situation. You acquire a filmstrip from a free/inexpensive source, and while it is useful, there are some rearrangements that you would like to make. First, cut the filmstrip apart at the frame line. Then acquire from your local photo store some half frame 2 × 2 slide mounts. Mount the filmstrip frames into the 2 × 2 masks, and you now have a set of slides that can be projected via the 2 × 2 projection system, and you can rearrange the order to your heart's content.

Filmstrips are another tool that you should consider when you are making your media selection—deciding which would be the best system to deliver your proposed message to your intended audience.

FILMSTRIP PROJECTORS

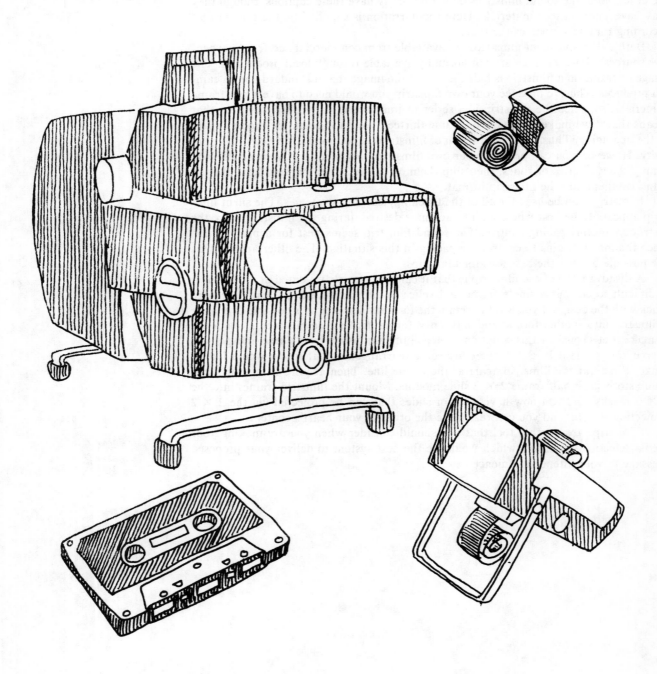

FILMSTRIP PROJECTORS

There are literally thousands of commercial and free/inexpensive filmstrips available that cover almost every curriculum area. To get these instructional materials to the intended audience we need an efficient and effective delivery system—the media to complement our materials. Perhaps because filmstrips are such a popular tool, there are a wide variety of filmstrip delivery systems available. These can be broken down into two major categories: 1) the projectors for delivery to a large group and 2) viewers for delivery to small groups or individuals. Both filmstrip projectors and viewers are available in either sound or silent formats.

The filmstrip projection system is quite simple. The filmstrip is inserted into a channel between the lens and the lamp, and the sprocket holes in the filmstrip are locked into the advance mechanism of the projector. There is normally an adjustment lever that will allow you to center the frames of the filmstrips of the screen. Once the filmstrip is loaded, framed, and the light turned on, all that is required is to rotate the advance lever or knob, and the next frame of the filmstrip will be displayed on the screen. The image is focused by adjusting the objective lens. If it is a sound filmstrip projector, there will be either a turntable (for the record) or a playback system (for the tape) as part of the equipment. Like our slide units, the sound filmstrips will have either an audible signal that will tell the operator when to advance to the next frame or an inaudible signal that will directly control the advance of the filmstrip projector. Actually, it is not uncommon to have the same narration on both sides of the tape or disc recording, with one side having the audible signal and the other having the inaudible signal.

Some of the newer filmstrip projectors have a cassette system for carrying the filmstrip. This has always been a major problem in using filmstrips. After the showing, the filmstrip is backwards and must be rewound. If this is not done carefully, it will result in tears and scratches on the filmstrip. While the new cassette system helps even it has not solved the rewind problem of the filmstrip.

In addition to the filmstrip projector, there are also filmstrip viewers. These are designed for small group or individual instruction. Rather than the image being enlarged and projected on a screen, here the image is displayed on a surface built into the viewer. Perhaps the simplest viewers are those designed for the silent filmstrips. They are nothing more than a light source and a built-in screen similar to the one shown on the opposite page. If they are used for sound, they become more complicated with the need for the audio playback system. But even these are much simpler than the projection system and thus usually less expensive.

There are even filmstrip delivery systems which can double as either a projector or a viewer, giving it more flexibility. These units are often used for individual instruction in learning centers.

MULTIMEDIA IN EDUCATION:

SEQUENTIAL ▭▭▭▭▭▭

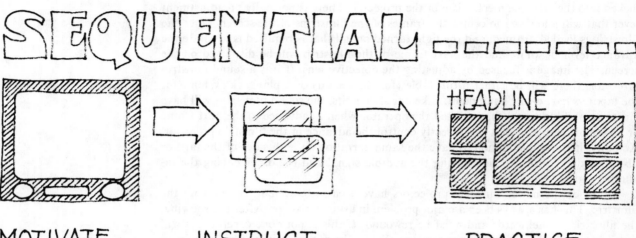

MOTIVATE   INSTRUCT   PRACTICE

SIMULTANEOUS ▬ ▬ ▬ ▬

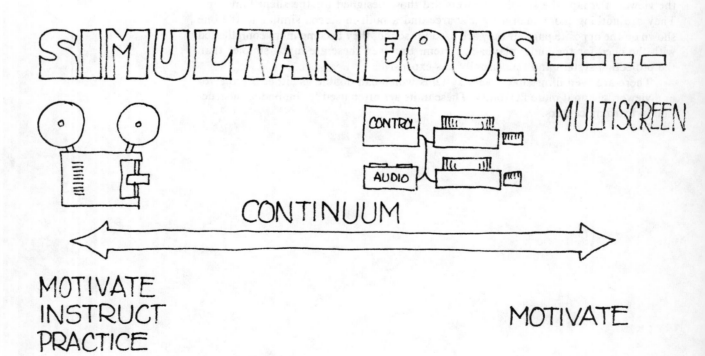

MULTISCREEN

CONTINUUM

MOTIVATE
INSTRUCT
PRACTICE

MOTIVATE

MULTIMEDIA IN EDUCATION

The term multimedia is used to describe a situation in which two or more media are used to transmit information. There are two types of multimedia that are suitable for instruction. The first is called sequential multimedia and the second simultaneous multimedia. They are quite different in form, and they are quite different in function.

SEQUENTIAL MULTIMEDIA

The type of multimedia experience that is called sequential is the type that is most commonly found in the classroom. Basically, the sequential multimedia program has a single concept or topic, such as the westward movement or oceanography. It utilizes a series of media experiences sequentially to motivate, instruct, provide practice for, and even evaluate the learners. For instance, it might use a video tape to introduce the topic and motivate the student. This might be followed up with a series of overhead transparencies to provide the instruction. Then a bulletin board might be designed to provide an appropriate practice activity. This is an example of various media that are used in sequence.

As you can see, it is impossible to tie sequential multimedia to a specific teaching/learning strategy. Rather, since it contains a variety of media, it is a matter of picking the right media for the desired strategy. Not too long ago the acquisition of sequential multimedia programs was limited to local production. But these have proven so popular and so effective that instructional packages are now available from many commercial sources and even some free/inexpensive sources.

SIMULTANEOUS MULTIMEDIA

The simultaneous multimedia is basically the use of two or more media simultaneously. Actually, this definition creates a continuum of possible multimedia experiences. At the simple end of the continuum we have things like motion pictures (picture and sound) or slide-tapes (slides plus a tape recording). At the complex end of the continuum we have the media that are more usually considered as multi-media or even multi-image. In this case we have a variety of delivery systems that are normally hooked into some sort of control system. This might be a series of slide projectors that are connected to a computer. When they are linked with an appropriate audio tape, this system will present a kaleidoscope of images onto one or more screens simultaneously. The control system will operate the slide projectors and create a montage of changing images that can be quite effective.

Normally these multimedia programs (at the multi-image end of the continuum) are locally produced. If there are any available from commercial sources or from free/inexpensive sources, I am not aware of them. Of course, at the other end of the continuum they are available from all sources. These simultaneous multimedia presentations are just that, presentations. While they can transmit information, they appear to be much more effective if they are used to motivate rather than to instruct. They are a specialty program for a special purpose.

MULTIMEDIA PRODUCTION:

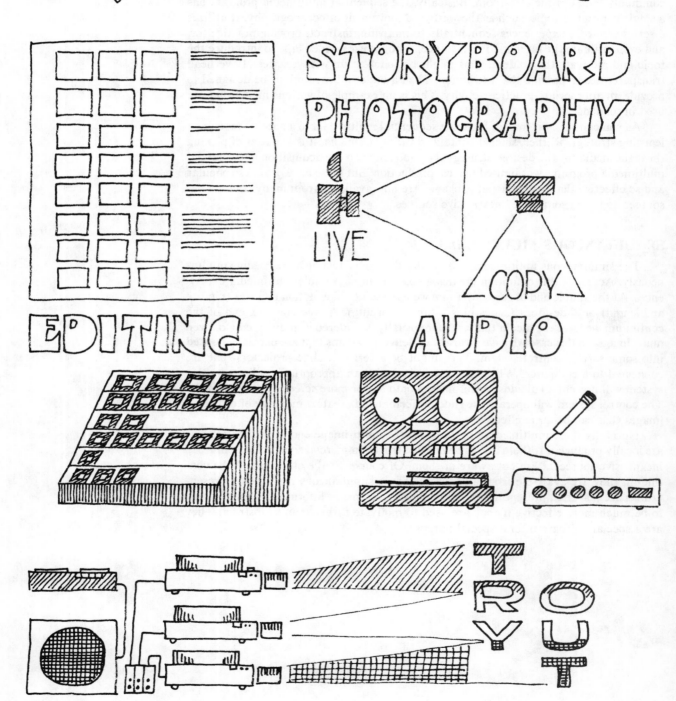

STORYBOARD

PHOTOGRAPHY

LIVE

COPY

EDITING

AUDIO

TRY OUT

MULTIMEDIA PRODUCTION

The production of multimedia or multi-image productions is very complicated, actually, too complicated to cover in detail here. But there are some general suggestions that we can make in this limited space. First, the simultaneous multimedia production, like all complex productions, begins with a need and objectives. Precise statements of what you expect the learners to be able to do as a result of their exposure to this medium are the beginning point. Once the objectives are set, then a content outline suggests both the content that will be delivered and the order and sequence of the content. An audience description suggests what audience characteristics you need to consider in the design, production and delivery of the message.

Once the planning documents are developed, our next concern is with the development of a storyboard. The one shown on the opposite page is a design for a three screen multi-image production. Note that there are three spaces for the images and, of course, a space for the script and/or music ideas. From this you develop the script and identify the slides that are to be produced. There are techniques for producing rather spectacular photographic effects. Panorama shots may match all three images so that they are one complete picture spread across all three screens. Other techniques will allow you to divide the slides into multiple images and create a montage on even a single screen. Obviously, techniques of both live and copy photography can be employed to make the visuals that you will present to the audience.

The editing process is even more important in this type of production than it is in a simple slide tape. Here, you first select the pictures on the basis of quality and communication. It is not unusual for a professional to throw away five slides for every one that he keeps for insertion into the program. In addition to evaluating the quality and content of the slides, the editing process is your opportunity to place them in the order and sequence desired. This is more difficult when you are dealing with multiple images on multiple screens.

The next step is the creation of the audio portion of the program. I have found that this is a very important consideration. Even with excellent visuals a poor audio track will create a less than acceptable end product. In addition to carrying the narration and/or music, the audio track can also be designed to carry the control system. One producer I know of records the audio on track A of a stereo system and commands to the operator on the B track. Thus, the operator can plug a headset into the audio recorder and hear the commands that control the operation of the projectors. For example, "Ready on one, take one. Ready on two and three, take two and three." However, more often than not the control unit is a much more complicated system that can involve thousands of dollars of equipment designed to deliver the slide changes that are called for in the script and storyboard. As you can see, these simultaneous multimedia production can become quite complicated and perhaps this is why they are not often used in the classroom.

MOTION PICTURES IN EDUCATION:

MOTION PICTURES IN EDUCATION

Motion pictures are a complex media that can be used for presentation, interaction, independent study and even drill and practice. Normally, the presentation made is most appropriate for this media, especially when they are used to introduce or review a topic or unit of instruction. There are a few motion pictures that are designed specifically to generate an interaction in a group of students. These are often referred to as trigger films, and they establish a problem without suggesting a specific solution, leaving this to the class discussion that is to follow. While these motion pictures could be used for independent study and drill and practice, there are other media that are more appropriate and more cost effective for these teaching/learning strategies.

Motion pictures are available from commercial sources and free/inexpensive sources. For that matter, they comprise perhaps the largest collection of instructional materials. These free/inexpensive films are normally produced by business and industry to serve as good public relations messages. However, some of these have strong instructional value. These are lent to teachers on a three to five day basis, and all the user has to spend is the postage to return these films to the distributor. Since they can be sent at book rate, this is not as costly as you might think. The films listed in the NICEM Index to 16mm Films can be purchased, but the cost is beyond most teachers. A 20-minute film might cost between $300 and 500. This means that since the average teacher cannot purchase them, there have to be film libraries that do the buying and then rent the films to the instructors. Libraries such as the Central Arizona Film Coop are cooperatives of schools that have combined their purchasing power to acquire these expensive materials. They are then rented to the coop members for a nominal fee and to others who are not members for a slightly higher fee. The major disadvantage of renting films is the simple fact that to get the films you want you have to put your order in many months in advance. This is especially true if the film is popular. Even with multiple copies the film libraries cannot fill orders on short notice.

In addition to commercial and free/inexpensive sources films can also be produced locally. Usually this local production is in an 8mm format, and quite often the films are silent. However, the fact that they are audience specific and task specific gives them a potential impact that commercially produced films just don't have.

There are some changes occurring that may present problems for the classroom film. With the advent of the video tape recorder schools can purchase a playback unit for approximately the same cost as a motion picture projector. If the content was available on video tape, there would probably be fewer film sales and rentals. A second technological innovation, the video disc, promises even more problems. Here the video disc can be produced at a much lower per/unit cost, and it can utilize a delivery system that is approximately the same cost as a motion picture projector. At the present time film is still an important media, but the future may substitute electronic distribution.

MOTION PICTURE PROJECTORS:

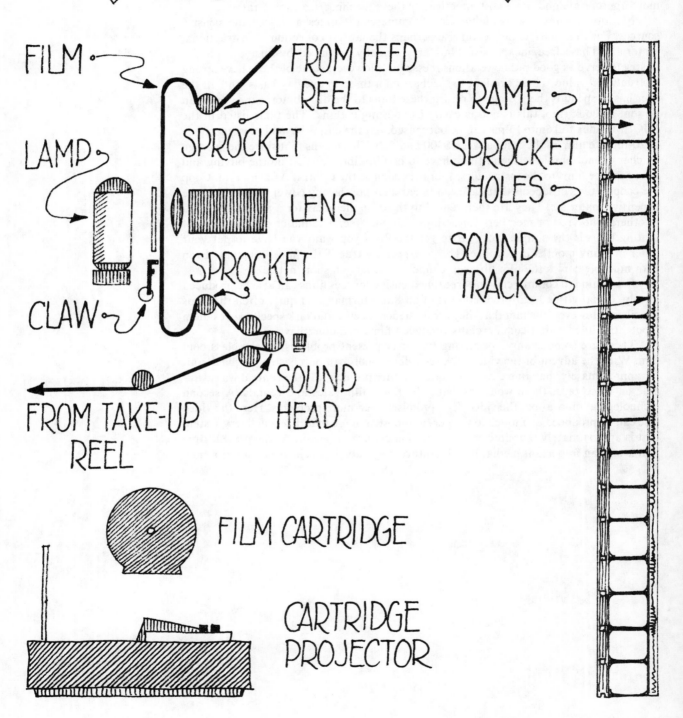

FILM

FROM FEED REEL

SPROCKET

LAMP

LENS

CLAW

SPROCKET

SOUND HEAD

FROM TAKE-UP REEL

FILM CARTRIDGE

CARTRIDGE PROJECTOR

FRAME

SPROCKET HOLES

SOUND TRACK

MOTION PICTURE PROJECTORS

The motion pictures used in education and business have generally been standardized in the 16mm format. While there are some 8mm films that can be used for educational purposes, they are the exception rather than the rule. The 16mm projector designed to deliver these films to the intended audience may be either manual load or auto load units. The auto load is much easier to operate, but it has some real limits. We will concentrate on the manual load projectors. There is a diagram of a typical loading and operating system on the opposite page.

The film comes off the feed reel at the top of the system and first engages a sprocket unit. This utilizes the sprocket holes in the film to pull the film from the feed reel. The film then goes into the top loop which allows the continuous speed of the film to be changed to the intermittent, motion necessary for projection. The film passes through the film channel between the lamp and the lens system. A claw pulls one frame into position, where it remains for projection, then the claw pulls the next frame into position for projection. To ensure that the image is not projected during the transition, the shutter closes as one image is being replaced with another and opens as the frame is in place for projection. The film continues on into the bottom loop, which establishes the proper distance between the image and its corresponding sound and also serves as a clutch to allow for the change from intermittent motion to the continuous motion that is required for the rest of the system. The sprocket at the bottom pulls the film through the projector and onto the sound head. An exciter lamp shines a narrow beam through the sound track on the film and into an electric eye. The differing amounts of light are recorded as different electrical signals are translated into sound through an amplifier. Finally, the film moves onto the take-up reel.

Problems in projection can occur at many different points. If there is an image but no sound, it probably means the exciter lamp in the sound head is burned out. If there is sound but no picture, it probably means the projection lamp has burned out. If the image is jumping up and down on the screen, it means that you have lost either the top or bottom loop and they must be reestablished. If there is a discrepancy between the image and the sound, it probably means that the bottom loop is the wrong size and the exact distance between picture and sound on the film must be reestablished. And, of course, if you have neither picture nor sound, you should check to make sure that the projector is plugged into the wall.

It is interesting to note that this means that when you are watching a motion picture, nothing is moving on the screen. The film is nothing but a series of sequential still pictures, and thus the image on the screen is also a series of still pictures projected in rapid succession. The perception of movement takes place within us. We "see" motion because the images are presented so quickly that they are blended together into the illusion of movement. It is this basic principle that allows us to create animated films.

MOTION PICTURE PRODUCTION:

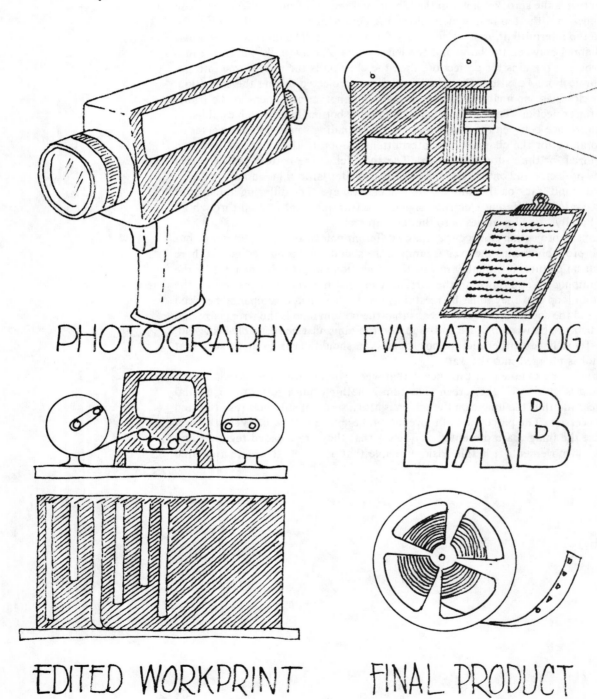

PHOTOGRAPHY

EVALUATION/LOG

LAB

EDITED WORKPRINT

FINAL PRODUCT

MOTION PICTURE PRODUCTION

Motion pictures are a complex instructional material, and as such they require the planning, design and production techniques that are appropriate for complex media. This means the development of: 1) planning documents, 2) design documents, and 3) production documents before we are ready for the actual production.

Planning documents consist of a content outline, an audience analysis, and a statement of objectives. The content outline, as the term implies, is an outline of the content to be included in the message. It shows not only the content but also the sequence in which the content will be presented. It answers the question, "What do you want to say?" The next question, "To whom?" is answered by the audience analysis. This is simply a description of the audience that emphasizes the characteristics that will influence the design and production of the materials. The last question, "With what effect?" is answered by the set of instructional objectives that are clear, concise communications of what the learners will be able to do as a result of the message.

The design documents are, first, a treatment. This is a written description of what the proposed message will sound and look like. Once the client has agreed to the treatment, this is translated into a storyboard. The storyboard is a combination of sketches (representing the various scenes), written descriptions of the scene, and an indication of the narration or concept that goes with the scene. If this is a sound film, you will next prepare a complete script for the production.

There are even production documents that will ensure success. The shooting schedule organizes the production and often suggests the order and sequence in which the various scenes will be shot. It is common practice to shoot scenes in a different order than that depicted in the storyboard to accelerate the production process. A prop and equipment list will ensure that the right materials are on hand for the scene that you are shooting.

With these documents out of the road you are ready to actually shoot the production. Begin with a knowledge of your equipment. Read the operators manual that goes with your camera and make sure you completely understand its operation. Watch the composition and don't be afraid to shoot long at the beginning and ends of the scenes. This extra footage will be important when it comes time to edit the film. Produce all of the required footage by making sure you have shot the scenes called for in the storyboard.

The editing process is where you recombine the scenes into their proper order. This is preceded by viewing the footage and evaluating the action and composition. When you are satisfied, you cut the scenes apart and put them in the sequence suggested by the storyboard. These are then spliced together and viewed for continuity. It is a rough cut, and you will want to make more precise cuts to match action and to create the impact that you desire. The final edit results in a print that can be copied for other prints or used in the classroom. If the film is a sound film, the process is a little more detailed.

GRAPHIC MOTION PICTURES

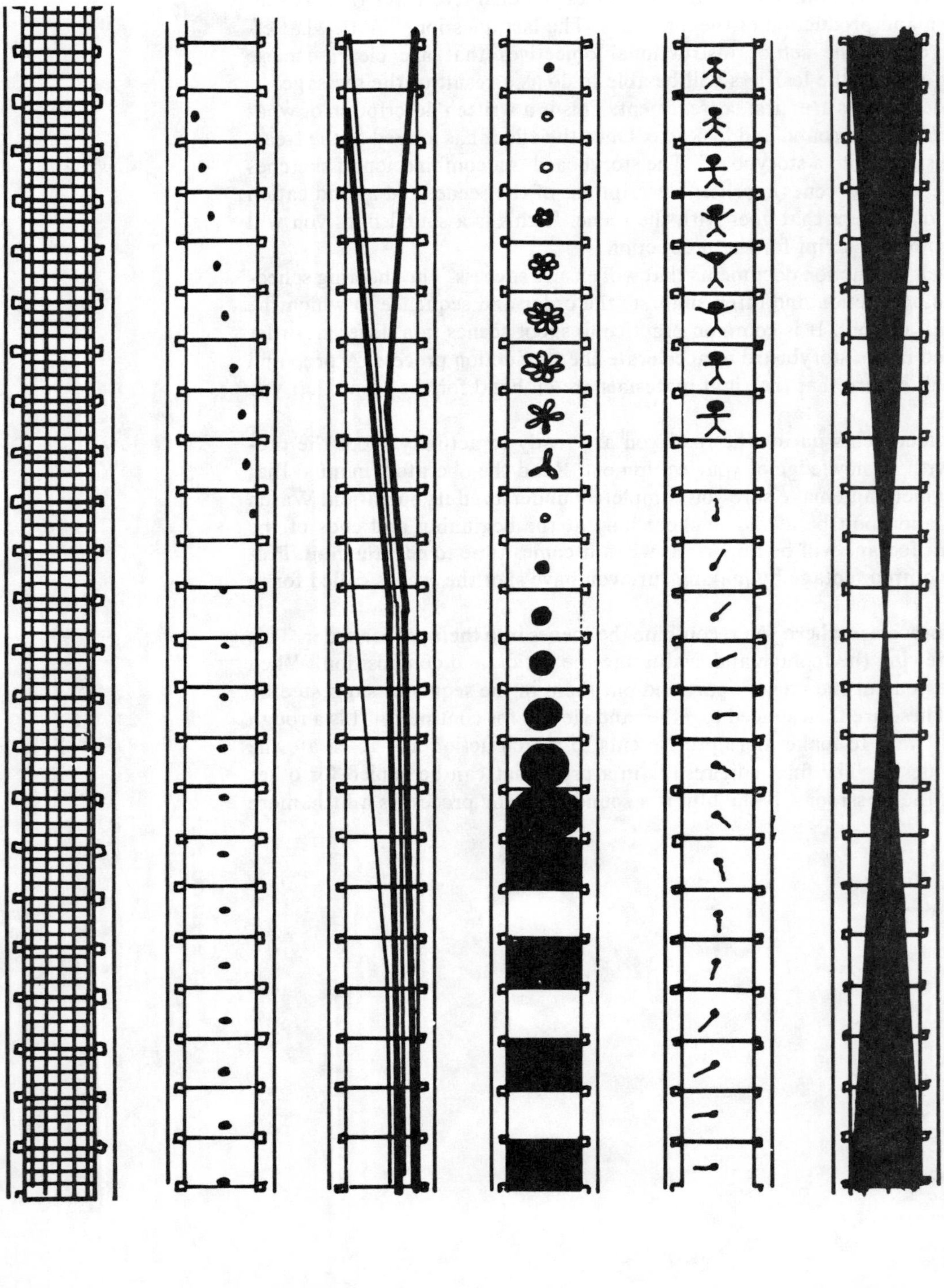

GRAPHIC MOTION PICTURES

It is possible to produce a motion picture without resorting to the use of a motion picture camera. Norman McLaren developed a technique for drawing directly on 35mm film that results in animated images that move on the screen. This technique utilizes the same medium used to draw on transparencies, to create motion sequences on 16mm film. This process does, normally, utilize a special film called matte lader. This is a 16mm film that has been chemically treated on one side so that it is rough. This rough surface will accept pencil, ball point pen, felt pen, and pen and ink images.

Now our concern is simply the creation of motion patterns. On the opposite page there are diagrams of strips of 16mm film. The first indicates the type of pattern you might use *under* your film to create these motion patterns. Note that normally there are no frame lines on the matter film, and you have to approximate the frame or image area. It is roughly the area bounded by two adjacent sprocket holes. This is the area that will be projected on the screen and the area in which we will create our series of still pictures.

The second diagram on the opposite page shows some dots in these frames. In the first example (top) the dot will appear on one side of the screen and rapidly move horizontally to the other. How fast will it move? Well, 16mm film moves through the projector at the rate of 24 frames per second. This motion pattern lasts for 11 frames, so it will last for slightly less than half of a second. The bottom example will project as a dot moving from the top of the screen to the bottom in 14 frames, or slightly over one half second.

The diagonal lines on the third diagram will project as lines that move horizontally across the screen in the first part, then join together and stay together. The fourth diagram shows a metamorphosis from a dot into a flower. Note that the dot (or center of the flower) stays in the center of the screen and does not really move. If you want part of the illustration to stay the same, it must be drawn in the same area of the frame each time. Here the dot begins to grow leaves, and eventually the leaves drop off, leaving only the dot. With technique we can make a square change into a triangle or a fish change into a bird. In the bottom of this diagram we see a dot moving toward us and eventually filling the screen. The fifth diagram shows someone exercising and, below, the hand of a clock or dial rotating around a center post. The last diagram shows a fade in and a fade out. These represent just a small part of the exciting images that can be created by this graphic technique for producing motion pictures.

If you can't get the matte leader, you can always get old commercials from the local television station and bleach off the images (with a 50% solution of ammonia and water) to give you a clear sheet of film on which you can draw these images. Norman McLaren's films are available for rent, and these can generate exciting visual ideas for creating your own motion pictures without a motion picture camera.

AUDIO --- UTILIZATION:

PRESENTATION

INTERACTION

INDEPENDENT STUDY

PROGRAMMED INST.

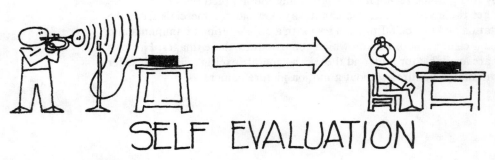

SELF EVALUATION

* WITH AND WITHOUT OTHER MEDIA

236

AUDIO UTILIZATION

Audio for instruction is available in two quite different formats. The earliest system was the record player and disc recordings or records. The materials are generally available from both commercial and free/inexpensive sources. There is even a listing called the Schwan Record Catalogue that lists all of the records available. It also lists the disc recordings that might be appropriate for instruction. Many of the record companies will supply a catalogue of their recordings that are suitable for classroom use. However, it is next to impossible to produce these records locally—the recording equipment is just too expensive.

While these disc recordings can be used for all teaching/learning strategies, they seem to be most appropriate for presentation and possibly interaction. They could be used for self-instruction and drill, but there are other systems that are better and more cost effective.

The second type of audio system is the tape recorder and tapes. Here we have a definite advantage over the disc recordings in that with the tape recorder we can do just that—record the sounds of the world around us. In addition to having the potential for local production, audio tapes are also available from commercial and free/inexpensive sources. There is probably more information now available on tape than there is on disc recordings.

Like the disc recordings, the audio tape recordings can be used for: 1) presentation, 2) interaction, 3) independent study, and 4) drill and practice. Unlike the disc recordings, the audio tapes can be designed to fit all of these applications. Tape recordings can be purchased or acquired, made to tell stories, recreate historical events or present excerpts from famous literature. These are excellent for presentation to large groups. Tapes can also be designed specifically to generate an interaction activity, usually following the tape. I remember one teacher who recorded exciting segments of famous stories that were designed to get students to the library to read the outcome. This was a type of interaction. However, the more normal interactive situation is to raise questions that the learners can deal with in a group discussion following the tape stimuli.

Audio tapes can also be designed specifically for self-instruction. In this case they present information (audio information of course), ask the learner to make a response (covert or overt), and provide feedback as to the accuracy of the response. These can be designed for either remedial activities or for enrichment. Tapes can also be used successfully for drill and practice. To many teachers this is the best use of audio tape. As the tape delivers the drill, it frees the teacher to work with individuals who might be having problems. There is another strategy that works well with audio tape, self-evaluation. Given an example of what their efforts should sound like, students can record their reading, speech, music, etc., and then compare their efforts with the model. This allows students to evaluate their own performance and removes some of the problems from the instructor.

AUDIO EQUIPMENT:

BALL

AUDIO EQUIPMENT

There is a wide range of audio equipment available for both the production and playback of instructional materials. First, let's consider the equipment used for the playback of disc recordings. The standard classroom record player will handle the playback of most instructional records. However, if you want the playback to be for only part of the class, you may need to plug a listening center into the record player. This unit mutes the speaker for the record player and provides 6–12 headset units that students can use to listen to the audio information without disturbing the rest of the class.

Tape recorders come in a much wider range of forms and functions. First, there are the cassette and the reel-to-reel tape recorders. The cassette system is easier to load and perhaps to use. It is also portable in the sense that it can operate off battery power, and it is normally much smaller than the reel-to-reel systems. However, the reel to reel system generally will give you much better recording quality as part of a production system. Most reel-to-reel tape recorders will allow you to record a second of audio information on 7 1/2″ of tape that is about 1/2″ wide. The cassette recorder will record the same second of information on only 1 7/8″. Obviously, if we can put the same signals over a wider area, we can get greater fidelity. Unfortunately, many of the schools are replacing their old reel-to-reel systems with cassettes and not recognizing the former's value as recording systems.

In addition to the variations in tape formats, the tape recorders are also available in different recording formats. The standard recording format records on half the tape, and you can put a single track on each side of the tape. Some tape recorders operate in a stereo format and have four separate tracks on each tape.

Then, of course, there are tape recorders that have special functions. You can purchase tape duplication systems that will allow you to make cassette copies of a master tape. Many of these transfer the audio information at more than the normal speed for playback. Then there are audio tape recorders that are specifically designed for slide-tape productions. These tape recorders will not only play back the audio tapes that have the inaudible pulse signal (to advance the slide projector), they will also record the inaudible signal onto the tape that works with the slides.

These variations in tape recorders only begin to scratch the surface. For example, there is a class of audio media called magnetic card readers. These utilize cards that have a strip of audio tape laminated to the bottom edge of the card. Fifteen to thirty seconds of information can be recorded and played back on these cards. They also have space where words or pictures can be inserted to supplement or reinforce the audio information. These magnetic card readers are normally used for drill and practice, but they can also be adapted to self-instruction without too much difficulty.

AUDIO PRODUCTION:

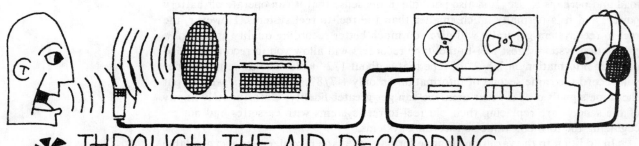

�֍ THROUGH THE AIR RECORDING.

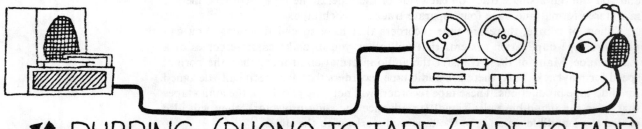

✤ DUBBING (PHONO TO TAPE/ TAPE TO TAPE)

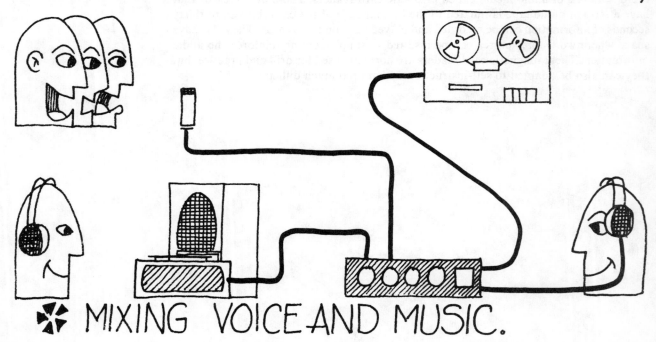

✤ MIXING VOICE AND MUSIC.

AUDIO PRODUCTION

With the advent of the audio tape recorder, the instructional developer was given the tools to produce audio materials locally. There are many applications and techniques for this local production.

The normal type of recording is often referred to as through the air recording. In its simplest form this is an individual speaking into a microphone that is connected to the tape recorder. However, you can add music and sound effects by simply playing another tape recorder or a record player in the same room, and its sound will also be picked up by the live mike. There are problems in this type of recording. The environment may intrude upon the tape. The sound of traffic (cars and/or planes), the sounds of equipment (clocks or the tape recorder itself), and the inadvertent sounds of your talent may end up on the tape and destroy the audio effects that you are trying to create.

It is especially important to eliminate environmental sounds when you are transferring audio information from a record to a tape or from one tape to another. It is quite possible to do this by simply connecting the output of the record player to the input of the tape recorder as shown in the diagram on the opposite page. Since there is no microphone used, there is no chance to pick up the noise in the environment. However, you must recognize that in this transfer process you may be violating copyright and infringing upon the ownership of the audio materials you are transferring.

A more complicated recording system simulates the old radio broadcasts. Here, the talent is located in an environment that can control the environment sounds. Their mikes are fed into an audio mixer. The music and sound effects can be fed into another channel of the mixer via wires. The output of the mixer can then be fed into a good quality reel-to-reel tape recorder. The audio director controls the program, and it is produced "live". This does not require expensive equipment and provides an opportunity to rediscover the radio techniques that produced those great programs your parents may remember.

A more normal approach to mixing is to first record the narration onto an audio tape. Then record the music and sound effects onto a second tape. Then feed these two tapes through a mixing system to produce a master audio tape.

If this is to be used as an audio instructional material, the tape is ready for playback. If this is to be used as part of a slide-tape program, the reel-to-reel tape is transferred to a cassette using a special tape recorder, and the inaudible signals that will advance the slide projector are put directly onto the tape.

This is just a surface look at the various audio production systems and techniques. As with any production equipment, it is essential to know the equipment, so read the instruction manuals and practice. You will find that locally produced audio materials can be both teacher and student made. Involving your students in audio production can be an interesting experience.

TELEVISION UTILIZATION:

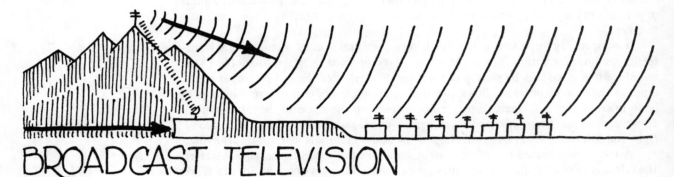

BROADCAST TELEVISION

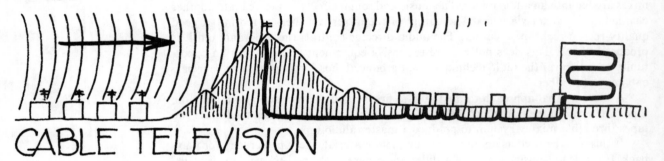

CABLE TELEVISION

PRESENTATION

INTERACTION

INDEPENDENT STUDY

SELF EVALUATION

TELEVISION UTILIZATION

There is no real question of the value of television as an instructional tool. By the time the average student graduates from high school he will have spent 15–20,000 hours watching TV. During that same time he only spends 11,000 hours in school. Television is a major force in educating our young people. Basically, there are three types of television that can be employed in instructional settings.

Broadcast television is the term used to describe the programs that are delivered through the air to your home or classroom. These broadcast signals can be picked up by any television receiver tuned to the proper channel or frequency. While these are available to all, they may not be available at the proper times. Broadcast television operates on its own schedule, not the schools' or the instructors' schedule.

A second type of television delivery system is cable. Cable also provides a number of different programs that might be effectively incorporated into an instructional program. Many of the channels that are available deal specifically with educational information, and it is more likely that the programming you want would be available when you can effectively use it. However, to receive these cable signals you must be wired into the system. In most cable systems the city has required that the schools have a drop that will allow them access to the cable signals. But the bad news is that few schools have wired the signal from the drop into the individual classrooms.

The third type of television delivery system is the video tape. These tapes are played back on a simple video tape recorder and into a television monitor that is part of the system. Here, the instructor has complete control over the delivery of the materials and can both time it to the instructional situation and even stop and start it as the needs of the class require. These video tapes can be acquired from commercial sources (purchase or rental) and from certain free/inexpensive sources (on a return basis). But perhaps more importantly, they can be locally produced. This local production can be either video taping of existing materials from broadcast or cable sources, or it can be the production of local scripts and ideas.

These video tapes, like motion pictures, can be used for all of the teaching/learning strategies. Television appears to be best suited to presentation and interaction activities. Using television for independent study and drill and practice is possible but probably not very cost effective. There are other media that would be more appropriate. There is one teaching/learning strategy that is becoming more and more popular and appropriate for television, self-evaluation. Psychomotor skills such as sports, music, and even art can be evaluated via TV. Video taping a tennis player allows you to play back his actions and point out problems, or it allows him to evaluate his own performance. When television is linked with other media such as computers, the applications become even important. New developments in video technology promise even more educational and industrial application in the relatively near future.

TELEVISION EQUIPMENT:

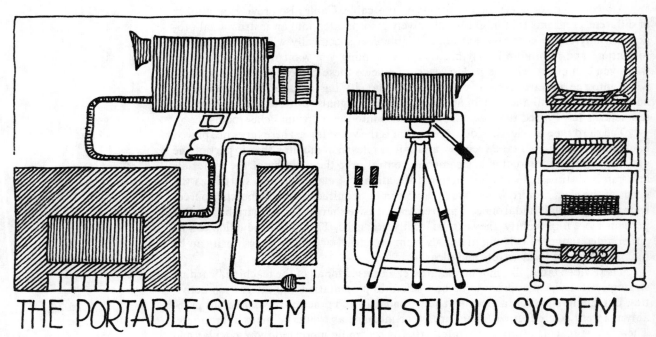

THE PORTABLE SYSTEM   THE STUDIO SYSTEM

THE MULTICAMERA SYSTEM

TELEVISION EQUIPMENT

When we are talking about television equipment, we must first consider the application. One set of equipment is used for playback, and another set is used for production. Let's look at the playback equipment first. For receiving broadcast television all you need is a television receiver. For picking up cable signals you not only need a television receiver, you also need a hook up to the cable and a special tuner to tap into the wider variety of signals that are available. To play back video tapes you need a television receiver and a video tape recorder or player. You also need the cables that will connect the elements in the system. This system used to play back video tapes can also be used to record programs off the air (broadcast) or off the cable. A general rule of thumb to remember is that the size of the television receiver should match the size of the audience. Thus, to serve 25 students you need a 25" set. The 25" dimension is the diagonal measurement of the screen. While there are video projection systems, these are either too expensive, or they do not normally meet the needs of the classroom.

Television equipment that is used for production is a little more complicated. Basically, there are three types of television production systems: 1) the portapak systems, 2) the single camera studio systems, and 3) the multicamera production systems. The portapak system consists of a video tape recorder and a camera. The camera also contains a built in mike for recording the audio as the camera is recording the video portion of the program. The video tape recorder contains the batteries that give this system its name—portapak. There are other components that can be added to the system. Naturally, you can add a large monitor for playback. For checking during production, the video tape recorder plays the signal back through the eyepiece of the camera. You can also add a mike to the system and bypass the built-in microphone. There is also an AC/DC converter that will allow you to operate the system from AC power and also to recharge the batteries.

The single camera system is the one most commonly found in the public schools. This system consists of a camera mounted on a tripod (and occasionally a wheeled dolly), and a cart containing the monitor/receiver, video tape recorder and other accessories to the system. You can add an audio mixer that will allow you to use more than the single mike that can be plugged into the video tape recorder. A cassette audio tape recorder can also be fed into the mixer to allow you to add music and sound effects to your productions.

The last system is a multicamera system. This, as the name implies, has two or more television cameras whose signals are sent to a video switcher located in a console. This allows the technical director to switch from one camera to another or to produce the special effects the director calls for. The various audio inputs (mikes and tape recorder) are fed into an audio mixer also located in the console. The audio and video signals from the console are fed to a video tape recorder and then to a line monitor that tells you what is being produced.

DEVELOPING MEDIA

The complex media that we have looked at represents just a beginning. Photographic and electronic technology is increasing at such a rapid rate that it's almost impossible to predict what media will be available for the classrooms of tomorrow. Already the computer has made a major impact on education. It has reached the point where most of the major computer companies will almost give you a computer, because they know that there is more money to be made in the sales of the software systems that feed these computers. These computer programs are becoming so important that there are national listings of locally produced programs that can be shared within the educational community. Companies such as Apple have catalogues that list literally thousands of computer programs that could be used in the classroom.

Another developing media is the video disc. Plagued with a number of different formats, the development of this system has been delayed. However, its potential is fantastic. It may well be the end of the 16mm film. The cost of mass production of films, video tapes, and other media into this format is very cost effective. You will be able to buy a film for almost what it costs to rent it today. These video discs contain thousands of bits of information, and that fact leads us to another development.

When the computer is linked with the video disc or with the video tape recorder, we have the potential for a fantastic interaction. A self-instructional program can be designed, for almost any subject matter, that will respond appropriately to the responses of almost every learner. This system is still in an experimental mode, but even now major producers of instructional materials are developing instructional materials for this as yet untried media.

But technology is not only inventing new delivery and production systems, it is also improving the systems that we already have. In the area of television the 1/2″ video systems are almost as good as the professional systems that cost ten times as much. Video tape recorders are getting smaller and cheaper and have capabilities that were only dreams just a few years ago. A video tape recorder that started as big as a room is now small enough to fit into a brief case, and it can record hours of information in full living color.

Television signals are bouncing off sattelites and reaching all parts of the world simultaneously. Cable has the potential for making a community a real, viable social group. It can provide hundreds of channels of information, and through sheer numbers can begin to feed the needs of individuals. The president of Sony Corporation sees a new type of television broadcasting for the future. He calls it narrow-casting, to signify that it is different from what's currently available. He perceives that cable will be able to provide programming specific to the needs of special small groups.

It's getting to the point that all you have to do is tell an engineer what you want a system to do, and he will build it for you, and if it's viable, he will market it to the world.

NOTES

NOTES